Parties and Unions in the
New Global Economy

Pitt Latin American Series

George Reid Andrews, General Editor

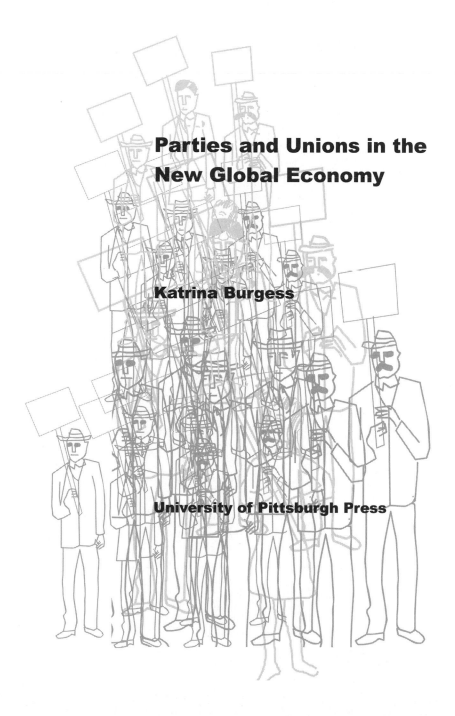

Parties and Unions in the
New Global Economy

Katrina Burgess

University of Pittsburgh Press

Published by the University of Pittsburgh Press, Pittsburgh, Pa., 15260

Copyright © 2004, University of Pittsburgh Press

Manufactured in the United States of America

Printed on acid-free paper

10 9 8 7 6 5 4 3 2 1

LIBRARY OF CONGRESS CATALOGING-IN-PUBLICATION DATA
Burgess, Katrina.
    Parties and unions in the new global economy / Katrina Burgess.
      p. cm. — (Pitt Latin American series)
    Includes bibliographical references and index.
    ISBN 0-8229-5825-2 (pbk. : alk. paper)
      1. Labor unions—Spain—Political activity. 2. Political parties—
    Spain. 3. Spain—Politics and government—1975– 4. Spain—
    Economic policy. 5. Labor unions—Mexico—Political activity.
    6. Political parties—Mexico. 7. Mexico—Politics and government—
    20th century. 8. Mexico—Economic policy. 9. Labor unions—
    Venezuela—Political activity. 10. Political parties—Venezuela.
    11. Venezuela—Politics and government—1935– 12. Venezuela—
    Economic policy. I. Title. II. Series.
    HD6487.5 .B87 2003
    322'.2—dc21
                                        2003014535

To my parents, whose support and encouragement made it possible for me to write this book

Contents

Tables and Figures

Tables

Figures

Acknowledgments

The initial inspiration for this book came from a presentation by a friend and colleague, Omar Encarnación, on the transition to democracy in Spain. At one point in his talk, he noted that the Socialist government's economic reforms were straining relations between the Spanish Socialist Worker's Party and its historic ally in the labor movement, the General Workers' Union. Although I knew very little about Spain at the time, I was struck by the similarity to events in Mexico, where another labor-backed party, the Institutional Revolutionary Party (PRI), was adopting reforms that threatened relations with its labor allies. I did some more research and learned that labor-backed parties around the world were embracing policies that contradicted their traditional platforms and subjected one of their core constituencies—organized labor—to painful sacrifices.

The first question that occured to me was: why would a political party bite the hand that feeds it? The answer proved fairly obvious. Labor-backed parties sought new sources of nourishment because workers and unions could no longer provide them with the same organizational and political support as in the past, and because changes in the international economy and domestic social structures encouraged them to adopt market reforms and cultivate alternative constituencies. But a more puzzling question remained: why did the leaders of party-affiliated unions react so differently to comparable reforms by their party allies? Drawing on the cases of Mexico, Spain, and Venezuela, I set out to answer this question and to explore its implications for the representation of working people in the political arena.

The people who made it possible for me to write this book are too numerous to mention, but I would like to acknowledge the special contributions of a few. I am particularly grateful to Nancy Bermeo, John Waterbury, and Miguel

Centeno at Princeton University. They provided me with both substantive guidance and moral support in the formative stages of this project. I would also like to thank several people who read and gave me useful feedback on one or more of its many incarnations: Jeremy Adelman, Javier Corrales, Elisabeth Friedman, Stephan Haggard, Steve Levitsky, Sandy McCaw, the participants in the 1996–1997 dissertation workshop at the Center for U.S.–Mexican Studies at the University of California, San Diego, and members of the 1999–2000 Global Political Economy Research Colloquium (G-PERC) in the Global Affairs Institute at Syracuse University's Maxwell School of Citizenship and Public Affairs.

This book would not have been possible without the financial, institutional, and personal support I received during my fifteen months of fieldwork. My research was funded through grants from the Department of Politics, the Program in Latin American Studies, and the Center for International Studies at Princeton University. I also received a grant from the Council for European Studies at Columbia University for a preliminary field trip to Spain. In Mexico, I spent a semester in the Departamento de Estudios Internacionales at the Instituto Tecnológico Autónomo de México (ITAM) in Mexico City, where Rafael Fernández de Castro made me feel especially welcome. I am also grateful to Graciela Bensusan, Rolando Cordera, Enrique de la Garza, and Jaime Serra Puche for giving me valuable contacts. In Venezuela, I was based at the Instituto de Estudios Avanzados (IESA) in Caracas and was given access to archival resources at CENDES and the Universidad Central de Venezuela (UCV). Rolando Díaz, Steve Ellner, Francisco "Pancho" Iturraspe, and César Olarte were particularly generous with their insights and contacts. I am also grateful to Vicky Murillo for sharing many of her sources in the Venezuelan labor movement. In Spain, I was a guest scholar at the Centro de Estudios Avanzados en Ciencias Sociales at the Instituto Juan March in Madrid and had access to archival resources at the Fundación Largo Caballero. Among the people who opened doors for me while sharing their knowledge were Francisco Fernández Marugán, Manuel Garnacho, José María Maravall, and Ludolfo Paramio. Finally, I want to thank the many other people who granted me interviews in the three countries.

Several institutions provided me with the time and space to write up my findings after completing my field research. In 1995–1996, I was a member of the Princeton Society of Fellows, funded by the Woodrow Wilson Foundation at Princeton University. In 1996–1997, I spent a year as a visiting research fellow at the Center for U.S.–Mexican Studies at the University of California, San Diego. Most recently, I spent two years as a William R. Rhodes Postdoctoral Fellow at the Watson Institute of International Studies at Brown University, where I completed this manuscript. I am very grateful to the Department of

Political Science and the Maxwell School at Syracuse University for giving me the leave and supplementary financial support to take advantage of this last opportunity.

At the University of Pittsburgh Press, I would like to thank Cathy Conaghan for encouraging me to submit the manuscript, Nathan MacBrien for being a very supportive and responsive editor, and Deborah Meade for her careful work on the manuscript. I am also grateful to Kevin Middlebrook, Robert Fishman, and an anonymous reviewer for their excellent suggestions as reviewers for the Press.

My final thanks go to the people who have lent me personal support on the long journey to completion of this project, particularly Abby Allen, Peter Andreas, Chuck Call, Elisabeth Friedman, Martha Little, Jeannie Sowers, Omar Valerio, Pam York, and Corrine Yu. Last, but certainly not least, I am indebted to Luisito for applauding my accomplishments while reminding me that there is more to life than writing a book.

CHAPTER 1
Introduction: Choosing Sides

"Down with garbage contracts!" This was the cry of millions of Spanish workers who went on strike on December 14, 1988 to protest the government's
economic reforms, particularly a proposed law that would enable employers to
hire young workers under temporary contracts at less than the minimum
wage.[1] Not only was it the first general strike since Spain's transition to
democracy in the 1970s, but it also pitted the governing Spanish Socialist
Workers' Party (PSOE) against its longtime ally in the labor movement, the
General Workers' Union (UGT), for the first time ever. In the months following the strike, commentators spoke of a "divorce" between the PSOE and the
UGT that marked a watershed in Spanish politics.

Five months later, Venezuelan workers followed the Spanish example and
held a general strike against the government's austerity policies. The strike's
main organizer was the Confederation of Venezuelan Workers (CTV), which,
like the UGT, had long been affiliated with the governing party, Democratic
Action (AD). In contrast to what had happened in Spain, however, the strike
in Venezuela did not lead to a divorce between the CTV and AD. Not long after the strike, AD leaders began to support the CTV's opposition to the government's reforms. Although they subsequently reimposed limits on antireform votes and mobilizations by the CTV, they never rallied strongly behind
their own government. In May 1993, AD legislators voted with the opposition to seek the impeachment of President Carlos Andrés Pérez, who had
taken office as the AD candidate in 1988, in the wake of two attempted military coups and ongoing social unrest. These events ultimately led to a transformation of the Venezuelan political system that threatened to destroy the
party-union alliance.

The nationwide mobilization of workers in Spain and Venezuela contrasted

1

sharply with the "sounds of silence" emanating from Mexico (Middlebrook 1989), where the Confederation of Mexican Workers (CTM) reluctantly cooperated with market reforms by its longtime ally, the Institutional Revolutionary Party (PRI). Although CTM leaders complained bitterly about the government's policies, they never mobilized workers against them. Instead, they collaborated on industrial restructuring in return for control over collective contracts, signed a series of anti-inflation pacts with business and the government, supported the negotiation of a free trade agreement with the United States and Canada, and campaigned for PRI candidates in elections. Collusion between the PRI and the CTM ultimately contributed to widespread disillusionment with the political system and a series of profound changes that, as in Venezuela, undermined the party-union alliance.

These vignettes from Spain, Venezuela, and Mexico illustrate a widespread change in the structure of interest representation in countries with historically strong alliances between parties and unions. For much of the twentieth century, unions were the most prevalent and influential instrument of collective action among subaltern groups, particularly in Latin America and Europe. They mobilized thousands of workers and helped them ascend the socioeconomic ladder. They also forged alliances with major political parties in at least two dozen countries. In the process, they often played vital roles in shaping the political regimes and economic development strategies that defined the societies in which they operated.

The centrality of unions as mediators between workers and the state began to decline as economic conditions and identities became more fluid in the late twentieth century. Heightened global competition, the collapse of Bretton Woods, and the information revolution all contributed to the rise of more flexible forms of economic organization. Capital became more mobile, the service sector exploded, manufacturers began to target niche markets with specialized products, small workplaces proliferated, and the skills and experience of workers became increasingly heterogeneous. Meanwhile, employers sought to reorganize production to confront "an unprecedented degree of economic uncertainty deriving from a need for continuous rapid adjustment to a market environment that seems to have become permanently more turbulent" (Streek 1987, 61).

These changes merged with the spread of mass-consumer culture, increased geographical mobility, the entry of previously marginalized groups into the labor force, and the emergence of "new social movements" organized around identity, citizenship rights, and community issues to erode worker self-identification with "the working class" (Pérez-Díaz 1987, 124). Identities fragmented and multiplied while the traditional base of union support declined as a share of the workforce. In addition, rising educational levels and access to the mass media, particularly television, reduced the control of unions and parties over political and economic information. As a result, unions lost much of their universalist appeal, confronted new and complicated issues in the workplace, and had to compete with other sources of information and identity among workers. They also became less able to deliver working-class support to their party allies, particularly during times of economic hardship.

In this context, even labor-backed parties had strong incentives to renege on their commitments to labor when in office. First, international competition and changes in industrial production undermined both the rationales and the resources for state intervention in the economy. Instead, governments found themselves under significant pressure to reduce the size of the state, liberalize price and factor markets, hold the line against domestic inflation, and enhance incentives for private investment.[2] As governments raced to create favorable conditions for firms to compete in an increasingly global and volatile economy, the "welfare state" gave way to the "competition state" (Cerny 1990). In the process, neoliberal technocrats gained influence within cabinets and government bureaucracies.

Second, the same uncertainties that led employers to seek more flexible forms of production encouraged parties to pursue more flexible strategies of coalition building. In a context of economic uncertainty, fragmented interests, and shifting identities, parties could no longer afford to be locked into commitments to a particular group, especially one likely to resist market opening. Moreover, most labor organizations could no longer deliver the kind of electoral support and legitimation the parties needed, particularly in an environment of fickle voters and media politics. Thus, labor-backed parties experienced pressures to diversify their coalition away from organized labor and appeal directly to individual voters, bypassing unions as intermediary organizations.

Faced with these conditions, many labor-backed parties adopted economic reforms in the 1980s and 1990s that were anathema to their traditional programs and strained their relations with unions and workers. Beyond the three countries discussed here, these parties included the Labour Parties in Britain and New Zealand, the Peronist Party in Argentina, the National Revolutionary Movement in Bolivia, Solidarity in Poland, the African National Congress in South Africa, and the social democratic parties in Germany, Sweden, and Austria. In many cases, the party's turn to the market provoked an identity crisis for both organizations and further undermined structures of interest representation in which unions had played a starring role. Party-affiliated union leaders often found themselves pulled in strategically contradictory directions. Either they remained loyal to the party by cooperating with the reforms, or they remained loyal to workers by resisting the reforms and, if necessary, abandoning the alliance. In short, they became caught in a "loyalty dilemma" in which they had to choose sides.

As we have seen in Mexico, Spain, and Venezuela, not all party-affiliated unions reacted in the same way to the party's perceived betrayal. This book seeks to explain the variation in their responses, particularly across cases in which they lacked sufficient leverage to halt or reverse the reforms.[3] This puzzle is important for three reasons. First, as suggested above, the fate of party-union alliances is inextricably linked to the structure of interest representation—and therefore the quality of democracy—in many countries. Whether these alliances survive, mutate, or die influences the mechanisms by which workers are either linked to or marginalized from the state. It also affects the future of labor-backed parties, many of which have played critical roles in their countries' politics. For each of these parties, its evolving relationship with labor will have a decisive impact on its identity, coalitional strategies, and electoral prospects, often with implications for the party system as a whole.

Second, even though these unions could not fundamentally alter governmental reform programs, they all had sufficient bargaining power to extract some important concessions, including getting certain reforms placed on the back burner. The nature and extent of these concessions were partly results of the unions' ability and willingness to challenge party authority. Thus, in order to explain the policy choices of labor-backed governments, we need to understand the strategic interactions that took place within the party-union alliance, as well as the fate of the alliance itself.

Finally, the strains placed on party-union alliances in recent years raise intriguing questions regarding the choices that organizational leaders are likely to make when they are placed in loyalty dilemmas. Any leader who is answerable to both followers and allies (or, for that matter, superiors in a hierarchical chain) is susceptible to becoming caught in the kind of conundrum faced by party-affiliated labor leaders. What determines whose side they choose? This book offers a conceptual framework for tackling this question. Although my explanatory variables are specific to party-union relations, my focus on relations of power and autonomy has relevance across a diverse range of cases.

Mexico, Spain, and Venezuela represent very different responses by labor leaders faced with similar challenges. All three countries were governed by parties with historic ties to the labor movement in the 1980s and early 1990s. In Mexico, the PRI extended its half-century reign as the country's ruling party under the leadership of Miguel De la Madrid and Carlos Salinas. The PRI had been organically linked to the CTM since the 1930s. In Spain, the PSOE returned from decades of exile to govern as a hegemonic party between 1982 and 1993 under the leadership of Felipe González. The PSOE had been closely associated with the UGT since the 1880s. In Venezuela, AD regained the presidency in 1984 after five years in the opposition and governed until 1994 under the leadership of Jaime Lusinchi and Carlos Andrés Pérez.[4] AD had dominated the CTV since the 1940s.

These parties all adopted reforms in the 1980s and early 1990s that imposed painful sacrifices on workers and unions. Their reforms included cuts in government spending, anti-inflation measures, price deregulation, privatization of state-owned enterprises, industrial restructuring, trade liberalization, flexibilization of the labor market, and welfare reform. In all three countries, the reforms subjected workers to wage austerity, unemployment, decreased job security, and cuts in social services. They also diminished the mediating capacity of unions by shrinking the size of the public sector and expanding the influence of neoliberal technocrats in policymaking circles. Moreover, the reforms appeared to signal a permanent shift by the parties away from their historic commitments to state-led growth and redistribution. Rather than presenting the reforms as short-term measures to rejuvenate the economy, their governments embraced them as necessary, if difficult, adaptations to a changed global environment.

Relatedly, the balance of power between the party and the union clearly favored the party in all three cases. The unions represented a relatively small share of the total workforce, were constrained by high rates of unemployment and/or underemployment, and faced obstacles to mounting unified labor opposition, especially in strategic sectors. A report by the International Labour Organization found that union membership as a share of the nonagricultural labor force was 31 percent in Mexico in 1991, 7.3 percent in Spain in 1985, and 25.9 percent in Venezuela in 1988 (ILO 1997–98).[5] These low affiliation rates hindered the unions' capacities to impose major economic costs on governments and to withhold meaningful numbers of votes from parties. As a result, they lacked sufficient leverage to block or significantly alter the parties' policy agendas.

In all three countries, both the party and the union were highly centralized. National leaders generally made the key decisions, and lower-level leaders generally obeyed their orders. Although internal splits occurred, they were unusual. In the rare event that a serious intra-organizational division took place, it almost always played out at the national level. Thus, each of the three cases involved similar processes of decision making whereby national leaders had the last word. Because their decisions served as a proxy for those of the organization as a whole, the fate of the alliance rested largely on their strategic calculations regarding the appropriate responses to the party's moves and countermoves.

Finally, despite these commonalities, labor leaders in each case responded very differently to the party's adoption of painful reforms. Their responses can be viewed as points along a continuum. At one extreme is the CTM's collaboration with the reforms, which translated into a sustained commitment to its alliance with the PRI. At the other extreme is the UGT's resistance to the reforms, which took the form of defection from its alliance with the PSOE. In the middle is the CTV's vacillation between collaboration and resistance, which strained but did not break its alliance with AD.

The divergent responses of disaffected labor leaders faced with similar pressures can be explained by two variables: (1) the relative power of the party and workers to punish labor leaders for disloyal behavior; and (2) the party's capacity to act autonomously from its own government. The first variable shapes the incentives of labor leaders to choose sides when the party adopts painful reforms and thereby places them in a loyalty dilemma. Their choice reflects who has the power to punish them most severely for betrayal. This power is a function of four institutional arrangements: (a) the legal framework governing industrial relations; (b) the structure of the labor movement; (c) the type of party system; and (d) the party's mechanisms for filling party posts.

The second variable determines whether the party can rescue labor leaders from their loyalty dilemma once it has been created. If the party is able (and willing) to oppose its own government and join labor in resisting the reforms, labor leaders will no longer have to choose between loyalty to the party and loyalty to workers. Instead, they can oppose the reforms with the party's blessing. But the party can only provide such relief if it has the capacity to act autonomously from its own government. This capacity derives from two institutional arrangements: (a) the location of supreme authority within the party; and (b) the spaces for intraparty dissent. If these arrangements give all or some of the party sufficient autonomy to challenge its own government, labor leaders may not have to engage in disloyal behavior at all. But if the party lacks this autonomy, they will have to choose sides.

Different relations of power and autonomy explain the divergent responses of disaffected labor leaders in Mexico, Spain, and Venezuela. Both the PRI and the PSOE lacked sufficient autonomy from their own government to join labor in resisting the reforms, which meant that labor leaders in Mexico and Spain had to choose sides. But they made very different choices because the threats of punishment came from opposite directions. CTM leaders enjoyed significant protection from backlash by workers but were vulnerable to punishment by the party. By contrast, UGT leaders were relatively protected from retaliation by the party but were vulnerable to punishment by workers. Not surprisingly, CTM leaders remained loyal to the party while UGT leaders defected from the party-union alliance.

Venezuela presents yet another scenario. CTV leaders faced credible threats of punishment from both the party and workers, which created incentives for them to vacillate between cooperation and resistance. As described earlier, they held a general strike against the reforms but then retreated back to a more collaborative approach. Their restraint cannot be entirely explained by their fear of punishment by the party, however. In contrast to both the PRI and the PSOE, AD had sufficient autonomy to challenge its own government. It exercised this autonomy at a critical moment in party-union relations, thereby enabling CTV leaders to resist the reforms without behaving disloyally toward AD. Although the party eventually reimposed limits on the CTV's resistance, this period of relief gave labor leaders additional incentives to preserve the party-union alliance.

CHAPTER 2

Exit, Voice, and Loyalty in Party-Union Relations

Political parties and labor unions began to forge alliances with the advent of industrialization and mass politics in the late nineteenth and early twentieth centuries (Pizzorno 1978; Marks 1989; Collier and Collier 1991). Although the earliest unions tended to be apolitical or anarchist, unions and parties discovered shared interests as workers developed a class consciousness, the state increased its involvement in the economy, and working-class support became a valuable commodity in the struggle for political power. These conditions laid the foundations for an exchange whereby the union would help the party win or maintain control of the state in return for the party's commitment to use state intervention to channel benefits to labor. Although labor-backed parties with no political representation often advocated radical intervention in the form of socialism or communism, participation in electoral politics usually led them to moderate their programs in favor of using state power to promote the interests of workers in the context of a capitalist economy (Esping-Andersen 1985; Przeworski and Sprague 1986).

In several countries, particularly in Europe and Latin America, this exchange produced stable, institutionalized alliances that resembled "regimes" as understood by international relations scholars. Stephen Krasner defines regimes as "sets of principles, norms, rules, and decision-making procedures around which actors' expectations converge" (1983, 2). Although he and his colleagues apply the concept of regimes to nation-states in the international arena, it can be extended quite naturally to organizations in the domestic arena. A defining feature in both cases is the non-unitary character of the central actors. Like nation-states, parties and unions have complex internal structures, identities, and constituencies. They can enter into regularized patterns of interaction, but they do so as collective entities rather than as individuals. Thus, they must take into account more than their individual preferences; they must also be sensitive to the demands and expectations of their followers. In addition, these central actors are relatively few in number, which means that any one of them can have an impact on institutional outcomes.

Like regimes, party-union alliances are structured by principles and norms.[1] The principles elaborate their shared vision of society, and the norms govern the terms of exchange and the management of conflict within the alliance. Whereas some principles and norms will be explicit and formalized, others will consist of informal yet mutual understandings that have evolved out of repeated interactions between the party and its labor allies. Principles and norms establish bonds of "loyalty" among the participants. Being loyal entails living up to one's explicit and implicit commitments within the alliance. Once bonds of loyalty have been established, participants become more inclined to trust their exchange partners to behave in ways that are favorable to their goals and interests.

Because parties and unions are collective entities rather than unitary actors, their leaders are bound by more than one set of loyalties. Labor leaders have commitments to both the party and workers. When the alliance is functioning well, these bonds of loyalty are mutually reinforcing. But if the party adopts reforms that harm workers, labor leaders are pulled in strategically contradictory directions. They find themselves in a "loyalty dilemma" in which they must choose between supporting the reforms, thereby remaining loyal to the party while behaving disloyally toward workers, or resisting the reforms, thereby remaining loyal to workers while behaving disloyally toward the party.[2]

Exit and Voice in Party-Union Relations

Borrowing from Albert Hirschman's seminal work, *Exit, Voice, and Loyalty* (1970), I contend that labor leaders faced with a loyalty dilemma will choose among three strategies: (1) demand-making that conforms to the norms governing their interaction with the party *(norm-based voice)*; (2) demand-making that violates the norms governing their interaction with the party *(norm-breaking voice)*; or (3) defection from the alliance *(exit)*.[3] Hirschman posits exit and voice as alternative responses by customers of a firm or members of an organization to a decline in the quality of the goods and services they are receiving. Exit occurs when they abandon their relationship with the firm or organization altogether. Voice occurs when they make "any attempt to change, rather than to escape from, an objectionable state of affairs" (30). Hirschman finds that exit is the most likely response because it is relatively costless and straightforward. Once an individual has gathered information about alternative products and organizations, he or she can exit without investing in political resources or organizing collectively. Voice, by contrast, "is costly and conditioned on the influence and bargaining power customers and members bring to bear within the firm from which they buy or the organization to which they belong" (30).

Labor leaders face an analogous set of choices when the party places them in a loyalty dilemma. Unlike the atomized individuals in Hirschman's model, however, they are likely to find voice less costly than exit. Exit is discouraged by the uncertainty and risk associated with abandoning regularized patterns of interaction (Stinchcombe 1968, 123). Voice, meanwhile, is facilitated by the norms of behavior and channels of communication already built into the alliance. Conforming to established norms is likely to be much less costly than violating them, and uncertainty surrounding the application of voice is likely to be lowered by previous episodes of responsiveness by the party.

In addition, the small number of actors in a party-union alliance is likely to raise both the resonance of voice and the costs of exit. In part, this is true because exit by a single actor (for example, the union) will lead to a collapse of the alliance, whereas organizations or firms can usually withstand the defection of numerous members or customers. Assuming the party still wants to preserve the alliance, this possibility lends greater weight to the threat of exit, thereby enhancing the effectiveness of voice. By the same token, exit itself cannot be undertaken quietly or inconspicuously. It is inevitably a loud, political act. Combined with the greater creativity required to exit, these factors are likely to make voice the default option for labor leaders faced with a loyalty dilemma.

Because of alliance norms, however, these leaders have the possibility of more than one kind of voice. The default option, which I call norm-based voice, involves tactics that conform to the norms that have emerged to govern the management of negotiation and conflict in the alliance. But if these tactics fail to elicit the desired response, disaffected labor leaders can choose a second option that falls short of exit. This option, which I call norm-breaking voice, violates alliance norms but does not constitute abandonment of the relationship. In fact, it is likely to coexist with norm-based voice on other issues or at other moments of time. Thus, while risky, norm-breaking voice does not dispense entirely with the regularized patterns of interaction that have historically served these leaders so well. It is only when this kind of voice falls on deaf ears that they are likely to resort to exit.

Exit ends the union's commitment to the norms that have guided its interaction with the party and therefore constitutes the ultimate act of disloyalty toward the party. But it does not mean that labor leaders stop negotiating with the party or the government. As Hirschman recognizes, there are cases in which "the alternative is . . . not so much between voice and exit as between voice from within and voice from without (after exit)" (1970, 104). This situation exists when the deteriorating products are public rather than private goods, which means "there is no *escape* from consuming them unless one were to leave the community by which they are provided" (101). Among the public goods delivered by parties in government are policies that generally affect workers and unions. Neither labor leaders nor their followers can escape the consequences of these policies, regardless of whether or not they are allied with the party. Thus, they are likely to engage in "voice after exit" and continue to negotiate deals with the party in government. But rather than being embedded in diffuse commitments of mutual support, these deals will take the form of ad hoc, issue-specific, and highly contingent exchanges between nonaffiliated organizations.

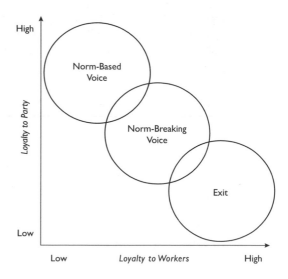

Figure 2.1 Different Combinations of Loyalty and Disloyalty

As illustrated in figure 2.1, each of these three strategies implies a different combination of loyalty and disloyalty on the part of labor leaders. If they limit their resistance to norm-based voice even after the party has refused to meet their demands, they behave loyally toward the party but are disloyal to workers. If they move to norm-breaking voice, they engage in discrete acts of disloyalty toward the party while partially restoring their loyalty to workers. If they resort to exit, they commit the ultimate act of disloyalty toward the party while demonstrating their loyalty to workers.

Divergent Responses by Disaffected Labor Leaders

As illustrated in figure 2.2, labor leaders in Mexico, Spain, and Venezuela made very different choices among these three strategies when faced with a loyalty dilemma. In Mexico, from 1982 to 1994, CTM leaders continued to choose norm-based voice even after the party failed to modify its reforms. In the process, they remained loyal to the party while betraying workers. In Spain, UGT leaders moved from norm-based voice (1982–1984) to norm-breaking voice (1985–1988) and then to exit (1989–1993) in response to the party's refusal to meet their demands. Unwilling to betray workers, they committed the ultimate act of disloyalty toward the party by abandoning the alliance altogether. In Venezuela, CTV leaders chose norm-based voice between 1984 and 1988, and then, in 1989, experimented briefly with norm-breaking voice before retreating in 1990 back to norm-based voice. Their vacillation produced a mix of loyalty and disloyalty toward both partners, although the party temporarily alleviated their loyalty dilemma by taking labor's side against its own government.

These divergent responses raise two questions. First, why did labor leaders in all three countries respond initially with the same strategy of norm-based voice? I have already suggested an answer: labor leaders were initially reluctant to abandon the alliance because of the high costs of exit relative to voice and their hopeful expectations regarding the party's behavior. This phenomenon is related to what some scholars call the "Nixon-in-China syndrome" whereby reform losers are willing to give their allies in government the benefit of the doubt despite assaults on established norms or principles (Rodrik 1994, 213). In such a situation, trust and expectations significantly affect the calculus by which actors assess their interests. Those who believe that short-term sacrifices will be compensated by long-term gains are less likely to invest political capital in fighting the sacrifice-inducing policies. It is only when they realize such gains are not forthcoming that they rebel against their former friends.

The second and more complicated question is: why did the strategies of labor leaders diverge over time? I find the answer in two variables: the relative power of the party and workers to punish labor leaders for disloyal behavior,

	Norm-Based Voice	Norm-Breaking Voice	Exit
Mexico (CTM Leaders)	1982–1994		
Venezuela (CTV Leaders)	1984–1988 ⟶ 1990–1993 ⟵	1989	
Spain (UGT Leaders)	1982–1984 ⟶	1985–1988 ⟶	1989–1993

Figure 2.2 Labor Leader Responses to Market Reforms

and the party's capacity to act autonomously from its own government. The first variable shapes the incentives of labor leaders to choose sides in a loyalty dilemma. Labor leaders who are exposed to punishment by the party but protected from backlash by workers are likely to resolve their loyalty dilemma in favor of the party. By contrast, labor leaders who are protected from punishment by the party but vulnerable to dissent and defection by workers are likely to resolve their loyalty dilemma in favor of workers. The power of the party and workers to punish labor leaders varies depending on how certain institutional arrangements are configured.

The punishing power of the party and workers has a decisive impact on the fate of a party-union alliance until and unless the party intervenes to resolve the loyalty dilemma. The adoption of market reforms is not the party's last act; rather, it initiates a dynamic interaction between the party and the union that may alter the loyalty dilemma itself. The party's elected officials could reverse their reforms in favor of more labor-friendly policies, thereby erasing the contradiction between support for the party and support for workers. Alternatively, the party could oppose its own government and join labor in resisting the reforms, which is a more likely outcome in countries where unions lack the leverage to induce the government to make fundamental changes in its economic policies. Even in the absence of policy changes, this situation would eliminate the loyalty dilemma because labor leaders could now side with workers without behaving disloyally toward the party.

The likelihood of the latter outcome depends on a second variable: the party's degree of autonomy from its own government. Like the power to punish, party autonomy is grounded in institutional arrangements. If party leaders or militants are able (and willing) to join labor in resisting the reforms, labor leaders will no longer be in a loyalty dilemma and therefore do not have to worry about being punished for disloyal behavior. But if party leaders or militants cannot (or will not) challenge their own government, labor leaders must choose sides. Their choice will depend on an assessment of who can punish them more severely for disloyalty.

Institutional Foundations of Punishing Power

Punishment occurs when one actor withholds or withdraws something of value to another actor. Most labor leaders place a high value on access to leadership posts, union financing, their union's importance in the labor movement, control over union decisions, and influence over government policy. Some labor leaders may also value leadership privileges, such as elected office, independently of their impact on other desired outcomes. I find that the relative capacity of the party and workers to withhold or withdraw these induce-ments depends on four institutional arrangements: (1) the legal framework governing industrial relations; (2) the structure of the labor movement; (3) the type of party system; and (4) the party's mechanisms for filling party posts.[4] Whereas the first two affect the punishing power of both the party and work-ers, the last two are of relevance primarily to the party.

The legal framework, which includes the labor code and union statutes, has a major impact on the punishing power of the party because it establishes the extent of state intervention in labor affairs, including union formation, leader-ship selection, union financing, collective bargaining, strike activity, scope of membership, and dispute settlement. A party governing under a labor code that gives the state extensive authority in these areas will have more power to punish labor leaders than a party governing under a labor code that restricts state involvement in union affairs.

The legal framework affects the punishing power of workers by shaping their access to voice and exit. Workers who are covered by a labor code and union statutes that give them a meaningful role in selecting union leaders, protect them against retaliation for expressing dissent, allow them to switch allegiances to a competing union, and enable them to control inducements that labor leaders may want to deliver to the party—such as wage restraint, industrial peace, or working-class votes—will have significant power to pun-ish labor leaders for disloyal behavior. By contrast, workers who are covered by a labor code and union statutes that create high barriers to exit and deny them the capacity or freedom to express dissent, select leaders, and control induce-ments will have little leverage against disloyal leaders.

Another institutional arrangement that shapes the punishing power of both the party and workers is the structure of the labor movement. María Vic-toria Murillo (2001) identifies two key features of this structure: union com-petition for members and party competition for union leaders. Although both features are partly products of the legal framework, they also reflect historical struggles within the labor movement. The first feature, which "refers to the ri-valry among unions for the representation of workers in the same sector" (16), primarily affects the punishing power of workers. If a union has a monopoly of representation in its respective domain, workers will have nowhere else to go if they become disgruntled with their leaders. By contrast, if the union faces competition—and the labor code allows it—workers can punish disloyal labor leaders by exiting to a rival union.

Party competition, which refers to the distribution of partisan affiliations in the labor movement, primarily affects the punishing power of the party. As Murillo notes, party competition interacts with union competition. A party

with a monopoly of partisan affiliation but only one ally in the labor movement will have less power to punish than a party with multiple and competing allies, which can threaten to shift inducements to rival unions. This interaction works somewhat differently in the case of a labor movement divided
along partisan lines. If partisan competition takes place *within* a hegemonic
union, the party will not be able to employ divide-and-conquer strategies and
may be constrained from punishing disloyal labor leaders because of incom-
plete control over union affairs. If partisan competition takes place *among* competing unions, the party's power to punish will depend on the capacity and
willingness of rival parties to offer the same inducements to labor leaders that
the party is threatening to withhold.

There are two other institutional arrangements that affect the party's capacity to manipulate inducements of value to labor leaders. One is the type of
party system, which involves the number of parties, the degree of electoral
volatility, and the advantages that accompany a party's control of the state.[5] A
hegemonic party that has been in power for many years will control greater resources than a party that has spent decades in exile or must share power with
other parties. Likewise, a party with the discretionary authority to withdraw
benefits once granted will enjoy significantly more power to punish than a
party restricted to using inducements as a bargaining chip only prior to their
delivery. Both of these factors are affected, moreover, by the benefits that ac-
crue from the party's control of the state. Controlling a weak state in an economy dominated by private interests will bring the party far fewer resources
than controlling a strong state capable of imposing its will on domestic and
foreign actors.

Another institutional arrangement that affects the party's power to punish,
although less crucially, is the party's set of mechanisms for filling party posts.
Affiliated labor leaders are likely to have an interest in two kinds of posts: appointments to the party's governing bodies and candidacies for elected office.
If party leaders control access to these posts, they will have the power to punish disloyal labor leaders, particularly those who place a high value on leadership privileges. But if labor leaders, voters, the party rank-and-file, or other
actors control such access, party leaders will be unable to withhold these inducements as punishment for disloyalty.

Institutional Foundations of Party Autonomy

Two institutional arrangements shape the party's degree of autonomy from
its own government: the location of supreme authority within the party and
the intraparty spaces for dissent. The location of supreme authority affects the
capacity of the chief executive elected under the party's banner to control the

party after taking office. If he or she serves as the party's highest authority, the party will be severely constrained from acting autonomously from the government. But if this authority is located elsewhere, such as the party's national executive committee, the party may be able to pursue an independent course of action, at least temporarily.

Even if the chief executive is the party's highest authority, the party may still be able to alleviate labor's loyalty dilemma if internal dissidents or factions can mount an independent challenge to the government and thereby redefine what constitutes loyalty to the party. This possibility is determined by mechanisms such as electoral rules affecting the influence of minority groupings, rules governing party factions, penalties for violating party discipline in the legislature, and control of party finances and candidacies. If these mechanisms favor dissent or factionalism, labor leaders may be able to cultivate allies within the party who can block or at least question the policies of the government and/or the party leadership.

Power and Autonomy in Mexico, Spain, and Venezuela

Different configurations of these institutional arrangements in Mexico, Spain, and Venezuela produced different responses by disaffected labor leaders. In Mexico, CTM leaders were forced to choose between the party and workers because the PRI lacked sufficient autonomy to challenge its own government. They sided with the party because they feared punishment by the party more than punishment by workers. This decision translated into a strategy of norm-based voice throughout the reform period. In Spain, UGT leaders also faced a united front of the party and the government, but they were more vulnerable to punishment by workers than by the party. Thus, they moved from norm-based voice to norm-breaking voice to exit during the reform period.

Venezuela is the only case in which the party had sufficient autonomy to take an independent stand against its own government. The party initially chose not to exercise this autonomy, which left CTV leaders in a loyalty dilemma. Faced with credible threats of punishment from both workers and the party, CTV leaders vacillated between collaboration and resistance. At one point CTV leaders and experimented with norm-breaking voice, but the experiment was short-lived because AD joined them in opposition to the Pérez administration, alleviating the loyalty dilemma. Although the party subsequently reimposed limits on the CTV, this experiment facilitated the CTV's retreat back to norm-based voice by providing an opportunity for loyal combativeness and extracting several pro-labor concessions from the government.

CHAPTER 3
Loyalties Under Stress

For much of the twentieth century, labor-backed parties and their union allies enjoyed a relatively favorable socioeconomic environment for sustaining mutually reinforcing bonds of loyalty. First, the parties could make credible commitments to deliver benefits to unions and workers in the context of Keynesian demand management, limited global competition, and the Bretton Woods system of fixed exchange rates. These conditions gave governments a compelling rationale to use public investment, public sector employment, and welfare spending to counteract fluctuations in demand and increase the purchasing power of workers. In addition, macroeconomic stability and trade protection made employers more willing to negotiate higher wages and benefits, provide job security, and accept rigid work rules. In this context, labor-backed parties constructed Keynesian welfare states in western Europe and demand-driven models of import substitution industrialization (ISI) in Latin America. Although they sometimes retreated from their commitments in times of economic crisis, they usually returned to pro-labor policies once the crisis had passed, thereby reinforcing labor's expectations that the party would remain loyal.

Second, unions could deliver the support and cooperation of workers to the party. Fordist mass production generalized the interests of the working class, created a relatively large group of semiskilled workers in key manufacturing sectors, and focused collective bargaining on quantifiable issues such as wages, benefits, and working hours (Howell and Daley 1992–93, 5–6; Pontusson 1992, 26–28; Regini 1987, 89).[1] Although Fordism made only partial inroads in Latin America, many of these same advantages existed in the areas of natural resource extraction and public monopolies such as electric utilities, telecommunications, and railroads, which often employed a sizable share of the formal workforce.[2] As a relatively homogeneous group in stable work roles, these workers tended to identify strongly with each other and with the union claiming to represent them (Pérez Díaz 1987, 120). They also tended to be geographically concentrated, which reinforced class identities and made it easier for the union to monitor compliance with economic and political directives. In addition, they relied quite heavily on the union for economic and political information. These conditions helped the unions deliver on their promises to the party, even during times of economic hardship.

The party-union alliances in Mexico, Spain, and Venezuela were constructed in this context. They each grew out of battles against more conservative elites, which led first to creation of the party and then to creation of the union, largely at the initiative of party leaders. In Mexico, the alliance between the PRI and the CTM emerged from a struggle among competing generals to determine who would reconstruct the political system after the Mexican Revolution. In 1929, Plutarcho Elías Calles founded the National Revolutionary Party (PNR) to impose central control over potential challengers to the postrevolutionary order. Far from being a creation of the PNR, the CTM grew out of a showdown between Calles, who had run the state from behind the scenes since 1928, and Lázaro Cárdenas, who became president in 1934 and challenged Calles's authority by supporting a wave of strikes. The CTM was founded in 1936 after Cárdenas prevailed over Calles, but it was not until Cárdenas transformed the PNR into the Party of the Mexican Revolution (PRM) in 1938 that the alliance was truly forged. In contrast to the PNR, which was little more than a club of Calles loyalists, the PRM adopted the slogan of "workers' democracy" and incorporated unions directly into its organizational structure. The CTM hailed the PRM as Mexico's "first truly popular party" (CTM 1942, 484) and began to construct a dense network of exchanges with the party, which became the PRI in 1946.

In Spain, the alliance between the PSOE and the UGT emerged out of a struggle against a dictatorial regime in the late nineteenth century. A group of Madrid printers created the PSOE in secret in 1879 and then refounded it as a legal organization after the government restored the right of association in 1881. From the beginning, PSOE leaders believed that they should have an ally in the labor movement. After differences with the anarchists derailed an effort to unify all Spanish workers in 1882, the Socialists created the UGT in 1888 out of an alliance between the Socialist printers' unions and other nonanarchist groupings (Brenan 1978, 217). The founder of both organizations, Pablo Iglesias, defended a policy of "concentric circles" whereby the party would serve as the inner core for political action, and the union would serve as the larger mass organization (Maravall 1992, 7). Although the PSOE was in government only briefly during the 1930s, it developed dense organizational linkages with the UGT and consistently promised to adopt pro-labor policies if given another chance to govern. After surviving over three decades of exile and repression under General Francisco Franco, both organizations staged a remarkable comeback inside Spain during the 1970s.

In Venezuela, as in Spain, the alliance between AD and the CTV grew out of a struggle against a dictatorial regime. Rómulo Betancourt and other members of the "Generation of '28" founded AD in 1941 as part of an ongoing struggle to topple the military government of Juan Vicente Gómez.[3] When political liberalization began to take place after Gómez's death in 1935, AD leaders encountered "an organizational vacuum full of potential recruits" in the country's growing working class (Levine 1978, 86). They rushed to fill this vacuum by organizing their own unions loyal to the party. But, unlike the PSOE, they did not unify their labor allies into a single, national organization until after they had taken control of the state. Two years after joining with junior military officers to stage a pro-democracy coup in 1945, AD leaders presided over the creation of a national labor confederation that unified nearly all of Venezuela's unions, the majority of which supported AD. Although this confederation collapsed after a counter-coup by Marco Pérez Jiménez in 1948, the restoration of democracy ten years later enabled AD and the other major parties to create the CTV in 1959. The confederation and the party developed a complex set of linkages over the years.

Although the principles and norms that sustained these party-union alliances varied across cases, they all involved a bargain whereby the union served as a key pillar of support for the party in return for the party's delivery (or promise) of extensive benefits in the socioeconomic, political, and organizational arenas. These bargains created virtuous circles of loyalty among the party, unions, and workers. The favorable conditions for sustaining these virtuous circles began to deteriorate in the late twentieth century, however. Labor-backed parties found themselves managing serious economic crises in an international context that was no longer amenable to state-led development. Many of them responded with economic reforms that created loyalty dilemmas for their labor allies.

The PRI, the PSOE, and AD were not exceptions. Beginning in the 1980s, they abandoned their historic commitment to state interventionist policies and imposed austerity and market reforms on their economies. The stress these policies placed on party-union alliances turned out to be qualitatively different than in the past, since the parties were rejecting alliance principles as well as many of their exchange obligations. Rather than reinforcing labor's loyalty by confirming expectations that the parties would retreat from painful policies, as in earlier episodes of alliance stress, these policies placed labor leaders in loyalty dilemmas. They had to decide whether to remain loyal to their parties despite dramatic, and most likely irreversible, declines in the benefits they accrued from the alliances.

Breaking the Virtuous Circle of Loyalty

Table 3.1 divides the reforms adopted by the PRI, the PSOE, and AD into four policy areas: stabilization, deregulation, industrial restructuring, and social welfare reform. The table then scores the degree of market reform in each country in four policy areas. The scores for each type of reform range from 0 (no reform) to 3 (extensive reform). The higher a country's total score, the more overall reform took place. Thus, Mexico experienced the most reform (31), followed by Spain (26), and then Venezuela (23). Although the degree of reform is not equivalent to the level of hardship experienced by workers and unions, all four types of reform exposed organized labor to painful sacrifices.[4] Stabilization brought declines in real wages and social spending; deregulation and industrial restructuring threatened employment and job security; and social welfare reform jeopardized the quantity and/or security of workers' benefits. By pursuing these reforms, the parties broke the virtuous circles of loyalty that had previously sustained their alliances with labor. As a result, their labor allies had to choose between loyalty to the parties and loyalty to workers.

From Stabilization to Structural Reform in Mexico

The PRI's development strategy of import substitution industrialization began to develop serious problems in the 1970s in the form of chronic trade and fiscal deficits, inflationary pressures, and industries incapable of responding effectively to increased global competition. At first, the PRI was able to paper over these cracks with high oil revenues and massive foreign loans. But the whole edifice came crashing down when these external resources dried up in the early 1980s. Plummeting oil prices, rising interest rates, and an abrupt halt in international lending brought Mexico to the brink of default on its foreign debt and plunged the country into its worst recession since the 1930s. In 1982, the economy contracted for the first time in fifty years, annual inflation approached 100 percent, and real wages declined by over 5 percent (Grayson 1990, table 9; Lustig 1998, table 2.4, table 3.2). Thus, when Miguel De la Madrid took office in December 1982, he faced the task of bringing the Mexican economy under control.

Immediately after his inauguration, he announced a "shock treatment" of devaluation and austerity, which was laid out in the Program of Immediate Economic Reorganization (PIRE). Despite its initial success in containing the fiscal and current account deficits and restoring moderate economic growth in 1984, the PIRE failed to resolve the crisis. Prices continued to escalate, and even the PIRE's modest gains vanished when falling oil prices contributed to another balance-of-payments crisis in mid-1985. To make matters worse, Mexico City suffered a devastating earthquake in September 1985, which placed additional stress on public finances.

The government responded by combining another round of harsh austerity measures with structural reforms. Hoping that cheaper foreign goods would put a ceiling on domestic prices, De la Madrid and his advisors began to liberalize Mexico's trade regime. They removed import licensing requirements on about 37 percent of the total value of Mexico's imports in July 1985, launched a unilateral tariff reduction program in early 1986, and joined the General Agreement on Tariffs and Trade (GATT) in August 1986 (Bennett 1988, 1989–91). To dampen objections from the private sector, they also promised to merge, liquidate, or sell nonstrategic firms in the public sector. Between 1982 and 1988, the government liquidated, privatized, or decentralized over seven hundred public enterprises (Lustig 1998, 105). Although most of these firms were of minor importance, they included a huge steel conglomerate

Table 3.1 Type and Degree of Market Reform, 1982–1994

Policy area	Reform	Mexico	Spain	Venezuela
Stabilization	Devaluation	3	2	3
	Wage austerity	3	2	3
	Fiscal austerity	3	2	1
	Tight monetary policy	3	3	1
Deregulation	Trade liberalization	3	3	3
	Price liberalization	2	2	3
	Foreign investment deregulation	2	1	2
	Labor market flexibilization*	2	3	1
Industrial restructuring	Privatization/liquidation	2	2	1
	Rationalization	2	3	2
	Financial reform	2	1	1
Welfare reform	Elimination of general subsidies	3	0	2
	Pension reform	1	2	0
TOTAL SCORE		31	26	23

Notes: Scoring for degree of policy change: 3 = high; 2 = medium; 1 = low; 0 = none or not relevant.
*These scores include de facto as well as de jure labor market flexibilization.

(Fundidora Monterrey), a diesel engine firm (DINA), and parts of the sugar industry (Schneider 1990, 331; Alvarez Béjar 1991, 42). The government also replaced general subsidies for staples such as tortillas with targeted subsidies that reached a much smaller number of consumers (Lustig 1998, 86).

These reforms resolved the balance-of-payments crisis and helped restore Mexico's credibility with external lenders, but inflation continued to spiral upward, reflecting a further deterioration in Mexico's external position and the questionable effectiveness of tariff reduction in controlling prices. When a stock market crash and another peso devaluation in October 1987 threatened to unleash hyperinflation, the government added a third ingredient—a comprehensive incomes policy—to its mix of austerity and structural reform. In December 1987, representatives from government, business, labor, and the peasantry signed an Economic Solidarity Pact *(Pacto)* that mandated a flexible exchange rate, continuing fiscal austerity and trade liberalization, moderate price increases, and wage increases far below the rate of inflation (CSE 1994, 285). Although intended as a temporary measure to break the inflationary cycle, the government renegotiated the *Pacto* periodically over the next decade.

The *Pacto* finally halted the inflation that had been plaguing Mexico since the early 1980s. Mexico's yearly inflation rate fell from 154 percent in 1988 to 24 percent in 1989 to 7 percent in 1994 (INEGI 2000). Greater price stability contributed to an economic recovery during the first year of the new administration of Carlos Salinas. Rather than backing away from market reform as the crisis subsided, however, Salinas accelerated it. Convinced that a sustainable recovery depended on integrating Mexico into the global economy and shifting the locus of growth from the public to the private sector, he adopted a comprehensive package of structural reforms while maintaining strict macroeconomic discipline.

Many of these reforms took the form of deregulation and industrial restructuring. Between 1989 and 1994, Salinas liberalized Mexico's foreign investment regulations, sold off more than three billion dollars' worth of public enterprises (including two leading airlines, a historic mining company, and the telephone monopoly), reprivatized the commercial banks, deregulated parts of the trucking, fishing, pharmaceuticals, mining, commodities, finance, and telecommunications industries, and negotiated a North American Free Trade Agreement (NAFTA) with the United States and Canada. These reforms prompted major restructuring in the private sector, as firms laid off workers and renegotiated more flexible collective contracts in an effort to compete in a more open economy.

Salinas also reformed several aspects of Mexico's social welfare system. First, he continued De la Madrid's practice of replacing general subsidies available to all workers with targeted subsidies for the very poor, most of whom were in the informal economy. Second, he created the National Solidarity Program (Pronasol), a new social welfare program that bypassed traditional party and organizational channels to deliver benefits directly to poor consumers. Finally, he sought to create private insurance schemes for pensions and workers' housing. Although he withdrew an ambitious proposal to transform Mexico's entire social security system, he proceeded with plans to create the System of Retirement Savings (SAR), an individual pension fund administered by private banks to complement the existing financial structure of the Mexican Social Security Institute (IMSS). He also reformed the National Worker Housing Institute (Infonavit) to establish more technocratic criteria for distributing housing construction contracts and assigning workers' housing credits.

The PRI's reforms had a devastating impact on the living standards of workers, particularly during the De la Madrid administration. Between 1983 and 1988, real wage income per worker fell by over 40 percent, and the real minimum wage lost nearly 50 percent of its value. Not surprisingly, the share of income going to the middle sectors, including organized workers, declined for the first time since 1963, from 52.9 percent in 1984 to 49.2 percent in 1989 (Lustig 1998, 78–79 table 3.2). The situation improved somewhat during the Salinas administration, but most workers did not regain the ground they lost in the 1980s. Table 3.2 shows that both the minimum wage and contracted wages continued to decline, despite the dramatic fall in inflation, after

Table 3.2 Real Daily Income in Mexico, 1980–1995 (1995 pesos)

Year	General Minimum Wage	Average Contractual Wage	Average Manufacturing Income
1980	47.66	60.51	162.26
1981	48.35	61.83	169.11
1982	42.73	67.67	166.26
1983	35.42	49.09	127.66
1984	33.22	47.22	119.67
1985	32.76	47.43	121.50
1986	30.30	54.17	112.68
1987	28.11	67.89	112.93
1988	24.63	41.88	110.61
1989	23.15	40.47	120.44
1990	20.98	38.50	124.74
1991	20.04	38.92	132.13
1992	19.15	37.74	143.41
1993	18.86	37.72	149.50
1994	18.86	37.14	155.33
1995	16.43	29.76	133.60

Adapted from Dávila Capalleja 1997, tables 10.2, 10.3.

Table 3.3 Annual Unemployment in Mexico, 1982–1994

Year	Unemployment Rate (%)
1982	4.2
1983	6.3
1984	5.7
1985	4.3
1986	4.3
1987	3.9
1988	3.6
1989	3.0
1990	2.8
1991	2.6
1992	2.8
1993	3.4
1994	3.7
1995	6.3

Adapted from Lustig 1998, table 3.3; Zedillo 1997, archive 038.

1988. The *Pacto* played an important role in enforcing wage austerity even in the context of economic recovery.

Trends were similar, if less dire, on the job front. From 1982 to 1988, total industrial employment fell by 6 percent, resulting in a net loss of 305,000 jobs. Although the open unemployment rate averaged only 4.6 percent during this period, implicit unemployment reached 20.5 percent in 1985.[5] The rate of industrial job growth picked up considerably between 1989 and 1991 but then declined in all sectors except construction. By 1993, the manufacturing sector had experienced a net loss of 180,00 jobs since 1982 (Nacional Financiera 1995). Table 3.3 shows the impact of these trends on the rates of unemployment and underemployment, both of which worsened in the early 1990s after a few years of improvement. In addition, the share of urban workers working in firms with fewer than six employees grew from 38.6 percent in 1987 to 42.2 percent in 1994 (INEGI 1995).

Finally, Mexican workers suffered from drastic cuts in social spending, particularly in the 1980s. Between 1983 and 1988, real social spending declined by an annual average rate of 6.5 percent, resulting in a cumulative decline of 40 percent per capita during this period (Lustig 1998, table 3.7). Although real per capita social spending was 3 percent higher between 1990 and 1993 than it had been between 1982 and 1989, it remained 26 percent below the level it had been between 1980 and 1982 (USAID 1996). Moreover, a sizable share of the increased social spending went to programs targeted to the rural and urban poor, many of whom worked in the informal sector and presumably did not belong to unions. Between 1989 and 1994, the average annual rate of growth of spending in the traditional areas of education, health, and labor was less than 3 percent, compared to 6 percent for total social spending (Lustig 1998, table 8.5).

Austerity and Restructuring in Spain

The economic crisis in Spain came on more gradually than in Mexico but had similar causes and symptoms. Just as Spain was making a transition to democracy in the mid-1970s, the global energy crisis converged with structural rigidities inherited from the dictatorship of Francisco Franco. Unable to adjust quickly, the economy experienced growing rates of inflation and unemployment, high current account deficits, industrial overproduction, and stagnant levels of growth and investment. The first democratic government, led by the conservative Union of the Democratic Center (UCD), took steps to liberalize the financial system, increase the government's tax base, reduce inflation, and increase labor market flexibility. But the challenge of consolidating a still-fragile democracy, along with party infighting and a weak position in parliament, inhibited the UCD from addressing the most serious rigidities inherited from Franco (Bermeo 1994).

Particularly in the context of worldwide recession, the UCD's limited reforms were not sufficient to turn the Spanish economy around. Between 1977 and 1982, the economy stagnated, investment continued falling, fiscal and trade deficits increased, annual inflation persisted at around 15 percent, and unemployment rose from 7.4 percent to 16.5 percent (Segura 1990, 59–60; Lopez-Claros 1988, 5). Notwithstanding the UCD's progress in modernizing public finances and containing the inflationary spiral, the PSOE inherited an economy in serious trouble when its candidate, Felipe González, won the national elections in October 1982.

The Socialists adopted a market-oriented program that aimed to overcome the economic crisis and prepare Spain for entry into the European Economic Community (EEC). First, they sought to overcome internal and external disequilibria by controlling inflation, promoting exports, and reducing the budget deficit. Second, they sought to upgrade the productive apparatus through industrial reconversion, energy sector adjustment, labor market flexibilization, and reform of public enterprise and social security. Although they pursued these reforms most rigorously between 1983 and 1985, they continued along the same path even after Spain signed a treaty of adhesion to the EEC in 1985 and began to grow rapidly in 1986.

In an effort to bring inflation down to the EEC rate, the Socialists restricted the money supply, limited public sector salaries, pressured unions to hold down real wage increases, and kept social spending as a share of the gross domestic product (GDP) constant through 1989 despite a marked increase in the number of retirees and unemployed workers (Fernández Marugán 1992, 179, 189). After three years of poor macroeconomic performance, these policies bore fruit. Inflation fell to single digits, the current account returned to surplus, and the economy grew by an average annual rate of five percent between 1987 and 1989 (Köhler 1995, 311). Rather than switching to expansionary policies, however, the Socialists continued to pass relatively austere budgets and to pressure unions to negotiate wages below the expected rate of inflation.

The Socialists also embarked on a program of industrial restructuring. The

1984 Law on Reconversion and Reindustrialization targeted 791 firms in eleven sectors for reconversion, with an estimated loss of 830,000 jobs. The Socialists hoped to soften the blow to workers and communities by creating the Fund for the Promotion of Employment (FPE) to provide unemployment benefits and retraining to excess workers, and Zones of Urgent Reindustrialization (ZURs) to assist hard-hit regions (Navarro 1990, 116–18; Fernández Marugán 1992, 157). Approximately 85 percent of the anticipated job losses took place by the end of 1987, with two-thirds occurring in the steel, shipbuilding, and textile sectors (Lopez-Claros 1988, 19). Another round of reconversions began in 1987 in the specialty steel and mining sectors.

The Socialists complemented their reconversion program with steps to streamline the National Institute of Industry (INI), which accounted for 15 percent of the country's industrial production at the end of the Franco regime. Between 1983 and 1985, they focused on halting the practice of using the public sector to rescue failing private firms.[6] After 1985, they directed their efforts toward privatizing existing state-owned enterprises. Between 1984 and 1986, they sold off or dissolved more than thirty firms (Bermeo 1990, 140). They subsequently adopted plans to privatize large firms such as Iberia (airline), Repsol (oil), Argentaria (banking), and Teneo (industry) (Dehesa 1994, 132).

The Socialists also sought to enhance the competitiveness of Spanish industry by deregulating the labor market and containing the costs of social security. In 1984, the parliament passed a law that created fourteen different kinds of employment contracts, most of which involved short-term work, exempted employers from paying full wages and benefits, and did not protect workers against dismissal (Palacio Morena 1991, 317–19). The following year, the parliament passed a pension reform that increased the period during which workers had to contribute, raised the amount of income on which they had to make contributions, and tied the size of pensions to average wages over the last eight years rather than the last two. In 1988, the government attempted and failed to adopt a Youth Employment Plan (PEJ) to provide employment for 800,000 youths over a three-year period by reducing employers' social security contributions and fixing wages at the statutory minimum (Rhodes 1997, 116). Finally, in late 1993, the government approved a labor law reform that liberalized restrictions on dismissals and effectively resurrected the PEJ (Rhodes 1997, 108–9).

As in Mexico, the party's reforms imposed painful sacrifices on workers, particularly at the beginning of the reform period. As illustrated in table 3.4, real wages declined by nearly 6 percent from 1983 to 1986, a loss from which workers did not recover until 1991.[7] In the process, the share of national income earned by salaried workers fell from 53.2 percent in 1982 to 50.3 percent in 1987 (Sabando Suárez et al. 1989, 58). Even after real wages began to recover in 1987, their annual rate of growth remained far below the high profit rates enjoyed by business and the 5 percent growth rate of the overall economy.

Table 3.5 shows that unemployment among Spanish work-

Table 3.4 Inflation and Wage Increases (%) in Spain, 1983–1992

Year	Annual Inflation	Contracted Wage Increases	Real Wage Increases
	(a)	(b)	(b–a)
1983	12.2	11.44	-0.76
1984	11.3	7.81	-3.49
1985	8.8	7.9	-0.9
1986	8.8	8.23	-0.57
1987	5.2	6.51	1.31
1988	4.8	6.38	1.58
1989	6.8	7.77	0.97
1990	6.7	8.33	1.63
1991	5.9	7.96	2.06
1992	5.9	7.27	1.37

Data from MTSS 1983–1992; *Anuario El País* 1993.

ers was much higher than for workers in Mexico. Partly as a result of industrial restructuring, the unemployment rate grew from 16.2 percent in 1982 to 21.9 percent in 1985. It fell back to around 16 percent in the early 1990s only to return to levels above 20 percent in 1993. Although these figures should be treated with caution given the prevalence of unemployment insurance fraud in Spain, the job prospects of Spanish workers, particularly those under the age of 25, clearly suffered. Moreover, employment became more precarious. In the two years after the 1984 labor law reform, limited duration contracts grew by 24 percent, part-time contracts by 44 percent, and apprenticeship and training contracts by 51 percent (Lopez-Claros 1988, 26–27). As a share of total employment, temporary contracts increased from 15.6 percent in 1987 to 30 percent in 1990 and 33 percent in 1992 (Tuñon de Lara 1992, 503).

In contrast to their Mexican counterparts, who had no unemployment insurance, Spanish workers received some compensation for being laid off, especially if they were in sectors undergoing industrial reconversion.[8] The resources devoted to unemployment compensation grew by 24.9 percent between 1985 and 1986 and by at least 10 percent each year through 1989 (Bermeo 1994, 618). Reflecting the dramatic growth in unemployment, however, the

Table 3.5 Annual Unemployment in Spain, 1982–1996

Year	Unemployment Rate (%)
1982	16.2
1983	17.7
1984	20.6
1985	21.9
1986	21.5
1987	20.6
1988	19.5
1989	17.3
1990	16.3
1991	16.3
1992	18.4
1993	22.7
1994	24.2
1995	22.9
1996	22.2

Data from MTAS 1982–1996; *Anuario El País* 1983–1992

share of jobless workers covered by unemployment insurance fell from 48.7 percent in 1980 to 26.3 percent in 1983 and remained below 40 percent until 1990 (Burgess 1999, fig. 2).The number of beneficiaries of public pensions, education, and health services increased by 8.2 million between 1982 and 1989, but the quality of these benefits in many cases declined. With regard to pensions, the 1985 reform contributed to an increase in the number and volume of employee contributions and a decline in the annual average rate of growth of disability pensions from 8.5 percent between 1981 and 1985 to 2.5 percent between 1985 and 1986 (Lopez-Claros 1988, 27). In other words, workers had to pay more into the system at the same time that they were receiving fewer benefits.

From Stop-and-Go Austerity to Radical Reform in Venezuela

In Venezuela, as in Mexico, serious cracks in the government's economic strategy began showing in the 1970s but did not become chasms until oil prices collapsed and interest rates in the United States skyrocketed in the early 1980s. The downward slide began in earnest during the administration of Luis Herrera Campins, of the Social Christian Party of Venezuela (COPEI). Between 1979 and 1982, gross fixed investment by the private sector plummeted, the economy grew by an annual average of only 0.7 percent, Venezuela's foreign debt grew to $35 billion, and average income fell by 18 percent (Palma 1989, 191; Chávez 1988, 29; Valecillos 1992, 142). Between 1979 and 1984, the number of people living in urban slums increased by 44 percent, reaching 56 percent of the total urban population (Naím 1993, 43–44).

Faced with a serious balance-of-payments crisis in early 1983, Herrera Campins allowed the bolívar to float against the dollar, causing a 75 percent drop in purchasing power in just one day (Ellner 1993, 65). Soon thereafter, he imposed price and exchange controls. Although these controls helped contain inflation, the country continued to do poorly on other macroeconomic indicators. In 1983, the economy shrank by 5.6 percent, imports fell by more than half, and open unemployment rose from 7 to 10 percent (Palma 1989, 194, 200). When AD's Jaime Lusinchi took the reigns of power from COPEI in February 1984, he found himself at the helm of a deeply troubled economy.

Like De la Madrid in Mexico and González in Spain, Lusinchi adopted a strict stabilization plan upon taking office. Although unwilling to sign a formal pact with the International Monetary Fund (IMF), he adopted several of the IMF's recommended policies, including a tight monetary policy and a severe contraction in public spending, particularly in the area of public salaries.

As in Mexico and Spain, these policies had a salutary effect on the country's external and internal accounts. In 1985, the government ran a budget surplus and enjoyed a one-third increase in its international reserves. After only a year of austerity, however, Lusinchi diverged from the pattern established in Mexico and Spain, where the governments persisted with macroeconomic stabilization despite an easing of the crisis. Instead, Lusinchi returned to the AD's traditional policies of demand stimulation based on public spending and an increase in the money supply. Moreover, he never introduced structural reforms to address Venezuela's heavy dependence on oil exports and public financing.

These policies spurred an economic recovery during the last three years of Lusinchi's administration despite a 50 percent decline in oil prices in 1986. The economy grew at an average annual rate of 5.3 percent between 1986 and 1988, and the rate of open unemployment fell from 13.1 percent in 1985 to 7.3 percent in 1988. But this reactivation came at the price of growing public deficits, a deteriorating external position, and rising inflation. Between 1985 and 1988, the budget deficit grew to 9 percent of the GDP, and the current account went from a surplus of $3.6 billion to a deficit of $4.7 billion. Meanwhile, annual inflation increased from 11.6 percent in 1986 to 29.5 percent in 1988 (Palma 1989, 231, 226).

By the time AD won another presidential election in December 1988, the country was once again in crisis. AD's new president, Carlos Andrés Pérez, had little choice but to adopt stabilization policies that would impose sacrifices on Venezuelan workers. In February 1989, he signed a letter of intent with the IMF agreeing to correct the country's macroeconomic imbalances in return for approximately $4.5 billion over three years (Kornblith 1995, 80). This time, however, AD went beyond short-term austerity measures to announce a comprehensive reform package. Dubbed "the great turnaround" (el gran viraje), the program called for removing controls on prices and interest rates, liberalizing exchange rates, containing public spending, lowering barriers to trade, eliminating restrictions on foreign investment, privatizing state-owned enterprises, shifting from generalized to targeted subsidies, reforming the tax and financial systems, restructuring social security and pensions, and revising labor legislation.

Relying primarily on his executive decree powers, Pérez launched a significant portion of these reforms during his first two years. Soon after taking office, he eliminated exchange controls, liberalized nearly all prices, raised rates on public services, devalued the bolívar by 170 percent, and freed interest rates (Naím 1993). He also adopted numerous structural reforms. Besides reducing trade barriers and joining the GATT, he removed restrictions on foreign investment in all sectors except oil, mining, and banking (Navarro 1994, 13). He also privatized four commercial banks, the cellular telephone system, a shipyard, and several sugar mills and hotels by 1991. Finally, he shifted the focus of social policy to direct transfer programs, slashed the budget for traditional social services by 32 percent in 1989 and 1990, and eliminated indirect subsidies to firms producing staples such as corn flour, milk, sugar, poultry, and sardines (Márquez 1995; Naím 1993).

After a year of abysmal economic performance, these reforms eased the country's internal and external imbalances and helped spur a recovery.[9] While inflation remained above 30 percent, the economy grew by 6.5 percent in 1990 and 10.4 percent in 1991.[10] Like his predecessor, Pérez took advantage of these improved conditions to pursue more expansionary fiscal policies. But rather than returning to the country's traditional model of state-led growth, he coupled these policies with plans to deepen market reforms in the areas of privatization, severance benefits, tax laws, the social security system, and the banking sector.[11] In 1992, he persuaded Congress to pass legislation on privatization and central bank autonomy. He would have pursued the rest of his reform agenda had it not been stalled by growing social unrest, a brewing rebellion within his own party, two attempted military coups, and, finally, his premature departure from the presidency under charges of corruption in May 1993.

As in Mexico and Spain, the party's reforms in Venezuela imposed painful sacrifices on workers. Table 3.6 shows that workers' incomes fell quite dramatically, particularly between 1988 and 1990. In manufacturing, wages and salaries lost over 50 percent of their value from 1984 to 1994. By 1990, the real wage rate was estimated to be 50.2 percent lower than its highest historical level and below that of 1950. Moreover, wages and salaries accounted for only 39 percent of national income in 1992, compared to 50 percent in 1983 (Lander 1996, 62–63).

Workers also experienced significant job dislocation. Although employment registered net gains from 1984 to 1993, the unemploy-

Table 3.6   Real Income in Venezuela, 1984–1994 (1984 bolivares)

Year	Manufacturing Wages and Salaries	Total Wages, Salaries, and Benefits
1984	37,962	144,371
1985	36,704	146,663
1986	35,353	147,667
1987	31,959	153,545
1988	29,336	155,821
1989	24,566	136,322
1990	21,833	130,778
1991	22,154	140,339
1992	22,545	151,859
1993	21,397	143,052
1994	19,236	130,557

Adapted from http://www.ocei.gov.ve/estadistica/index.htm.

ment rate fluctuated between 7 and 13 percent during this period (see table 3.7). Between 1988 and 1992, the manufacturing share of total employment shrank from 18 percent to 16 percent, with some of the worst losses occurring in labor-intensive activities related to textiles, apparel, leather, food, beverages, and tobacco. In October 1991, the government's unemployment insurance agency reported petitions by 70,000 newly unemployed workers each month (Lander 1996, 61–63). In addition, the use of "atypical" kinds of labor contracts, particularly temporary contracts, became increasingly widespread (Iranzo 1991, 78–79).

Some of these layoffs and contract revisions resulted from industrial restructuring. In 1991, the SIDOR steel complex dismissed three thousand workers, and the National Port Institute liquidated its entire eleven thousand–person workforce. Nearly all of the blue-collar workers subsequently hired by the ports were on temporary contracts (*chanceros*) and did not belong to any union (Ellner 1999b, 122). Privatization of the telephone company, CANTV, led to a reduction of the workforce from 23,000 to 19,600 in the three years after the company was sold in 1991 (Ellner 1999b, 127).

Finally, workers suffered from an overall decline in social spending. Between 1983 and 1990, social spending per capita declined by nearly 40 percent in real terms while social service delivery was plagued by corruption and inefficiency. Although AD refrained from reforming severance benefits or the social security system, the lack of funds and services in public education and healthcare significantly affected Venezuelan workers. Moreover, monthly pensions grew by an average annual rate of only 1 percent in *nominal* terms from 1984 to 1989. Even with a nominal increase of 84 percent in 1990, they lost 65 percent of their value in real terms in these six years.[12]

Table 3.7 Annual Unemployment in Venezuela, 1982–1994

Year	Unemployment Rate (%)
1982	7.1
1983	10.1
1984	13.0
1985	13.1
1986	11.0
1987	9.2
1988	7.3
1989	9.9
1990	10.4
1991	9.5
1992	7.7
1993	6.7
1994	8.7

Adapted from International Labour Organization 2003, Venezuela 3A.

Workers, Unions, and Party Competition

As these narratives suggest, workers in Mexico, Spain, and Venezuela had good reasons to feel betrayed by the parties in government and to demand that union leaders take action against the reforms. By the same token, labor leaders had good reasons to resent the parties' roles in jeopardizing their mediating capacities and organizational privileges by shrinking the state and unleashing market forces. Because of alliance norms, however, they could not take dramatic action against the reforms without behaving disloyally to their parties. In short, they found themselves caught in a loyalty dilemma.

I have argued that the variation in labor leaders' responses to such dilemmas can be explained by the relative power of the party and workers to punish them for disloyal behavior and the party's capacity to act autonomously from its own government. But it is important to consider other variables that might explain the divergent trajectories of labor leaders, particularly the depth and nature of hardship experienced by workers; the degree to which unions suffered a loss of power and privilege; and the availability of a leftist alternative in the party system. As we will see, these variables do not stand up to the empirical evidence. Each one varies across the cases in interesting ways, but none correlates as we might expect with the three outcomes.

It might be reasonable to assume that the divergent responses by labor leaders to the party's adoption of market reforms correlate with the degree of suffering by workers. In these three countries, however, the relationship is roughly the opposite of what we would expect: *more* suffering correlates with *less* combativeness. Spanish workers endured far less sacrifice than their Mexican and Venezuelan counterparts with regard to wages and social welfare. Even where they suffered more, namely on the job front, the differences with Mexico and Venezuela are not as great as the official figures would suggest.[13] Spain uses a less restrictive definition of "unemployed" than the other two countries, particularly Mexico.[14] Additionally, workers in Mexico and Venezuela (until 1989) could not afford to be unemployed for any length of time because did they not have access to unemployment insurance.[15] Thus, the more relevant figure for these countries is underemployment, which was very high during the reform period.[16]

The picture does not become much clearer when we factor in the extent of the party's reforms. The finding that reforms were greatest in Mexico, then Spain, then Venezuela might explain why UGT leaders reacted more vehemently to the party's reforms than CTV leaders, but it cannot account for the decidedly noncombative response of CTM leaders. Moreover, UGT members continued to be among the main beneficiaries of compensatory social spending by the government, in contrast to members of the CTM and the CTV. Spain is the only country that channeled compensation primarily to formal workers, particularly those in reconverted industries who tended to be unionized, rather than to the urban poor, who tended to work in the informal economy and not be incorporated into unions.

We face the same puzzle when we disaggregate the reforms. Mexico took a moderate approach to reforms more likely to elicit a combative reaction by the unions (e.g., pension reform and labor market flexibilization), but so did Spain and Venezuela.[17] A possible caveat is that Spain was the only country to revise its labor law to allow for more temporary contracts. But, once again, a closer look at the reality in Mexico and Venezuela reveals more hardship than formal indicators would suggest. Despite the lack of labor law reform in Mexico and the adoption of an anti-market reform in Venezuela, firms in these countries engaged in substantial flexibilization of the labor market through contract renegotiations on a case-by-case basis. Moreover, this kind of flexibilization directly affected unionized workers, whereas most of the labor market reforms carried out in Spain exposed new workers to job insecurity while preserving the rights and privileges of established workers, who were the most likely to be unionized and to vote in factory council elections (Burgess 1999). This evidence suggests that the extent to which each party's reforms imposed hardships on workers cannot explain the divergent responses of disaffected labor leaders.

A second possible explanation is that labor leaders were responding primarily to assaults on their own powers and privileges rather than to workers' sacrifices. Once again, however, we do not find the expected correlation in these three countries. CTM leaders remained within the alliance despite PRI-backed challenges to their hegemony in the labor movement and threats to their quotas of political power. By contrast, UGT leaders defected from the alliance despite the PSOE's support for UGT hegemony and repeated offers of public office and/or high-level positions within the party.

Venezuela is the one case in which combativeness correlates positively with changes in union prerogatives. CTV leaders were most combative after losing influence over key positions when Pérez took office in early 1989. They retreated to a more cooperative strategy when the AD's congressional delegation supported a law increasing labor representation on the boards of state-owned companies and Pérez restored the Venezuelan Workers' Bank under CTV control. As we will see, however, the causal story behind these strategic shifts goes beyond changes in union prerogatives and can be told more effectively with variables that work in all three cases.

A third possible explanation for the divergent responses by disaffected labor leaders is the strength of the left in the party system. Perhaps the willingness of these leaders to risk a collapse of the party-union alliance correlated with the availability of alternative party allies more sympathetic to their antireform cause. But this hypothesis does not hold up to the evidence in these cases either. Both AD and the PSOE faced very limited electoral competition during the 1980s, particularly from the left. Although left parties existed—most notably the United Left (IU) in Spain and Causa R in Venezuela—they had no realistic chances of winning control of the government. Yet their labor allies pursued very different strategies. In Venezuela, CTV leaders responded as one might expect: no alternative, no exit. In Spain, by contrast, UGT leaders exited *despite* the lack of a strong left alternative. They did not even make an effort to build ties with the IU, preferring instead to maintain autonomy from all political parties. In addition, CTV leaders did not move any closer to exit when a new left challenger, Causa R, gained strength in the early 1990s. To the contrary, they viewed Causa R as a threat to their prerogatives rather than as a potential ally.

The only party to experience a real electoral challenge from the left in the 1980s was the PRI, but this option did not prompt the CTM to switch allegiances. In July 1988, Cuauhtémoc Cárdenas, the son of the CTM's first benefactor, Lázaro Cárdenas, ran against the PRI, which suffered its narrowest victory in history. He went on to found the Party of the Democratic Revolution (PRD), which became one of the PRI's two main challengers in the 1990s.[18] Yet rather than viewing the *cardenistas* as potential allies, CTM leaders treated them as their worst enemy, despite strikingly similar rhetoric against the PRI's market reforms. In fact, the emergence of a left option pushed CTM leaders even closer to the PRI technocrats.

Since none of these variables can account for the divergent trajectories of labor leaders in Mexico, Spain, and Venezuela, we are left with the relations of power and autonomy discussed in chapter 2. Not only do they correlate as hypothesized with the outcomes, but they also help explain the puzzling findings with regard to worker sacrifice, union privileges, and party options. In the case of worker sacrifice, Mexico's alliance could withstand harsher reforms because CTM leaders were heavily protected from dissent from below. In Spain, by contrast, the alliance was very sensitive to shifts in the workers' well-being because UGT leaders were vulnerable to punishment not only by union members but also workers in general. In Venezuela, CTV leaders enjoyed sufficient protection to tolerate a dramatic decline in worker well-being but feared losing their grip on the labor movement when riots against Pérez's policies signaled much deeper disaffection among workers than they anticipated.

We find a similar story with regard to union prerogatives. CTM leaders could afford to give priority to leadership privileges over workers' benefits because they were protected from workers' dissent. Given the party's extensive power to punish them—as well their historically grounded expectation that the party would ultimately retreat from an assault on their privileges—they were unwilling to move beyond norm-based voice even when Salinas threatened to reduce their prerogatives. UGT leaders, by contrast, valued policies favorable to workers over leadership privileges because they were vulnerable to workers' dissent. Rather than be associated with reforms they viewed as unnecessarily draconian toward workers, they unilaterally sacrificed one of the few prerogatives the PSOE could offer them—seats in parliament. Finally, CTV leaders valued leadership privileges as highly as CTM leaders, but they were more able to rely on allies within the party to help them defend these privileges against attempted assaults by the government.

Finally, relations of power and autonomy also help explain why the availability of a leftist alternative in the party system did not shape the strategies of labor leaders as expected. CTM and CTV leaders viewed the emergence of leftist rivals to the PRI and AD more as a threat to their privileges and power than as an opportunity to represent workers more effectively. Thus, as indicated by the CTM's reaction to the *cardenistas* and the CTV's reaction to Causa R, they were likely to close ranks behind their traditional allies rather than switch allegiances to more pro-worker parties. For UGT leaders, a leftist alternative did not pose a serious threat, but neither was it a prerequisite to exit. While they may have welcomed a stronger challenger from the left to pressure the PSOE to modify its reforms, they preferred to abandon their strategy of party affiliation altogether rather than risk punishment by workers by remaining in the alliance.

CHAPTER 4

Power and Autonomy in
Party-Union Relations

The relations of power and autonomy that shaped the incentives of labor leaders in Mexico, Spain, and Venezuela derived from both formal rules and informal practices. The formal rules were codified in political constitutions, electoral laws, labor laws, and party and union statutes. The informal practices emerged out of critical junctures in the country's political development—such as the Mexican Revolution and the transitions to democracy in Spain and Venezuela—and historical struggles within the labor movement. These rules and practices differed significantly in each country, producing variation in the power of the party and workers to punish labor leaders for disloyal behavior and the party's capacity to act autonomously from its own government.

Power to Punish

Disaffected labor leaders in Mexico, Spain, and Venezuela faced very different threats of punishment for disloyal behavior. In Mexico, they enjoyed significant protection from challenges by workers but were highly vulnerable to the denial and withdrawal of inducements by the party. In Spain, they were relatively protected from retaliation by the party but heavily dependent on the approval of workers. In Venezuela, they faced credible threats of punishment from both sides, although the party had somewhat greater capacity to withhold inducements. As argued in chapter 2, these outcomes reflected four institutional arrangements: (1) the legal framework governing industrial relations; (2) the structure of the labor movement; (3) the type of party system; and (4) the party's mechanisms for filling party posts.

Pressure from Above in Mexico

In Mexico, these four arrangements maximized the punishing power of the PRI while minimizing that of workers. As the ruling party in an authoritarian regime with a highly interventionist labor code, the PRI had discretionary control over state resources and could intercede extensively in union affairs, employ divide-and-conquer strategies in the labor movement, and dictate labor's access to party posts. Workers, meanwhile, had few opportunities to exercise voice and exit against CTM leaders except when the PRI provided them.

The PRI's political dominance is well known. Between 1929 and 1982, it won an average of 85 percent of the vote in presidential elections (Klesner 1987, 129), along with every governorship and the vast majority of legislative, state, and municipal offices. Because of its grip on the legislature, the PRI also controlled the judiciary through the president's de facto power to appoint and dismiss judges. Although rival parties existed in Mexico, they controlled very few resources and had almost no ability to alter the policy decisions of the PRI. Nor was the PRI constrained by an independent judiciary that could enforce universal rights or hold party leaders accountable.

When combined with Mexico's statist development strategy, this dominance endowed the PRI with tremendous economic, political, and organizational resources with which to induce the loyal behavior of CTM leaders. These resources included selective benefits for workers, guaranteed access to public office, and privileged treatment relative to rival labor organizations. Just as importantly, the lack of checks and balances in the political system enabled the PRI to distribute and withdraw these resources on a discretionary and contingent basis. Once CTM leaders became accustomed to enjoying these resources, they had strong incentives not to risk their withdrawal as punishment for disloyal behavior. Thus, despite being "a creation neither of the state apparatus nor of its Party" (Garrido 1982, 101), the CTM quickly became one of the PRI's most loyal pillars of support.

The PRI also derived significant punishing power from Mexico's labor code, which gave the state extensive authority to intervene in labor affairs. The legal basis for this authority came from two documents: the 1917 Constitution, particularly Article 123, and the 1931 Federal Labor Law (LFT). The constitution laid the foundations for a system in which labor received rights and privileges that outweighed its market power but only so long as it operated within the parameters set by political elites. The most progressive labor code of its time, Article 123 guaranteed workers extensive rights and privileges. But it also empowered the state to influence the distribution of these benefits through its presence on tripartite bodies such as the arbitration and conciliation boards responsible for ruling on labor disputes (including the legality of strikes) and the commissions mandated to set minimum wages, administer workers' housing, and regulate profit sharing (*Ley Federal del Trabajo* 1990, 5–15).[1]

This system was reinforced in 1931 by passage of the LFT , which codified many of the provisions in Article 123. The LFT continued the practice of combining benefits for workers and unions with state authority to intervene in labor affairs, but it tipped the balance in favor of state authority. First, it enabled the state to intervene in the process of union formation. Although labor organizations could be formed without prior authorization, they had to be recognized by labor authorities before they could legally represent workers, negotiate a collective contract, or call a strike. Petitions for registration could be rejected if membership and information requirements were not met, and the registering agency could cancel a union's registration at any time if it was found to be violating these requirements (*Ley Federal del Trabajo* 1931, 111–12).[2]

The LFT also empowered the state to intervene in disputes between groups of workers vying for control of a collective contract. Workers had the right to ask the labor authorities to conduct a survey to determine which group was supported by the majority of workers and thereby had title to the contract. Although the outcome depended partly on the opinion of workers, it also reflected the whims of labor authorities, who not only had the power to decide whether the survey would be taken but controlled the process by which the responses were collected and counted (Bizberg 1990, 124; La Botz 1992, 47). Like the controls on union formation, this mechanism gave PRI governments the capacity to wrest membership and negotiating power away from unions that stepped out of line.

Finally, the LFT allowed the state to regulate strike activity, thereby diluting the mobilizing capacity of unions. To be recognized as legal, a strike had to be supported by the majority of workers and preceded by a formal petition (*emplazamiento*) specifying the goal and time of the strike action. Acceptance of this petition required that the petitioning union meet strict procedural requirements (*Ley Federal del Trabajo* 1931, 116–18). Even if the strike were allowed to proceed, the state had several measures of control over the outcome. First, the parties to the conflict were required to participate in conciliation efforts led by labor authorities. Second, employers (or an interested third party) could ask the authorities to declare the strike "nonexistent" within seventy-two hours of the strike's initiation (Middlebrook 1995, 69).[3] The PRI increased these restrictions on union mobilization when it reformed the LFT in 1941 to expand the penalties for illegal strikes, prohibit solidarity strikes as a union tactic, and tighten notification requirements for the declaration of strikes (Camacho 1980, 46).

A third source of the PRI's power to punish was its multiple and competing allegiances, which facilitated divide-and-conquer tactics to keep its labor allies in line. Lázaro Cárdenas was an early architect of these contending allegiances. Although he supported the unification of industrial unions in the CTM in 1936, he engineered the formation of the Federation of Public Service Workers' Unions (FSTSE) as a separate organization for public employees in 1937 and the National Peasants' Confederation (CNC) as a separate organization for peasants in 1938.[4] He also established different regulations for public employees and prohibited them from belonging to more than one confederation (Acedo Angulo 1990, 107–8).[5]

Cárdenas reinforced these divisions when he restructured the official party in 1938 to include four groupings: the Labor Sector, Peasant Sector, Military Sector (eliminated in 1940), and Popular Sector (initially for public employees) Although the Peasant Sector, represented by the CNC, enjoyed less organizational autonomy than the Labor Sector, it had more members and was therefore eligible to receive more candidacies for elected office. Moreover, the CTM dominated but did not monopolize the Labor Sector, and both the FSTSE and the powerful National Teachers' Union (SNTE) belonged to the Popular Sector. These divisions split the labor movement into competing groups that sought to outbid each other for special privileges from the PRI.

The CTM saw its leverage diluted even further when the party strengthened the Popular Sector in the 1940s. In addition to expanding the sector's membership beyond public sector unions to include self-employed workers and small entrepreneurs, President Avila Camacho presided over the creation of the National Confederation of Popular Organizations (CNOP) in 1943. In the midterm elections that year, the Popular Sector received over half of the of the party's seats in the new legislature, compared to one-third for the Peasant Sector and only one-seventh for the Labor Sector. In addition, the CNOP won the presidency of the Electoral College and the Chamber of Deputies (Collier and Collier 1991, 418). The Labor Sector never regained its place ahead of the Popular Sector, and the CNOP took over the CTM's role as the leading channel of party recruitment and mobilization.[6]

Camacho's successors also encouraged the formation of rival labor organizations among PRI-affiliated workers. In 1952, President Miguel Alemán supported the creation of the Revolutionary Confederation of Workers and Peasants (CROC). Like several other confederations, the CROC attracted unions that belonged to the PRI but rejected CTM membership. With the backing of President Adolfo López Mateos in the early 1960s, the CROC joined the National Workers' Central (CNT), which unified more than six hundred unions opposed to the CTM-dominated Labor Unity Bloc (BUO). When open rivalry between the CNT and the BUO threatened to undermine the effectiveness of the PRI's Labor Sector, President Gustavo Díaz Ordaz encouraged the two coalitions to unify under a single umbrella organization (Durand Ponte 1991, 89). On February 18, 1966, the executive committees of the CTM, the CROC, the FSTSE, the national autonomous unions (SNA), and several craft and regional unions formed the Labor Congress (CT).[7]

The Labor Congress institutionalized a system in which the PRI could shift allegiances within the labor movement without encouraging dissidence or abandoning its overall commitment to labor. The CT accounted for 73.5 percent of unions and 83.9 percent of unionized workers in 1979. With the exception of unions in nuclear power and telecommunications, all CT affiliates formally required their members to belong to the PRI (Durand Ponte 1991, 89, n. 4). At the same time, these unions retained their organizational autonomy and engaged in direct negotiations with the party and the state, often in competition with one another. Although the CTM dominated the CT, it never achieved a monopoly of representation. Consequently, the PRI could employ tactics of divide-and-conquer to keep the CTM in line without having to go outside the official labor movement for alternative interlocutors.

These divisions reduced the CTM's bargaining power within the party and encouraged competition rather than cooperation among subaltern groups. Although the sectors could conceivably form a united front, they were more likely to haggle over candidacies for public office, which the party distributed along sectorial lines. Even within the Labor Sector, the CTM had to protect its share of candidacies against encroachment by rival confederations, particularly the CROC and the Regional Confederation of Mexican Workers (CROM). By allowing the PRI to play one group off another, these divisions increased the incentives for "official" organizations to demonstrate their loyalty to the regime and expanded the options available to party leaders for punishing CTM leaders who challenged their authority.

Unlike the PRI, Mexican workers faced major constraints on their capacity to punish CTM leaders for disloyal behavior. As already mentioned, the state had the legal instruments to control dissent by intervening in the formation of unions and the mobilization of workers. When these mechanisms proved inadequate to quell workers' unrest, the PRI resorted to coercion (see chapter 5). But the PRI's preferred strategy for maintaining labor peace was to delegate control to the unions themselves. In accordance with the LFT, the state could grant incumbent leaders special protections from challenges to their leadership and condone the centralization of authority within unions. This system had the dual effect of reducing the power of workers to punish labor leaders for disloyal behavior while making the survival of these leaders contingent on their cooperation with the regime.

As long as CTM leaders kept a few lieutenants happy with opportunities for personal gain and patronage, they did not have to worry too much about losing control of the rank-and-file. Once a union received official recognition from the labor authorities, it gained the legal capacity to dominate the workplace. The LFT required employers to sign a collective contract with an officially recognized union when requested to do so, even if the union represented a minority of employees. This contract, once signed, applied to all workers, regardless of whether or not they belonged to a union (*Ley Federal del Trabajo* 1931, 29). Particularly when coupled with the state's practice of denying recognition to a second union in a single workplace, this provision gave officially recognized unions "an effective monopoly over the representation of rank-and-file interests" (Middlebrook 1995, 62).

The LFT also allowed for—but did not require—the creation of a closed shop through the incorporation of "exclusion clauses" into collective contracts (*Ley Federal del Trabajo* 1931, 30, 110). Reflecting the power bestowed on incumbent leaders by these clauses, employers tended to negotiate them only with "reliable" unions. An "entry clause" made union membership a prerequisite to employment, and a "separation clause" required the employer to dismiss any worker who lost his or her union membership. By linking union membership to employment, these clauses restricted the options of both voice and exit for workers. The entry clause eliminated the possibility of exit by a single worker to a competing union within the workplace. The separation clause made voice from within very difficult and risky. These clauses effectively protected incumbent leaders from defection or dissent from below, even in the event that workers (or lower-level leaders) became disgruntled with union policy.

The exclusion clauses also provided CTM leaders with opportunities to develop patronage networks. Many union bosses used their control over hiring and firing to cultivate personalistic ties with workers, sometimes even selling jobs in return for promises of compliance (Coppedge 1993, 255). Others capitalized on the controls offered by the exclusion clauses to negotiate "protection contracts" with employers. These contracts, which were often sold to the employer without the workers' knowledge, prevented organization of the workforce by a more militant union. They were most prevalent in small and medium-sized firms and were estimated to account for the majority of labor contracts in the Federal District in the early 1990s (La Botz 1992, 55).[8] More generally, the exclusion clauses created a strong association between union membership and access to special privileges, thereby enabling CTM leaders to win workers' support through the distribution of selective benefits.

Moreover, labor leaders favored by the PRI enjoyed wide latitude in managing the internal affairs of their unions. Despite a requirement that unions inform the government of any changes in their constitutions, by-laws, or leadership, they were legally free to prepare their own statutes and internal regulations, elect their officers, and formulate union policies. While consistent with democratic unionism, these provisions created opportunities for labor leaders to limit dissent from below, especially since they faced no legal requirements regarding the use of secret ballots in union elections, the frequency of union assemblies, or the structure of union authority (Middlebrook 1995, 66–7).

The PRI took advantage of this margin to overlook—and even encourage—the consolidation of power within the CTM by a leadership group, led by Fidel Velázquez, known as the "five little wolves" *(cinco lobitos)*. Their fragmented social base and political pragmatism made them ideal allies for the regime (Camacho 1980, 112). With the help of his main rival, Vicente Lombardo Toledano, Velázquez became secretary general of the CTM in 1941 and won reelection in 1943, despite a statutory prohibition against the reelection of members of the National Committee and the virulent opposition of more radical leaders (Medina 1978, 174; López Villegas 1990, 148).[9]

This victory was critical because it determined "the mechanism that would predominate: the force of the leaders or the democratic consultation of the bases" (Medina 1978, 177).[10] Despite its original billing as a temporary violation of union statutes, his reelection became a permanent mutation in favor of a leadership group backed by the ruling party. Except for a brief hiatus between 1947 and 1950, Velázquez retained the post of secretary general until his death in June 1997.

The *cinco lobitos* consolidated their hold on the CTM in the late 1940s. In addition to manipulating the delegate registration process for the CTM's March 1947 Congress, they engineered a statutory reform that replaced an electoral procedure linking voting shares to membership size with a one union–one vote rule. This reform greatly diminished the electoral weight of the SNA in favor of the small but plentiful unions loyal to the *cinco lobitos*

(Middlebrook 1995, 115). At the CTM Congress, the "five little wolves" pushed through another reform that created two classes of National Committee members: the first were those elected in the National Congress and the second were SNA representatives who had voice but no vote (Medina 1979, 130, 132, 142–43).[11] Ten months later, the *cinco lobitos* purged the CTM of competing leadership groups by expelling Lombardo and the Communists.

Taken together, these arrangements created a top-down, pyramid-like structure of authority, much like the structure of the political system. At each level, union leaders had only to maintain the loyalty of their immediate subordinates to preserve their power. This structure enabled the leader at the top of the pyramid, Fidel Velázquez, to coordinate the CTM's activities around the country and to mobilize and demobilize union members nearly at will.[12] In contrast to the political system, moreover, his subversion of the no-reelection rule in the 1940s enabled him to hold the reins of power in the CTM for nearly sixty years. Thus, the networks of patron-client relations that sustained the CTM were not nearly as fluid or crosscutting as in the political arena.

This authority came at a price, however. As already suggested, CTM leaders had room to behave disloyally toward workers only so long as they remained in the good graces of the PRI. Employers tended to negotiate exclusion clauses only with unions favored by the ruling party. Moreover, the provisions of the LFT and the party's dominance of the state enabled the PRI to expose previously protected labor leaders to voice and exit by workers. Instead of denying registration to a competing union, labor authorities could grant it. Or instead of quelling dissent within the workplace, they could cultivate it. They could also take away the internal autonomy usually enjoyed by labor leaders by interfering in leadership selection or union organization. Although PRI governments generally used these tactics against the CTM's rivals until the 1980s, their successful application sent the message that friends prosper while foes perish. Thus, the threat of worker dissent worked paradoxically to reinforce the CTM's loyalty to the PRI at the expense of its loyalty to workers.

Pressure from Below in Spain

In stark contrast to Mexico, the institutional landscape in Spain gave very limited punishing power to the PSOE while placing key inducements in the hands of workers. During Franco's long rein, the PSOE was in exile and had no chance of mobilizing the resources of the state. When democracy was finally restored, the PSOE gained access to the state but found its power constrained by a labor movement divided along party lines, an anti-corporatist labor code, and democratic checks and balances that reduced its capacity to withdraw inducements once granted. Workers, meanwhile, had significant capacity to punish labor leaders, primarily as a result of Spain's factory council system. The only institutional feature that strengthened the party while weakening workers was the centralization of authority within the party and the union. Party statutes enabled PSOE leaders to control the UGT's access to party posts, and union statutes largely protected UGT leaders from dissent from within the union. As we will see, however, these exceptions had only a marginal impact on the overall distribution of punishing power.

The PSOE spent most of its long history out of office. After a brief period of governing as part of a coalition government during the Second Republic (1931–1933), PSOE leaders were killed, forced underground, or obliged to flee into exile to escape the repressive backlash of General Franco, who defeated the Republicans in the Spanish Civil War. As Franco consolidated his power, control of the PSOE shifted to a group of exiles based in France.[13] They refused to allow Socialist participation in any institutions established by his regime, and the party inside Spain shrank to a few, committed militants, mostly in the former UGT strongholds of the Basque Country and Asturias (Mateos López 1986, 339).

Although shared experiences of repression and exile generated strong ties of solidarity among PSOE and UGT leaders, they did not enable the party to cultivate either "sticks" or "carrots" in its relationship with the union. As noted by a prominent Socialist and former secretary general of the UGT's chemical federation, Matilde Fernández, "Spain was in a freezer while, in other European countries, party-union relations were developing on the basis of a dialogue between autonomous organizations."[14]Although there was an extreme overlap between the leadership of the PSOE and that of the UGT, the party had little leverage over UGT leaders once normal political conditions resumed.

The PSOE finally returned to the political stage when Franco's death paved the way for a democratic transition in the 1970s. In the legislative elections of 1977, the PSOE catapulted from a party with almost no presence inside Spain to the country's second most powerful political force. Although the Union of the Democratic Center (UCD) won the elections with 34.3 percent of the vote and 46.8 percent of the lower house seats, the PSOE garnered a close second with 28.5 percent of the vote and 33.7 percent of the lower house seats (Share 1989, 44). After maintaining its second-place position in the general and municipal elections in 1979, the PSOE swept the general elections of October 1982, prompting one PSOE leader to proclaim, "we are going to install the PRI in Spain" (Gutiérrez and de Miguel 1990, 237).

Unlike in Mexico, however, the PSOE's ascendance as a hegemonic party did not bring a significant increase in its power to punish UGT leaders. In fact, the institutions constructed during the democratic transition inhibited the Socialists from punishing their labor allies for disloyal behavior. First, the 1978 Constitution and the 1980 Workers' Statute gave the state little authority to intervene in labor affairs. Intent on dismantling Franco's interventionist system of industrial relations, the PSOE supported provisions that severely limited the state's capacity to interfere in union formation, collective bargaining, strikes, and leadership selection.[15] Although a few vestiges of Franco's regulatory regime remained in the area of dispute resolution, the unions gained a significant degree of autonomy from the state.

Second, the PSOE did not share the PRI's capacity to manipulate the delivery of inducements to its labor allies. Despite ruling as a hegemonic party from 1982 to 1993, the PSOE remained subject to checks and balances within the political system, as well as the constraints accompanying Spain's entry into the European Economic Community in 1986. Particularly when inducements were mandated by legislation or the constitution, the PSOE could not easily withdraw them once granted. Nor did the PSOE have the option of redirecting inducements to other mass-based organizations linked to the party. The PSOE generally lacked well-institutionalized ties to civil society, and Spain's other major union, the Workers' Commissions (CCOO), was closely allied to the PSOE's rival on the left, the Spanish Communist Party (PCE).[16] Thus, the UGT was the PSOE's only game in town as far as intermediary organizations were concerned.

There was one area, however, in which the PSOE did have the power to punish its labor allies for disloyal behavior. Authority within the party became highly centralized in the late 1970s. Much of this authority was concentrated in the hands of González's close ally, Alfonso Guerra, who ran the party apparatus and served as vice president of the country from 1982 to 1991. By early 1990, he and his allies controlled the party executive and apparatus, the Socialist group in parliament, some key positions in government headquarters, seven ministries, three regional governments, two universities, and elements of the judiciary (Gillespie 1992, 9–10).

Guerra built this empire with the help of patronage networks based on his control over closed electoral lists and numerous party and government posts. By the mid-1980s, over 50 percent of the party's membership, including many trade unionists, "either held party or government posts or appeared as candidates for office on Socialist lists" (Share 1989, 127). Although members of the UGT executive did not hold positions in the cabinet, several of them served as deputies in the parliament. Since the González-Guerra team controlled access to these positions, they could presumably punish UGT leaders for disloyal behavior by leaving them off party lists for the next election. This dependence was greater at the lower levels of the UGT, where union leaders frequently held positions in both the party and the government. As we will see in chapter 6, however, UGT leaders unilaterally devalued these instruments of control by resigning their parliamentary seats rather than voting for provisions they viewed as disloyal to workers.

In contrast with the PSOE, Spanish workers had significant capacity to punish UGT leaders for disloyal behavior. Rather than reflecting internal union democracy, this capacity derived from a system of representation that held UGT leaders accountable to workers outside the union. Within the UGT, the national leadership enjoyed significant autonomy from lower-level leaders and workers. Authority in the UGT was highly centralized in the Confederal Executive Commission (CEC), and particularly in the position of secretary general (Führer 1996, 159–61).[17] Although union members voted directly for their leaders at the level of the firm, the UGT's governing bodies at the provincial and national levels were elected by delegates, whose selection became increasingly indirect toward the upper levels of the organizational hierarchy. Delegates came from two kinds of organizations: territorial unions and industrial federations. Within each category, the number of delegates each union could send was proportional to the size of its membership. Across the two categories, however, the share of delegates was divided evenly, giving a disproportionate influence to the weaker and more politicized territorial unions (Führer 1996, 151–52).

This organizational structure contributed to "sclerotic structures of power" within the UGT (Führer 1996, 155). Union members faced obstacles to removing high-level leaders from office, and the national leadership tended to dominate the outcome of the UGT Congresses held every three to four years.[18] This centralization of power was reinforced by the CEC's control over union finances and the organizational weakness of the UGT within the workplace. Both the industrial federations and the territorial unions depended on the CEC for economic subsidies, many of which came from the state (Führer 1996, 180). In addition, the UGT suffered from a small executive staff, a low number of cadres, and insufficient training and education for union activists (Escobar 1993, 8). When combined with the UGT's tendency to base union policy on national pacts, these factors conspired to limit the independent power of lower-level leaders within the UGT.

The centralizing tendencies within the UGT were strongly counteracted, however, by the dual system of worker representation that grew out of the transition to democracy in the late 1970s. Spain developed two legal mechanisms of workers' representation on the shop floor: the union section and the factory council. The union section consisted exclusively of union members and acted as "the extended arm of unions in the enterprise" (Escobar 1993, 37). The factory council, by contrast, was elected by *all* workers in the workplace, regardless of whether or not they belonged to a union.[19] Although union membership hovered between 10 and 15 percent of salaried workers in the early 1990s (Escobar 1993, 6), around half of all salaried workers voted in factory council elections. Among workers in firms where factory council elections took place, the participation rate rose to 80 percent (Miguelez Lobo 1991, 220).[20]

In contrast to other European countries, the factory councils had the right to organize strikes and bargain collectively.[21] Moreover, the union sections gained bargaining rights only through their presence on the factory councils. If a union gained an absolute majority of seats, the union section could negotiate directly with the employer. In the absence of such a majority, the factory council became the negotiating agent, as occurred in most large firms (Escobar 1993, 29).[22] Nor did the unionization of a factory council necessarily mean a strong union presence within the workplace. Often, the unions did not have enough activists to complete their closed electoral lists, so they included both union members and union sympathizers (Escobar 1993, 23).[23] Also, union sections rarely existed in firms with fewer than fifty employees, which accounted for over half of factory council delegates (*El Pais*, May 24, 1992).

The factory council system provided opportunities for dissent not only by union members, but also by workers in general. First, the factory councils enjoyed a high degree of autonomy from the external unions. Council members were not legally bound to follow union directives, and they often pursued independent strategies (Fishman 1984, 112; Bermeo 1994, 609). During the 1980s, factory councils called around half of the strikes in Spain (Martínez Lucio 1992, 513), and these strikes were often unauthorized by the union leadership, especially in sectors undergoing industrial restructuring (Rigby and Lawlor 1994, 269).[24] Thus, although workers and lower-level leaders were constrained from challenging the structure of authority *within* the UGT, they could undermine union policies through mobilizations and independent bargaining on the shop floor.

Second, and more importantly, workers could punish labor leaders for disloyal behavior at both the local and the national levels through their participation in factory council elections. Within the workplace, electoral performance determined access to leadership positions and the influence of the union section. Beyond the workplace, it determined: the right to negotiate provincial, regional, or national agreements; the legal capacity to convoke elections in any workplace; representation on the boards of public agencies; and access to state subsidies. Under the 1980 Workers' Statute, these privileges were reserved for unions that qualified as "most representative" by receiving more than 10 percent of all delegates at the national level or more than 15 percent of all delegates at the regional level (Escobar 1993, 20). Until 1994, the last two privileges were distributed proportionally among these unions on the basis of electoral results.

Although the UGT was never at risk of losing its most representative status, it faced stiff competition from the CCOO over institutional representation and government subsidies. The UGT was especially dependent on the latter, since around half of its income during the 1980s and early 1990s came from government sources. Although the state had discretionary control over some of these funds—the most important being education and training grants that accounted for 21 percent of the UGT's income in 1992 (*El Pais*, May 24, 1992)—others were distributed on the basis of electoral performance, including subsidies from the national budget, payments for union participation in state agencies, and union patrimony derived from the Franco period.

Combined with the limited the capacity of UGT leaders to distribute selective incentives to workers, this system of "voters' trade unionism" (Rigby and Lawlor 1994, 262) left them vulnerable to punishment in the form of opposition voting. As Ludolfo Paramio argues, workers in such a system are likely to "have an *instrumental* vision of the union, which they will support or not depending on its capacity to offer positive results in the short run" (1992, 531). Moreover, if "the electoral system is competitive, and the strength and resources of each union depends on its capacity to capture votes, it is easy to understand that union strategies will be strongly influenced by the perceptions of their potential electors" (532). Not surprisingly, UGT leaders placed an increasingly high premium on flexibility in their dealings with the government and the party so that they could respond quickly to shifts in these perceptions. In this context, the centralization of authority within the UGT worked to facilitate rather than inhibit movement from voice to exit.

Pressure from Both Sides in Venezuela

In Venezuela, the institutional landscape endowed both AD and the workers with power to punish labor leaders for disloyal behavior. AD gained leverage from its dominance of the political system (particularly in an oil-rich economy), the interventionist provisions of Venezuelan labor laws, and the party-based distribution of leadership posts within the CTV. Its punishing power was constrained, however, by competition from minority parties in the political arena and the labor movement and by the organizational strength of labor within the party. Meanwhile, workers found their voices muted by the legal framework but faced relatively low barriers to exit and could pose a real threat when minority parties refused to collude with AD to block resistance from below.

AD had more leverage over its labor allies than the PSOE but not as much as the PRI. Its first opportunity to govern came when party leaders joined with junior military officers to stage a coup against Venezuela's authoritarian government in October 1945. Over the next three years (the *trienio*), AD ruled as a hegemonic party, dominating both houses of Congress and refusing to share cabinet positions with any other parties.[25] AD used its newfound access to state power to distribute socioeconomic, political, and organizational re-sources to its labor allies and to privilege them over their rivals. AD's reign came to an abrupt end, however, when General Marco Pérez Jiménez reestab-lished military rule in 1948. Thrown once again into clandestine opposi-tion—and often sharing jail cells with members of rival parties—AD leaders concluded that their hegemonic aspirations had contributed to the collapse of democracy.

Eager to avoid a replay of this outcome, AD supported a system of power sharing with the country's other non-Communist parties after Pérez Jiménez fled into exile in January 1958. In October 1958, AD joined with the Social Christian Party of Venezuela (COPEI) and the Democratic Republican Union (URD) to sign the Pact of Punto Fijo in anticipation of elections later that year. In the pact, the signatory parties committed themselves to minimizing negative campaigning, accepting the results of the elections, and "forming a government of national unity with the participation of the three parties irre-spective of the election results" (Kornblith 1991, 70–71).[26] They also signed pacts to regularize industrial relations, appease the fears of the military and the church, and establish the limits of state intervention in the economy (López Maya, Calcaño, and Maingón 1989, 70–76). These pacts laid the foundations for a system in which AD and COPEI dominated at the expense of the left.[27]

Although these arrangements prevented AD from monopolizing the politi-cal system as it had during the *trienio*, the party continued to be Venezuela's most important political actor. After 1958, AD controlled the presidency for twenty-five of the next thirty-five years and always held the largest share of seats in Congress (Coppedge 1994, 10). Moreover, the provisions of Venezuela's pacted democracy guaranteed AD some access to state power regardless of which party controlled the presidency. Even after formal power-sharing arrangements collapsed just before AD suffered its first presidential loss to COPEI in 1968, AD and COPEI negotiated an "institutional pact" whereby they agreed to share power informally.[28]

As in Mexico, the party's hold on state power in Venezuela endowed it with substantial economic, political, and organizational resources with which to induce the loyal behavior of CTV leaders. Although AD did not have as much discretionary authority as the PRI to manipulate the political system, the state's access to vast oil rents gave AD tremendous leverage over economic outcomes, particularly through public spending and the creation of government jobs. The party used this leverage to distribute substantial benefits to workers and unions, as well as including the CTV in policymaking circles and privileging the CTV over its rivals in the labor movement.

AD also derived significant punishing power from Venezuela's labor code. Modeled after Mexico's LFT, the 1936 Labor Law combined entitlements for workers and unions with extensive state regulation of the labor movement. Its progressive features included social security, profit-sharing, regulation of and compensation for unjustified layoffs, special protection from dismissal (*fuero sindical*) for union leaders, and a requirement that 75 percent of all oil workers be Venezuelan (McCoy 1989, 38; Larrañaga n.d., 13). Its regulatory features empowered the Labor Ministry to register unions, resolve collective conflicts, and rule on the legality of strikes (McCoy 1989, 55).

Although the 1961 Constitution guaranteed the right of workers to form unions, all unions had to submit a petition for registration to a labor inspector, who could request changes in the union's statutes (Lucena 1982, 212–13). Because the labor inspectors enjoyed "ample room for interpretation" in their ruling on the petition (McCoy 1989, 55), they could delay or reject registration for unions that did not belong to the majority current or were opposed by regional interests (OIT 1991, 65).[29] They could also approve parallel unions within a single workplace or sector (Lucena 1982, 212).

Once registered, unions had to communicate to the labor inspector any changes in leadership or statutes within ten days of union elections, as well as to submit lists of members twice a year and to provide copies of union financial records to the labor inspector and union members (McCoy 1989, 55). Although the authorities rarely cancelled a union's registration once granted, they often colluded with employers to prevent a particular group of workers from taking control of a union or to encourage the formation of a parallel union with a more docile leadership (OIT 1991, 66).

The Labor Law also imposed strict regulations on strike activity, thereby limiting the bargaining power of unions. For example, unions had to exhaust a lengthy conciliation process before they could call a legal strike. In the event of a dispute, workers had to submit a "petition of conflict" *(pliego conflictivo)* to the labor inspector. This submission triggered the formation of a conciliation board composed of representatives of each of the warring parties and chaired by the labor inspector. The board would meet for a maximum of thirty days until its members either agreed unanimously to create an arbitration board composed of outside members or decided that conciliation was impossible.[30] In the former case, the arbitration board had to reach a decision in thirty days, and its decision was binding for at least six months. In the latter case, the labor inspector would issue a report, and the parties to the conflict could call a strike or lockout (McCoy 1989, 57).

Even if a strike met all of these requirements, the government could still declare it illegal upon determining that it "places the health or socioeconomic well-being of the people in immediate danger" (McCoy 1989, 57). In 1974, the government extended this provision to all strikes in transport, electricity, gas, water, telephones, communication, hydrocarbons and mining, medical services, and the distribution of basic necessities. The following year, Congress passed the Organic Law of Security and Defense, which established a "security zone" in which the armed forces could impose measures of exception to ensure the continued operation of key public services (López Maya and Werz 1981, 64; Ellner 1993, 58; McCoy 1989, 58).

Workers in the vast public sector had especially strict limits on their right to strike. White-collar workers were prohibited from bargaining collectively or striking, although the government issued a Regulation of Public Unions in 1971 that effectively allowed public sector unions to negotiate work conditions (OIT 1991, 122).[31] Blue-collar workers in the public sector enjoyed both rights, but they had to follow an even longer and more state-mediated process of conciliation and arbitration. Under a 1976 presidential decree, workers in state enterprises and autonomous institutes were required to discuss contracts in conciliation for a maximum of ninety days. If no agreement was reached, the dispute went to a higher-level commission composed of four representatives from the state and one from the CTV. The decision made by this commission could not be appealed (McCoy 1989, 58).

AD derived a third source of punishing power from the party-based distribution of leadership positions within the CTV. Both during the *trienio* and after the return to democracy in 1958, the CTV was organized along party lines. Moreover, the distribution of power within the CTV became a rough mirror image of the political arena. Whereas AD nearly monopolized the confederation during the *trienio*, it agreed to share power with minority parties when reconstructing the CTV in 1959. The CTV's first post-1958 executive included seven members of AD *(adecos),* three Communists, and two members each from COPEI and the URD (Ellner 1993, 13). Although the positions held by AD and the Communists reflected their historic ties to labor, COPEI and the URD gained a degree of representation that greatly outweighed their meager presence among organized workers (Collier and Collier 1991, 430). This imbalance worsened after the URD, the PCV, and the Movement of the Revolutionary Left (MIR) boycotted the CTV's Fourth Congress in December 1961. AD gained control of 70 percent of the party delegates, which left the remaining 30 percent for COPEI (Ellner 1993, 53).

This party-based system of leadership distribution gave AD significant leverage over its labor allies. First, it created organic ties between AD and individual labor leaders that made these leaders dependent on AD for their upward mobility within both the union and the party. In union elections, they relied on the party hierarchy for inclusion (and a favorable ranking) on closed lists, which AD and the other parties would often concoct *(confeccionar)* to prevent more radical rivals from winning seats. Moreover, elected positions "belonged" to the parties in the sense that that they could replace a suspended or expelled leader (Arismendi and Iturraspe 1990, 257). At the same time, the party hierarchy controlled labor's access to closed lists for legislative seats and strongly influenced the composition of party labor bureaus at the municipal, state, and national levels. As a result, AD labor leaders who dominated the CTV had strong incentives to support the party even if it violated the interests of workers or unions.

Second, this system discouraged the construction of a unified labor opposition. AD labor leaders languished or prospered depending on their party's performance relative to its rivals in the labor movement. Moreover, they had disincentives to form national industrial unions in strategic sectors. Even after the government amended the labor code in 1958 to allow collective bargaining by industrial sectors, individual labor leaders resisted "the readjustment of party quotas and power that would tend to occur as a consequence of the fusions implicit in restructuring" (OIT 1991, 59).[32] Thus, almost no restructuring took place at the national level, despite repeated calls by the CTV for the formation of national unions.[33] Because of this party-based fragmentation, AD had less need to adopt the kinds of divide-and-conquer strategies pursued by the PRI, leaving the CTV with a far more encompassing membership than the CTM.[34]

These three resources—political dominance, access to an interventionist labor code, and party-based ties with individual unionists—endowed AD with significant power to punish CTV leaders. But several other factors kept the party from maximizing this power. First, AD faced limited but real competition by minority parties as a result of the power-sharing arrangements established during the transition to democracy. The Suffrage Act of 1959 mandated proportional representation for seats in the Venezuelan Congress, state legislatures, and city councils. Likewise, the organization responsible for reconstructing the labor movement, the National Unified Labor Committee (CSUN), agreed that all subsequent union elections would be based on proportional representation for all parties with a significant following (Ellner 1993, 12).[35]

In the political arena, this system meant that AD had to negotiate with other parties to carry out its program and did not have the degree of discretionary authority available to the PRI for manipulating inducements to affiliated labor leaders. Although AD always had the largest share of seats in both houses of Congress, it had an absolute majority in only two out of five terms between 1959 and 1983 (Coppedge 1994, 10). In addition, AD included members of other parties in its first two cabinets and negotiated appointments in the legislative and judicial branches with rival parties. Thus, the party could not rule with impunity even when it controlled the presidency. As demonstrated most vividly by the government's intervention in the Venezuelan Workers' Bank during the COPEI administration of Luis Herrera Campins (see chapter 7), AD had even less control over inducements to labor while in the opposition.

In the labor movement, this system meant that AD did not "control" the CTV, since some CTV leaders belonged to rival parties, including the secretary general, who was second-in-command. As a result, even the most loyal AD labor leaders could not guarantee the CTV's cooperation with AD's agenda, since they had to negotiate it with non-AD leaders. Moreover, proportional representation lowered the opportunity costs to disgruntled labor leaders of defecting to a rival party. Several of AD's most prominent labor leaders took this course when they formed a new party, the People's Electoral Movement (MEP), in 1968.[36] Frustrated by the party's conservative turn and unwilling to recognize the triumph of Luis Beltran Prieto as the party's presidential candidate in 1967, they risked leaving the party to which they owed their careers.

Because of the CTV's pluralist composition, the founders of the MEP did not suffer the same dire fate as CTM leaders who tried to form a rival party to the PRI in the late 1940s. Rather than becoming completely marginalized, these former *adecos* retained control of important positions in the CTV executive, including the presidency (until 1970), two state federations, and several key industrial federations (López Maya and Werz 1981, 37). They controlled 31.7 percent of the delegates at the CTV's Sixth Congress in 1970, compared to 34.5 percent for AD.[37] Although AD was able to reverse many of these gains, the MEP remained an important minority player within the CTV, especially after AD's power-sharing arrangements with COPEI broke down in the 1980s. Moreover, the experience revealed that AD labor leaders had more options than their CTM counterparts to challenge the party without sacrificing all their influence.

A second factor that limited AD's punishing power was the organizational strength of labor within the party. AD's national Labor Bureau, which was composed entirely of important leaders in the CTV, enjoyed a degree of intraparty influence that neither the CTM nor the UGT could match. Because leadership selection within the party—including nomination of AD's presidential candidate—rested on the individual votes of convention delegates, regional and sectorial power brokers played pivotal roles through their control of large voting blocs (Coppedge 1994, 109). Like the CTM (and in contrast to the UGT), the Labor Bureau constituted the most unified and organizationally autonomous grouping within the party.[38] But, unlike the CTM, the Labor Bureau could translate this power resource into a swing vote in leadership selection at the highest levels. Thus, party leaders could not afford to run roughshod over the Labor Bureau, particularly just prior to internal elections.

The punishing power of Venezuelan workers was similarly intermediate. The workers had more power to punish labor leaders than workers in Mexico but less than workers in Spain. In Venezuela, as in Mexico, affiliated labor leaders enjoyed significant protection from workers' dissent. First, incumbent leaders controlled inducements that discouraged exit from an officially sanctioned union. The 1961 Constitution allowed collective contracts to include "union clauses" *(clausulas sindicales)* that provided unions with input into the selection of personnel. These clauses could take two forms: (1) a *clausula de enganche* that obligated the employer to select all or part of his workforce (normally between 70 and 80 percent) from lists provided by the union; or (2) a *clausula de preferencia* that established a preference for candidates proposed by the union but did not require the employer to hire them (OIT 1991, 85). Although union leaders did not have the authority to withdraw employment once granted, these clauses enabled them to favor loyal workers. Moreover, employers could negotiate such clauses selectively, thereby privileging cooperative unions.

Second, formal and informal practices diluted workers' voice at election time, particularly at the federal and confederal levels. Workers elected delegates who voted for the boards of regional and national federations, and delegates who voted for the executive committee of the CTV. Because the number of delegates each union could choose did not vary proportionally with the size of the union, the votes of workers in small firms carried far more weight than those of workers in large, strategic industries.[39] In addition, federations had "delegates for life" (*delegados natos*) who received automatic representation by virtue of having assumed a leadership position in the organization. Taken together, these mechanisms created a kind of "institutional fraud" that helped AD maintain its hegemony in the CTV even while losing support among strategic industrial workers and in militant sectors of the working class (Febres 1985, 297; Ellner 1993, 97).

In addition, the established parties frequently cooperated to avoid electoral competition and thereby block radical challengers. CTV statutes encouraged the political parties to agree on a single slate of candidates at all levels. According to the CTV's electoral regulation, "if in the first assembly the party factions arrive at a unanimous agreement for a single slate, this may be proclaimed at this same assembly, avoiding in this manner another meeting" (Arismendi and Iturrapse 1990, 246). This practice, which became known as the "CTV accord" (*acuerdo cetevista*), often reduced elections to "acts of approval of a prearranged deal" (Collier and Collier 1991, 621).[40] By presenting workers with only one choice at the ballot box, these arrangements eliminated their option of using party pluralism to punish incumbent leaders.[41]

When unable to control an election through an *acuerdo cetevista*, the CTV occasionally resorted to coercion. One of the most notorious examples took place in Venezuela's largest union, the Single Union of Steel Industry Workers (SUTISS), located in a state-owned steel complex in the industrial state of Bolívar. In 1979, a leftist slate headed by Andrés Velásquez won a landslide victory in the SUTISS elections. Two years later, the Federation of Metalworkers (Fetrametal) and the Federation of the State of Bolívar (Fetrabolívar), took advantage of a contract dispute to seize SUTISS and name a provisional commission composed of AD and COPEI members to run the union. The company fired the leftists on the SUTISS executive a year later, and new union elections were not held until 1987 (Ellner 1993, 156–57).

These mechanisms left AD labor leaders much more protected from workers' dissent than their Spanish counterparts. But their autonomy from the rank-and-file never matched that of CTM leaders. First, they did not have as much capacity to monopolize the workplace. The Venezuelan Congress removed exclusion clauses from an early draft of the 1936 Labor Law, and workers were even allowed to belong to more than one union until 1973 (Lucena 1982, 315, n. 15). Parallel unionism was therefore rampant at the local and regional levels, especially during periods when AD's hegemony came under attack in the political arena. In addition, non-unionized workers had the right to bargain collectively if they represented at least 75 percent of the workers in the firm (Lucena 1982, 212–13; McCoy 1989, 56).[42] Thus, at least some workers had the option of exiting from a union that did not serve their interests.

Second, party pluralism created the possibility for workers to punish incumbent leaders by supporting challengers from another party. Meaningful partisan competition meant that the union hierarchy could "less easily ignore or manipulate rank-and-file demands" (Davis 1989, 67). This competition intensified in the 1970s and 1980s, as New Unionism (*Nuevo Sindicalismo*) emerged as a radical challenger to the CTV, and the minority parties became increasingly unwilling to collaborate with the AD majority on the CTV executive. At the level of the firm, AD began to suffer serious challenges to its dominance in strategic sectors of the economy. Although its hegemony on the CTV executive remained secure, realignment among the minority parties placed additional pressure on AD labor leaders to outbid their rivals for workers' support.

This realignment was part of an overall breakdown in power-sharing arrangements between AD and COPEI. At the CTV's Ninth Congress in 1985, COPEI refused to negotiate a united slate for the CTV executive. This change did not harm AD's position, but COPEI lost control of the secretary general position to the MEP, which had a stronger tradition as a pro-worker party. Under the leadership of César Olarte, who became secretary general in 1985 and was reelected in 1990, the MEP became an important source of pressure on the AD majority for greater contestation against AD governments. Within the AD faction, this shift reinforced the power of ex-*mepistas* such as Juan José Delpino and Pedro Brito who placed a higher premium on union autonomy than some of their AD comrades.

Comparing the Power to Punish

Table 4.1 provides an index based on my narrative that compares the power of the party and workers to punish labor leaders for disloyal behavior across the three cases. The individual and average scores range from 3 (high) to 0 (negligible) and measure the contribution of each institutional arrangement to the punishing power of the party and workers. The balance refers to the difference between the punishing power of the party and that of workers. Thus, a

Table 4.1 Index of Punishing Power by Institutional Arrangement

Institutional Arrangement	Punishing Power	Mexico	Spain	Venezuela
Legal framework	Of party	3	0	2
	Of workers	0	2	1
Structure of labor movement	Of party	3	0	2
	Of workers	0	3	2
Political system	Of party	3	1	2
Control over party posts	Of party	3	3	2
Average	Of party	3	1	2
	Of workers	0	2.5	1.5
Balance	Party minus workers	3	−1.5	0.5

Scoring of punishing power: 3 = high, 2 = medium, 1 = low, 0 = negligible. Scoring of balance: >0 = party has more punishing power, <0 = workers have more punishing power.

positive score indicates greater punishing power by the party, whereas a negative score indicates greater punishing power by workers.

The index shows that Mexican labor leaders had strong incentives to favor the party over workers in the event of a loyalty dilemma. The PRI averaged the highest possible score of 3 because all four institutional arrangements contributed substantially to its power to punish labor leaders. Meanwhile, Mexican workers averaged the lowest possible score of 0 because the legal framework and the structure of the labor movement gave them negligible influence. Thus, on balance, the distribution of punishing power heavily favored the PRI. Not surprisingly, CTM leaders were much more willing to betray workers than to risk retaliation by the party.

Spanish labor leaders faced nearly as strong incentives as their Mexican counterparts but in favor of workers rather than the party. The PSOE received an average score of only 1 because, although it governed as a hegemonic party for ten years, its only real leverage came from the party hierarchy's control over party posts. In all other respects, the PSOE had very little power to punish UGT leaders for disloyal behavior. Spanish workers, on the other hand, received an average score of 2.5 because the only serious constraint on their punishing power was their limited voice within the UGT. Otherwise, they had significant leverage over UGT leaders as a result of the factory council system and stiff competition between the UGT and the CCOO. Thus, on balance, workers had significantly more punishing power than the party. Not surprisingly, UGT leaders preferred to behave disloyally toward the PSOE than to risk retaliation by workers.

Venezuelan labor leaders faced the most ambiguous incentives, since the balance of punishing power was only slightly greater than o. AD received an average score of 2 because all four arrangements endowed it with some power to punish labor leaders, but this power was constrained by partisan competition in the electoral arena and the labor movement. Similarly, Venezuelan workers received an average score of 1.5 because they faced constraints on their leverage as a result of the legal framework and the structure of the labor movement but had low barriers to exit and could capitalize on partisan competition in the labor movement to pose a credible threat to labor leaders. Thus, the distribution of punishing power slightly favored the party, but not by much. Predictably, CTV leaders vacillated between cooperation and resistance in an effort to dissuade both camps from punishing them for disloyal behavior.

Party Autonomy

The incentives for labor leaders to avoid punishment for disloyal behavior are relevant only as long as they are caught in a loyalty dilemma. Otherwise, they do not have to choose between loyalty to the party and loyalty to workers. In cases where labor lacks sufficient bargaining power to persuade the government to reverse its reforms, the most likely relief from a loyalty dilemma will come from the party's decision to defy its own government and join labor against the reforms. But such a decision is only conceivable if the party has sufficient autonomy to carry it out. Party autonomy reflects two institutional arrangements: the location of supreme authority within the party, and the spaces for intraparty dissent.

Party Capture in Mexico

The PRI had almost no autonomy to resist the actions of its own government. While endowed with the formal capacity to select its own leaders, set a political agenda, and nominate candidates for public office, it "never developed an institutional structure independent of the state apparatus" (Middlebrook 1995, 28). In fact, PRI autonomy was so nonexistent that Mexicans often referred to "the PRI-government" *(el PRI-gobierno)* as a single, undifferentiated entity. The chief executive, who was always a PRI candidate from 1930 through 1994, acted as the de facto commander of both the state and the party during his six years in office *(sexenio)*.[43] He chose a significant share of the party's leaders and could remove any PRI bureaucrat or politician who challenged his authority.[44] More importantly, he controlled the nomination of his successor. In a veiled practice known as the fingering *(dedazo),* each outgoing president selected his own successor, who was then formally nominated by the PRI. This system gave PRI leaders and their clients strong incentives to curry favor with the chief executive, particularly toward the middle of each *sexenio*.[45]

Presidential control over leadership selection was reinforced by severe limits on dissent and factionalism within the PRI. In the 1940s, the party reduced the capacity of organized sectors to nominate their own candidates, heightened the influence of party bureaucrats, and imposed strict party discipline on PRI deputies and senators (González Casanova 1981, 122–29; Pacheco 1991, 77–78). Besides generating the majority of legislative proposals, the chief executive dictated the party line in Congress. Divisions existed within the PRI, but harsh penalties discouraged the public airing of internal disputes. Combined with the PRI's dominance of the legislative branch, this discipline meant that presidential initiatives almost always became policy.[46] If party actors failed to alter these initiatives through internal negotiations, they had little choice but to throw their support behind the final outcome, however undesirable.

Party Subordination in Spain

The PSOE differed from the PRI in that it was not created as a government party; the PSOE had its own identity and institutional structure independent of the state apparatus. Nonetheless, it also answered to the chief executive when in power and was highly disciplined. As a result, it had very little autonomy to resist the actions of its own government.

The 1978 Spanish Constitution established a parliamentary system in which legislators were elected through a system of closed lists and voted the party line in the parliament. PSOE statutes required members of the Socialist Group in parliament to adhere to party discipline regarding their legislative action and votes (PSOE 1981, 52). The party leadership also deducted stiff fines from the paychecks of deputies who missed parliamentary sessions and committee meetings, thereby discouraging abstention as a form of silent protest against the government (Share 1989, 125).

The chief executive, who was also head of the dominant party, enjoyed significant autonomy from both his ministers and the legislature. Endowed with the title of president rather than prime minister, "he [was] no longer a *primus inter pares* but a real president as his official title indicates" (Bar 1988, 111). His powers of appointment and dismissal extended to the cabinet, hundreds of joint government and civil service posts, the civil governors in each province, the government delegates to the autonomous communities, and the heads of the Council of State and the National Institute of Industry (INI) (Donaghy and Newton 1987, 66). He also had final authority over whether to request a vote of confidence, dissolve the parliament, or call a referendum, all of which gave him leverage in his relations with parliament (Bar 1988, 112).[47]

As in Mexico, the decisive role of the chief executive in Spain was reinforced by controls on dissent and factionalism within the PSOE. Aware of the debilitating consequences of party divisions in the past, a group of Socialists led by Felipe González pushed through a reform of the party's internal structure at the PSOE's Twenty-eighth Congress in May 1979. The new rules established an indirect, strictly majoritarian, winner-take-all electoral system for delegates to party congresses and shifted voting on congressional resolutions from local groupings to regional blocs (Share 1989, 56).[48] The new rules also reinforced the party's intolerance for dissent, stipulating that a member could be expelled for making public declarations seen as damaging to the party image, for serious acts of indiscipline, for slandering another party member, or for provoking a major conflict within the party (Gillespie 1989, 346–47).[49] Finally, the rules denied the right of organized tendencies or non-organized "currents" to exist within the party.[50] When combined with the power of the chief executive, the PSOE's low levels of membership, and Gonzalez's popularity among the electorate, these rules severely limited the capacity of party actors to block the initiatives of their own government.[51]

Party Autonomy in Venezuela

Only in Venezuela did the party have sufficient autonomy to challenge its own government. The key difference was that control over the party resided with the National Executive Committee (CEN) rather than with the chief executive.[52] Upon taking office, an AD president held no formal post in the party leadership and had no direct control over the party organization (Coppedge 1994, 123). The CEN, meanwhile, controlled the placement of party candidates on closed lists for the Senate and the Chamber of Deputies, preselected the leader of the party's legislative faction, chaired all congressional committees held by AD, dictated the party line in Congress, and final authority over the formation of a multiparty coalition to pass legislation (Kelley 1986, 35; Myers 1986, 132).[53]

Not only were party militants dependent on the CEN for their legislative careers and decisions, but AD presidents had only limited influence over the nomination of their successors.[54] The party's nominating convention had both formal and de facto power to select its presidential candidate, and its delegates often voted down the president's choice (Coppedge 1994, 109, 122). Unlike the Mexican *dedazo*, which united the PRI behind the president, this system had the effect of splitting the party into open factions, one of which inevitably challenged the president and his inner circle.[55] Although this factionalism rarely translated into a frontal challenge to the president by AD's parliamentary group, it provided opportunities for disgruntled labor leaders to cultivate the support of more sympathetic elements within the party.

Ordinarily, party leaders did not act on their capacity to challenge their own government. To the contrary, they usually granted the president significant leeway to carry out his agenda. They customarily released him from party discipline while in office (Coppedge 1994, 65), and they rarely challenged presidential initiatives in Congress. In 1961 and 1974, AD even used its congressional majority to grant the president special decree powers (Crisp 1998, 5–7). But the possibility nonetheless existed that the CEN would defy an AD president in the event that he seriously compromised the party's interests, as occurred under Carlos Andrés Pérez in the 1970s. This possibility meant that the party leadership could conceivably ameliorate a loyalty dilemma by siding with labor against its own government.

Comparing Party Autonomy

Table 4.2 provides an index based on my narrative that compares each party's capacity to act autonomously from its own government across the three countries. The scores for supreme authority have only two possible values: 3 if it is located in the party apparatus and 0 if it is located in the chief executive. The scores for intraparty dissent range from to 3 (high) to 0 (negligible). The average scores range from greater than 2 (high) to less than 1 (low).

The PRI received the lowest average score of 0 because the president of the republic was the undisputed leader of the party and controlled a highly disciplined party machine that had been at the service of the state since its creation. The PSOE averaged a slightly higher score of 0.5 for having an institutional identity and structure independent of the Spanish state, but it still scored low because of the location of supreme authority in the chief executive

Table 4.2   Index of Party Autonomy by Institutional Arrangement

Institutional Arrangement	Mexico	Spain	Venezuela
Supreme authority	0	0	3
Intraparty dissent	0	1	2
Average score	0	0.5	2.5

Scoring of supreme authority: 3 = located in party apparatus, 0 = located in chief executive. Scoring of intraparty dissent: 3 = high, 2 = medium, 1 = low, 0 = negligible. Average scores: >2 = high, 1 to 2 = medium, <1 = low.

and its high degree of party discipline. In both cases, the party lacked the autonomy to join labor leaders in resisting the reforms and therefore was unable to alleviate their loyalty dilemma.

AD is the only party that scored high for party autonomy. Its average score of 2.5 is based primarily on the location of supreme authority in the CEN instead of the chief executive, which freed AD to stake out an independent position. In addition, the existence of influential factions within the party hierarchy provided labor leaders with potential allies and encouraged the incumbent leadership to bid for labor's support against rival factions by distancing itself from the government. Thus, while the party's hierarchical structure and the strict discipline imposed on AD legislators prevented it from receiving the highest score, AD had sufficient autonomy to oppose its own government and thereby brings its labor allies relief from their loyalty dilemma.

CHAPTER 5

Survival of the Postrevolutionary Alliance in Mexico

Mexico's party-union alliance, which grew out of the Mexican Revolution in the early twentieth century, rested on the principles of revolutionary nationalism and a set of norms generated by exchanges in the socioeconomic, political, and organizational arenas. These principles and norms faced unprecedented challenges in the 1980s and 1990s, when the PRI governments of Miguel De la Madrid (1982–1988) and Carlos Salinas (1988–1994) adopted reforms that violated the central tenets of revolutionary nationalism and imposed painful sacrifices on workers and unions. Because the PRI lacked sufficient autonomy from its own government to join labor in resisting the reforms, CTM leaders had to choose between loyalty to the party and loyalty to workers. They selected the former because the party had a much greater capacity to punish them for disloyal behavior. This choice translated into a strategy of norm-based voice throughout the reform period. Although CTM leaders threatened, cajoled, and made deals with the PRI in attempts to soften the blows of the reforms, they never deviated from alliance norms governing exchange and conflict management.

Principles of Revolutionary Nationalism

The vision of society that sustained the PRI-CTM alliance had its roots in the Mexican Revolution and the 1917 Constitution. The revolution began in 1910 as a middle-class revolt against the dictatorship of Porfirio Díaz, but it quickly turned into a popular rebellion. Led by mythic figures such as Emiliano Zapata and Pancho Villa, the revolutionaries broke the hold of traditional elites on Mexican society and paved the way for a mass-based politics. Although a more conservative faction prevailed over Zapata and Villa by 1916, the revolution became fixed in the popular imagination as a victory of the masses against injustice and oppression.

This image was reinforced by the 1917 Constitution, which emphasized the rights of the common people and empowered the state to intervene on their behalf. Among its most progressive provisions were Article 27, which mandated the redistribution of land to the peasants, and Article 123, which granted workers protections against dismissal, the right to organize and strike, minimum standards of occupational health and safety, job training, a prohibition against child labor, maternity leave, equal pay for equal work, a living wage, an eight-hour workday, overtime pay, housing, social security, and profit sharing (*Ley Federal de Trabajo* 1990, 5–15). Many Mexicans viewed these articles as an inheritance that could not be denied to them without betraying the revolution.

The symbolic and constitutional legacies of the revolution laid the basis for the doctrine of "revolutionary nationalism." Pragmatic and flexible, this doctrine included three principles: economic sovereignty, social justice, and national unity. All three principles were linked to an interventionist state. The principle of economic sovereignty implied resistance to imperialism. Among the most powerful symbols of this resistance were Villa's attack on New Mexico in 1916 and the expropriation of the foreign-owned oil companies by President Lázaro Cárdenas in 1938. These events affirmed Mexico's independence from its powerful northern neighbor and made freedom from foreign domination a key component of the revolutionary project.

The principle of social justice implied socioeconomic benefits and political representation for the organized masses. Whereas workers and peasants had been excluded and oppressed under previous regimes, they became the pillars of Mexico's postrevolutionary government. Not only did the constitution mandate their protection and support, but they also became incorporated into a reconstructed national identity. As portrayed in the murals of Diego Rivera and José Clemente Orozco, the revolution was glorified as a struggle by and for working Mexicans, whose claims for justice earned a central place in the postrevolutionary discourse.

Finally, the principle of national unity implied defense of postrevolutionary institutions by the members of "the revolutionary family" (*la familia revolucionaria*). When these institutions came under attack by foreign or domestic interests, the heirs to the revolution were expected to close ranks to protect them, even if it meant sacrificing other goals. In a few cases, such as the 1938 oil expropriation, this defense involved support for pro-worker policies. More often, however, it meant the moderation of labor's demands during moments of national crisis, as well as an encompassing, rather than sectarian, vision by the CTM. In the process, the principle of national unity tended to temper demands for social justice by mass-based groups incorporated into the system. Afraid of reopening the Pandora's box of popular revolt, *la familia revolucionaria* viewed public order as a prerequisite to realizing the other goals of the revolution.

Norms of Exchange and Conflict Management

The principles of revolutionary nationalism generated norms of behavior for the PRI and the CTM in the socioeconomic, political, and organizational arenas. The alliance was strengthened, moreover, by several episodes in which the party temporarily violated its side of the bargain but ultimately respected its commitments to the CTM in response to norm-based voice. Although these episodes placed significant stress on party-union relations, they ended up contributing to the sustainability of the alliance because they counseled patience by labor leaders in the event that the party strayed again from alliance norms. In effect, experience taught CTM leaders that the persistent application of norm-based voice was likely to restore the PRI's delivery of inducements, particularly in the political and organizational arenas.

Socioeconomic Bargain

Under the socioeconomic bargain, the party was expected to use state power to deliver material benefits to workers. Cárdenas firmly established this norm in the 1930s when he supported individual unions in their wage negotiations with employers, backed strike actions, and used state authority to push through settlements favorable to unions. Although the bargain was restructured in the 1940s to exclude PRI support for labor mobilization, the PRI continued to provide material benefits to workers and unions, especially between 1955 and 1973.

Many of these benefits were positive externalities of the successful adoption of non-inflationary ISI. In the 1950s, the government launched a strategy of "stabilizing development" that combined conservative fiscal and monetary policies with protectionist trade policies, extensive state regulation, and high levels of public investment. After an initial period of austerity, this strategy unleashed the "Mexican miracle" of rapid growth with low inflation. Between 1950 and 1970, Mexico's economy grew at an average annual rate of 7.8 percent while annual inflation remained around 3 percent (Lustig 1998, 14–15).

Stabilizing development brought substantial gains to workers. On the employment front, it generated millions of jobs in industries with relatively high rates of unionization. Between 1940 and 1969, the number of workers employed in the secondary sector of the economy (mining, petroleum, manufacturing, construction, and public utilities) grew at an average annual rate of 5 percent, from 826,000 to 3.4 million (Gregory 1986, 30). On the wage front, it contributed to a quadrupling of average real wages between 1952 and 1976 (Basañez 1990, 171). In real terms, industrial workers saw their wages and benefits grow by an average of 85 percent between 1960 and 1975. During this same period, the real urban minimum wage grew by an average of 110 percent (Gregory 1986, 232).

Workers also profited from policies specifically designed to raise their living standards. In the mid-1950s, the PRI revived the practice of using the extensive powers of the Labor Ministry to pressure employers to increase wages and benefits in collective contracts negotiated with unions. In addition, wage increases negotiated by collective contracts set the pace for increases in the minimum wage, which were determined every two years by the National Minimum Wage Commission (CNSM) established in 1962. As a result, some of the gains achieved by the unions reached non-unionized workers.

The PRI also provided non-wage gains to labor in the form of social security, health care, education, and subsidies on basic commodities and housing. Coverage by the Mexican Social Security Institute (IMSS) expanded from 4 percent of the workforce in 1952 to 25 percent in 1970, and most unions in nationalized sectors negotiated generous social security benefits in their collective contracts (Mesa-Lago 1978, 216–19). The PRI also fulfilled its constitutional mandate to require workers' participation in company profits and to create the National Worker Housing Institute (Infonavit). Although some of these programs reached non-unionized workers, union members tended to have privileged access.

Besides channeling benefits directly to workers, the PRI guaranteed unions representation in government agencies that had an impact on workers. Three agencies of particular importance to the CTM were the IMSS, the CNSM, and the Infonavit. Although other official unions received seats on the governing boards of these agencies, the CTM tended to control the largest share. As of 1979, the CTM controlled one out of the four labor positions in the IMSS and 55.6 percent of the labor representatives in the CNSM, with the remaining 44.4 percent divided among four other organizations (Zazueta and De la Peña 1984, 381–82).[1]

The CTM had even greater success in dominating labor's participation in the Infonavit. Although originally designed to grant financing to workers on the basis of technical criteria, the Infonavit quickly evolved into a source of patronage resources for the CTM. Besides becoming directly involved in housing construction, the agency shifted from a computerized system for assigning housing to one of "external promotions" whereby groups of workers selected by the unions, the private sector, or the government would submit development plans (including their choice of a construction company) to the agency for approval.[2] Soon thereafter, the CTM gained control of labor's representative on the Infonavit board and took charge of the union representing Infonavit workers with the help of the Labor Ministry (Aldrete-Hass 1991, 112).

Finally, the PRI contributed to the CTM's financial solvency. Besides receiving PRI subsidies to compensate for its lack of self-financing, the CTM built its national headquarters on expropriated land donated by the state, and staff members received two paychecks: one from the CTM and one from the PRI. In addition, President José López Portillo created the Workers' Bank *(Banco Obrero)* in 1977. The *Banco Obrero* not only provided banking services to workers and their families, but also extended low-interest loans to unions and confederations (Grayson 1989, 51, 55). Although many unions were shareholders, the CTM dominated the bank's administration (Middlebrook 1995, 222).[3]

Not coincidentally, the PRI created the IMSS, the Infonavit, and the *Banco Obrero* during periods of high inflation. This pattern established a norm whereby the PRI would compensate the CTM for falling real wages with new organizational privileges that enabled the CTM to channel selective benefits to its members. Because the power of CTM leaders rested more on the loyalty of a few subordinates than on the generalized well-being of workers, these programs played a crucial role in sustaining the party-union alliance during economic crisis.

For receiving these benefits, the CTM was expected to support the PRI's economic plan, particularly during hard times. First, the CTM contributed to wage moderation through formal participation in the CNSM, informal agreements with the government, and the exercise of influence over collective wage bargaining by CTM affiliates at the plant level (Collier and Collier 1991, 582). Although the confederation preferred to use these channels to transmit real wage gains to its members, it was willing to negotiate wage austerity in periods of high inflation. Second, the CTM helped create a favorable environment for private investment by choosing conciliation over mobilization. Besides discouraging strikes by its own affiliates, the CTM signed tripartite pacts to ensure labor peace and exercised a moderating influence through its control of the majority of labor seats on the special Boards of Conciliation and

Arbitration (JCA).[4] Among other things, these boards resolved individual and collective labor disputes and ruled on the legality of strike petitions (Middlebrook 1995, 61).

This norm of worker demobilization was sustainable partly because the CTM had access to an instrument of voice—"radical posturing"—that produced wage concessions while stopping short of mobilizing workers. As discussed in chapter 4, the Federal Labor Law (LFT) required that unions file a strike petition *(emplazamiento)* before holding a legal strike. Whenever the government attempted wage austerity, the CTM would file a rash of *emplazamientos* and threaten to mobilize its members. Usually, the CTM's militant stance would contrast with the unconditional support given by rival unions to the wage policy. Once the PRI responded with concessions, the CTM would withdraw the *emplazamientos* and reaffirm its historic alliance with the PRI.

The CTM successfully resorted to radical posturing after major devaluations of the Mexican peso in the mid-1950s and the mid-1970s (Collier and Collier 1991, 591; Zamora 1990, 540–56). The outcomes served the interests of both the CTM and the PRI. In both instances, the CTM recuperated legitimacy among its bases and the PRI avoided unified labor opposition against its policies while maintaining controls on wage growth. Moreover, the CTM's access to radical posturing as an effective instrument of norm-based voice lowered its incentives to resort to norm-breaking voice in times of alliance stress, thereby contributing to the stability of the party-union alliance.

Political Bargain

Under the political bargain, the party was expected to allocate a certain number of party posts and elected offices to CTM leaders. Once again, this norm had its origins under Cárdenas, who created a system of sectorial representation when he transformed the official party into the Party of the Mexican Revolution (PRM) in 1938. The organizations incorporated into the PRM's three sectors, including the CTM, became the PRM's sole channels of representation and were guaranteed party posts and candidacies. Even after losing influence in the mid-1940s, the CTM continued to be the most important union in the Labor Sector and to receive "power quotas" *(cuotas del poder)* in the form of candidacies at the local, state, and federal levels. Since the PRI won the vast majority of elections through the 1970s, these candidates almost always took office.

Although the CTM received a relatively small share of total PRI candidacies, it dominated those allocated to the Labor Sector. Between 1964 and 1982, it controlled an average of 60 percent of the Labor Sector's deputies in the Chamber of Deputies (Grayson 1989, 52).[5] Likewise, the CTM controlled eight out of twelve senate seats held by the Labor Sector in the late 1970s, with the remaining four divided among three other organizations (Zazueta and de la Peña 1984, 382, 371).[6] Between 1940 and 1988, one of the two senate seats in the Federal District was always held by Fidel Velázquez or one of his trusted colleagues (Middlebrook 1995, 105). The CTM was also the only member of the Labor Sector to have one of its leaders serve as governor until 1982.[7]

This norm of guaranteed positions for the CTM survived several episodes of alliance stress. The first episode occurred in 1946, when President Manuel Avila Camacho transformed the PRM into the PRI. As part of an attempt to centralize power within the party, Avila Camacho proposed a shift in the basis for affiliation and candidate selection from the sectors to individual militants. The reform ultimately foundered, however, on the resistance of the sectorial organizations, particularly the CTM, and the lack of real party structures outside the sectors. In anticipation of presidential elections later that year, Avila Camacho negotiated a pact that reaffirmed the role of the sectors.[8] Four years later, the PRI reformed its statutes to reinstate the system of internal elections based on assemblies of delegates chosen by the sectors.[9]

A similar pattern occurred in the mid-1960s, when the president of the PRI, Carlos Madrazo, attempted to replace the sector-dominated process of candidate selection in the municipalities with a series of primary elections open to individual party members (Middlebrook 1981, 18). Once again, the reform initiative failed in the face of fierce opposition by the CTM and other entrenched interests. Madrazo was forced to resign in 1965, and the sectors continued to dominate the selection process. The CTM was less successful in blocking an electoral reform in 1977, which threatened to reduce its *cuotas del poder* by ceding power to opposition parties. Nonetheless, the PRI compensated the CTM by increasing the total number of legislative seats and raising the CTM's share of PRI positions. In the 1979 elections, the CTM's share of all PRI deputies grew from 8.8 percent to 14.6 percent compared to the previous legislature, while its share of labor deputies increased from 59 percent to 65.2 percent (Grayson 1989, 52).

These experiences created the expectation among CTM leaders that the PRI would ultimately retreat from reforms that jeopardized their access to party posts and public offices. Rather than taking the risks associated with norm-breaking voice, CTM leaders had good reason to believe that norm-based voice would salvage the political bargain before the PRI had to face another presidential succession. These expectations (and their fulfillment) contributed to the survival of the PRI-CTM alliance in the early 1990s.

In return for its sectorial privileges, the CTM was expected to deliver two kinds of political "goods" to the PRI: the undivided loyalty of its members and active support for the PRI's political hegemony. The norm of undivided loyalty was cemented in the late 1940s, when the CTM's ex-secretary general, Vicente Lombardo Toledano, tried to form a new party, the Popular Party (PP), with a strong labor base and greater autonomy from the regime.[10] After initially tolerating Lombardo's plan, the CTM leadership clamped down on the PP, declaring, "it would weaken the electoral force of our [Confederation]" (CTM 1986a, 75). With the active support of President Miguel Alemán and the PRI, the CTM punished members who participated in the PP and expelled Lombardo (and the Communists) for having political loyalties to more than one master (Medina 1979, 137–39; Ramírez Cuéllar 1992, 211).[11] Rather than viewing the emergence of the PP as an opportunity to realize the ideological agenda of the labor movement, CTM leaders saw it as a threat to the prerogatives that were at the heart of their political bargain with the PRI.

Soon thereafter, the CTM adopted rules that closed off any remaining avenues of political pluralism. In 1951, the CTM approved a decree requiring PRI affiliation and militance by CTM members and their families (CTM 1986b, 590–91). This requirement, which was subsequently incorporated into CTM statutes, meant that exit by workers to a competing party could be punished by dismissal under the separation clause of the LFT (see chapter 4).[12] In addition, the CTM created a new position of Secretary of Political Action to encourage CTM members to participate in the PRI and to increase CTM representation in elected offices (Mussot López and González Cruz 1990, 235).

The norm of undivided loyalty facilitated the CTM's delivery of its second political "good" to the party: support for the PRI's political hegemony. Within the PRI, the CTM exercised a stabilizing influence during the transition from one administration to another. As discussed in chapter 4, the outgoing PRI president used the *dedazo* to choose the next candidate. Party militants would then unite around his choice and mobilize the party's machinery to bring the PRI another victory in the presidential elections.

The CTM, and particularly Velázquez, took the lead in circling the wagons around the president's nominee. Following a pattern established in the late 1930s, the CTM would endorse (and sometimes announce) the new candidate, and, in the process, undermine the candidate's intraparty rivals, particularly from the party's left wing. This contribution was vital in Mexico's dominant-party system, since the decisive moment in the transfer of power was "the selection and designation of the official candidate rather than the casting or counting of votes" (Corona Armenta 1995, 128). In a clear indication of the CTM's critical role in managing these transitions, Velázquez always assumed the presidency of the Labor Congress during the period of candidate selection.

The CTM also participated actively in PRI campaigns at the municipal, state, and national levels. In the months leading up to an election, the CTM distributed propaganda and organized mass demonstrations in favor of PRI candidates. Often, the CTM enticed workers to gather in the town square by offering them transportation and food. CTM leaders also helped the PRI buy votes and lambasted the opposition as enemies of the Mexican Revolution. On election day, the CTM delivered the working class vote—entire districts in some cases—to the party. Besides requiring CTM members and their families to vote for the PRI, the CTM frequently brought workers to the polls and, when necessary, helped local PRI officials doctor the results.

As in the socioeconomic arena, these norms placed limits on union behavior but did not prevent CTM leaders from engaging in radical posturing in pursuit of their interests. Prior to the allocation of PRI candidacies for an upcoming election, CTM leaders would often file a rash of strike petitions and issue threats to abandon the PRI. But once the candidacies were allocated and the election campaign began, the CTM would close ranks with the party and devote its energy to mobilizing votes for the PRI.

Organizational Bargain

Under the organizational bargain, the PRI was expected to support the hegemony of the CTM within the labor movement. As of 1979, the CTM represented 47 percent of unions and 27.4 percent of unionized workers, a larger share than any other organization except the FSTSE. It also had the widest distribution of membership within the Labor Congress (CT), accounting for the majority of CT-affiliated workers in twenty-three out of thirty-two states and in fifteen out of twenty-eight sectors (Zazueta and de la Peña 1984, 456, 470–71, 480–81). Moreover, the CTM dominated decision making within the CT, as reflected by its hold on the position of general coordinator and its frequent control of the presidency.

The CTM could not have been maintained its hegemony, however, without the active support of the PRI. The CTM's base in small, state-dependent unions was no match for the national autonomous unions (SNA) in strategic sectors such as petroleum, mining and metalworking, railroads, telecommunications, and public utilities.[13] Several PRI policies helped the CTM prevail over its rivals despite these strategic disadvantages.

First, the CTM's privileged access to seats on organizations with an impact on workers gave it both carrots and sticks in its competition with rival unions. Representation on the CNSM, the IMSS, the Infonavit, and the *Banco Obrero* provided the CTM with selective incentives and "became an important basis for many labor leaders' legitimacy within their own organizations" (Middlebrook 1995, 62). Moreover, the CTM's dominance of labor's seats on the special Boards of Conciliation and Arbitration enabled it to block leadership challenges and worker mobilizations by rival unions.[14]

When these mechanisms failed to contain threats to the CTM's hegemony, PRI governments would intervene directly in the affairs of dissident unions. This norm became established in the late 1940s, when several national autonomous unions organized a broad-based coalition that challenged both the CTM's hegemony and the PRI's economic policies. This dual threat prompted President Miguel Alemán to intervene directly in the affairs of the dissident unions. He began by supporting a challenge to the dissident leadership of the Union of Mexican Railroad Workers (STFRM) in 1948. With the PRI's backing, a rival leader, nicknamed *el charro* for his cowboy attire, took control of the STFRM and rewrote the union's statutes to centralize control over union governance. Alemán engineered similar purges in the oilworkers' union in 1949 and the mining and metalworkers' union in 1950 (Collier and Collier 1991, 415; Middlebrook 1995, 148–49).

These purges, which became known as *charrazos*, established a pattern of PRI opposition to dissident challenges.[15] Often with the CTM's complicity, labor authorities would use their control over union formation and organization to marginalize competing labor unions, impose compliant leaders, and restructure union statutes. If necessary, they also resorted to coercion, either deploying the police directly or turning a blind eye to fraud and intimidation by union thugs aimed at manipulating leadership selection or seizing control of a collective contract from a rival union. Although the PRI preferred more subtle methods of labor control, these tactics were crucial to defeating renewed challenges by dissident national autonomous unions in the late 1950s and mid-1970s.

As in the political arena, the norm of PRI support for the CTM survived an episode of alliance stress. Faced with a crisis of legitimacy following the PRI's violent repression of student demonstrators in 1968, President Luis Echeverría tried to restructure the party-union alliance by marginalizing the CTM and encouraging independent unions. Besides launching rhetorical attacks against the CTM's undemocratic practices, he permitted the legal recognition of unions not affiliated with official confederations and even supported attempts by dissident factions to win control of local unions (Middlebrook 1995, 224). He also attempted to bypass the CTM as a mediating institution by delivering social welfare benefits directly to workers.

Echeverría's flirtation with alliance restructuring came to a grinding halt, however, with the approach of the presidential succession. Once again, the PRI needed the CTM to manage the transition, particularly given a serious deterioration in Echeverría's relations with the private sector. Thus, the PRI returned to its traditional strategy of using the legal and coercive powers of the state to crush the dissident movement, which went from impressive proportions in 1975 to near-extinction by the end of 1976 (Aziz Nassif 1989, 178–79). Meanwhile, "the influence of Velázquez reached its maximum point in the moments of the selection of López Portillo as [presidential] candidate and during the first two years of his administration" (Camacho 1980, 70).

This episode of confrontation followed by reconciliation reinforced the CTM's expectation that the PRI would retreat from any attempt to eliminate its leadership privileges once the presidential succession approached. CTM leaders came to expect that the PRI's reliance on their support during the transition outweighed any desire it might have to "modernize" its relations with the labor movement. Because of this expectation, CTM leaders had little incentive to move beyond norm-based voice during periods of alliance stress.

In return for the PRI's support, the CTM was expected to help the PRI survive regime crises and to provide ideological legitimation. The CTM's backing for the regime proved crucial at moments of crisis such as the confrontation with foreign oil companies in 1937–1938, the dissident union movements of the late 1940s and late 1950s, the student demonstrations of 1968, the private sector offensive against Echeverría in the mid-1970s, and the nationalization of the banks by López Portillo in 1982. In some cases, the CTM mobilized its mass base against challenges from domestic or international forces on the right. Equally important, however, was the CTM's willingness and capacity to act as a bulwark against the left. By aligning itself with the PRI, the CTM prevented leftist forces from constructing a unified popular front against the regime. Within organized labor, this alignment was key to keeping the labor movement divided and thereby undermining the potential challenge posed to the PRI by the economically important—and sometimes more democratic—national autonomous unions.

The CTM also helped the PRI retain its legitimacy as the rightful heir to the Mexican Revolution. As a mass-based organization with an institutionalized presence within the party, the CTM bolstered the PRI's claims to represent the common people for whom the revolution was allegedly fought. The CTM tirelessly reinforced the symbolic links between the revolution and the PRI in speeches and political propaganda, as well as participating in the formulation of the party's programs and platforms, which were imbued with revolutionary nationalist rhetoric. The appropriation of this rhetoric by the PRI and its labor allies made it difficult for leftist opponents to challenge the regime on ideological grounds. Any rival to the PRI, however progressive, was an enemy of the revolution and thereby forfeited its political rights.[16]

Bargains in Crisis

From the 1940s until the early 1980s, a symbiotic relationship existed between the bargains of the PRI and the CTM and the economic and political models that prevailed in Mexico. This relationship proved unsustainable, however, in the face of growing pressures at home and abroad. Trends such as the exhaustion of ISI and increasing public indebtedness merged with international price shocks in the 1970s and early 1980s to bring the Mexican economy to its knees. In response, the PRI abandoned ISI in favor of market opening, which dealt a serious blow to the normative framework on which its alliance with the CTM had been based.

The PRI's bargains with the CTM became a mixed blessing in this new context. Although the party continued to rely on some features of its special relationship with labor, it was paying an untenably high price for others. Thus, the PRI attempted a balancing act between dismantling its old bargains with the CTM and offering CTM leaders enough goodies to keep them from jumping ship. This strategy was facilitated by a distribution of punishing power that significantly favored the party over workers. Not only did CTM leaders rely heavily on the PRI and its de facto leader, the president of the republic, for their career successes, but they also had sufficient autonomy from workers to accept leadership privileges in exchange for less favorable socioeconomic policies. Moreover, they had historically grounded expectations that the PRI would retreat from an assault on these privileges as the presidential succession approached. As a result, the PRI had room to retain their loyalty without seriously jeopardizing its market reform program.

In many respects, the CTM became more of a liability than an asset for the PRI in the 1980s and early 1990s. The privileges to which the CTM had become accustomed were not so readily accommodated in an environment of greater economic and political competition. In the economic arena, the goals of delivering real wage growth, stable employment, and generous social spending often clashed with those of controlling inflation and competing in the global marketplace. In the political arena, guaranteeing candidacies to CTM leaders often clashed with the requirement that candidates be electable. In a more competitive political system, the CTM lost much of its capacity to deliver large blocs of votes on election day, particularly due in part to the power of the media and other modern campaign tools to mobilize voters without the help of intermediary organizations such as unions. In this context, the

PRI had incentives to reduce its exchanges with the CTM and restructure its support coalition to match Mexico's new economic model and increasingly heterogeneous social structure.

Restructuring the Wage Bargain

One of the PRI's top priorities in the 1980s and 1990s was fighting inflation. After failing to control prices through more orthodox measures largely opposed by the CTM, the PRI adopted a pacted incomes policy in 1987 that required the CTM's collaboration. During both phases, a combination of sticks and carrots convinced CTM leaders to limit themselves to norm-based voice, despite a permanent loss in their influence over wage levels, not to mention a drastic decline in real wages. First, they were highly vulnerable to punishment by the PRI if they actually mobilized workers against wage austerity. Second, they could afford to accept leadership privileges as compensation because they were relatively protected from punishment by the workers who were suffering from the PRI's policies.

Upon taking office in December 1982, Miguel De la Madrid adopted an orthodox anti-inflation policy that consisted of unilateral wage restraints, drastic budget cuts, and trade liberalization. The CTM responded with its traditional tactic of radical posturing; it filed thousands of *emplazamientos* and warned that its collaboration with the regime was in jeopardy if the government did not grant higher wage increases (see table 3.2 for income levels; see table 5.1 for petitions filed). In contrast to the 1950s and the 1970s, however, the CTM's actions this time brought almost no concessions from the government.[17] Insisting that he would not be pressured "by old styles of negotiation" (*Proceso*, July 25, 1983), De la Madrid supported rival unions willing to back his austerity policies and took repressive measures against the few unions that refused to modify their wage demands.[18] Although these crackdowns were not aimed directly at the CTM, they "made it much more difficult for the CTM to build broad labor support for its policy positions" (Middlebrook 1995, 261).

Rather than taking the risk of carrying out its strike threats, the CTM acquiesced to the government's salary caps. In the process, real wages plummeted, and the CTM experienced a significant loss of decision-making authority. This loss of authority took two forms. First,

Table 5.1   Federal Jurisdiction Strike Petitions Filed by CTM, 1983–1998

Year	Petitions Filed
1983	9505
1984	6387
1985	6165
1986	8689
1987	12295
1988	5694
1989	4766
1990	4450
1991	4524
1992	4485
1993	5163
1994	5007
1995	5223
1996	5527
1997	5662
1998	5245

Adapted from STPS 1995, 2000

De la Madrid effectively transferred control over minimum wage levels from the tripartite CNSM to the economic cabinet.[19] Second, he reversed a traditional pattern whereby increases negotiated in collective contracts set the pace for minimum wage adjustments. With the short-lived exception of 1986 and 1987, minimum wage adjustments served as salary caps for increases in contracted wages throughout the 1980s.[20] Such policies "tended to erase . . . the boundary between unionized workers and non-unionized workers, eliminating or seeking to eliminate one of the central functions of the union and the collective contract: the negotiation of wages" (Ortega and Solís 1990, 225). In the process, the CTM lost much of its ability to deliver real wage gains to its members.

At the same time, however, the PRI adhered to the norm of granting CTM leaders a new fiefdom during periods of high inflation to enable them to distribute selective benefits to their followers. Early in his term, De la Madrid gave constitutional status and government funding to the "social sector" of worker-owned enterprises. As defined by the CTM, the social sector consisted of "all enterprises of a collective character, owned by a nucleus of workers or a union organization, without profit motives, integrated into all economic activities and oriented toward producing, commercializing, or consuming necessary goods and services of generalized use" (CTM 1986c, 203). Because the PRI's funding for the social sector was channeled through the CTM-controlled *Banco Obrero*, "the CTM, and in part the CT, prevented other unions, large or small, from benefiting from and initiating their own projects" (Aguilar García and Arrieta 1990, 702).

The nature and timing of the government's assistance reinforced the link between organizational rewards and CTM cooperation with market-oriented reform. In the midst of tensions over wage policy in February 1983, the government authorized a credit of five billion pesos for the social sector. The credit was formally announced just before May Day (Aguilar García and Arrieta 1990, 699). The government granted the *Banco Obrero* another five billion pesos to promote union enterprises in June 1985, just one month before the midterm elections (Zamora 1990, 128).

The number of CTM enterprises in the social sector grew by an average annual rate of 15 percent between 1982 and 1985. The unions with the greatest participation were in sugar, oil, petrochemicals, electricity, radio, cinematography, rubber, and graphic arts, along with several state federations. In 1985, four hundred CTM firms employed two hundred thousand workers and produced goods such as basic goods, clothing, shoes, and medicines that were distributed in 142 shops controlled by the CTM. Even after the social sector fell victim to privatization after 1985, the government extended another credit of twenty-one billion pesos to the CTM in 1987 (Aguilar García and Arrieta 1990, 698–703). These benefits came nowhere near to compensating workers for their generalized loss of income, but they provided CTM leaders with resources for sustaining the loyalty of key subordinates.

As described in chapter 3, the Mexican economy took a dramatic turn for the worse in late 1987 with the collapse of the stock market in October and a 40 percent devaluation of the peso in November. In response to escalating prices, the CTM filed thousands of *emplazamientos* and threatened to hold a general strike if the government did not grant immediate increases in both minimum and contracted wages. In a thinly veiled reference to the CTM's political bargain with the PRI, Velázquez warned that, without these increases, the working class "will not make it to the 1988 elections because they will have died of hunger" (*La Jornada*, November 21, 1987).

Rather than dismissing the CTM's radical posturing this time, the government took advantage of it to create the political space necessary for constructing a new anti-inflation policy. Even before the CTM launched its strike threats, a network of officials in the Ministry of Planning and Budget, the Bank of Mexico, and the Ministry of Finance had grown convinced of the need for negotiated price and wage controls (Kaufman, Bazdresch, and Heredia 1994, 377). For the purposes of this initiative, the CTM's resistance became a useful instrument for pressuring the private sector to cooperate. In stark contrast to previous years, the CTM's demands received support not only from the PRI delegation in the Chamber of Deputies but also from the PRI's presidential candidate, Carlos Salinas, who was a key ally of the financial technocrats (*Proceso*, December 7, 1987; *La Jornada*, December 10, 1987, December 12, 1987). According to Javier Bonilla, who was undersecretary of labor at the time, this support helped convince the private sector to come to the negotiating table.[21]

After difficult negotiations, representatives from government, business, labor, and the peasantry signed the Pact of Economic Solidarity (*Pacto*) on December 15, 1987. The *Pacto* mandated another devaluation of the peso, budget austerity measures, price and wage controls, and trade liberalization. Although intended as a temporary measure to break the inflationary cycle, the *Pacto*'s remarkable success prompted the government to renegotiate it periodically over the next decade.

While creating a new space for the CTM to participate in wage policy, the *Pacto* reinforced the centralization of wage bargaining in the hands of the economic cabinet. First, the CNSM became further marginalized in the wage-setting process. Although the commission retained its formal authority to establish minimum wages, its business and labor delegates were obligated to follow the guidelines established by the *Pacto*.[22] These guidelines, in turn, were generally decided by the economic cabinet and then delivered to the *Pacto* signatories for their approval.

Second, the *Pacto* retained the practice of using minimum wage adjustments as caps for wages negotiated in collective contracts (Woodruff 1997, 5–6). It extended increases in the minimum wage to contracted wages in December 1987 and March 1988, but then froze all wages between April and December 1988 (CSE 1994, 285–90). As manufacturing income began to diverge from the downward trend of the minimum wage, the *Pacto* explicitly prohibited further increases in contracted wages and, in 1993, explicitly required that collective wage bargaining "be resolved within the inflation rate guiding this Concertation" (297). Evidence suggests that these provisions caused earning differentials between unionized and non-unionized workers to narrow, particularly in the late 1980s (Woodruff 1997, 24).

The *Pacto* essentially brought the CTM's radical posturing over national wage policy to an end, even after a drastic devaluation of the peso in 1994.[23] Rather than filing a rash of strike petitions, the confederation chose to pursue its wage demands through the *Pacto*, which was renewed in early 1995 (Grayson 1998, 114). In part, this change resulted from the *Pacto*'s success in controlling inflation and thereby improving the conditions for real wage growth. But the CTM's less combative tactics cannot be explained entirely by improved economic conditions, since contracted wages in federal jurisdiction activities continued to stagnate, and all wages fell after the peso devaluation in 1994 (see table 3.2).

Rather than reflecting a major victory for organized workers, the CTM's tactical shift signaled its acceptance of a new wage bargain with the PRI. Essentially, the CTM traded a devaluation of its traditional mechanisms of wage setting for a formalized—and privileged—channel through which to engage in insider bargaining, which it always preferred to external pressure.[24] Perhaps most importantly, the *Pacto* made the CTM an indispensable partner in the government's economic program and thereby gave the CTM valuable leverage in its overall relationship with the PRI.

Challenging the CTM's Prerogatives

De la Madrid engineered a permanent reduction in the CTM's real influence over wage levels, but he did little to challenge the CTM's leadership privileges. Carlos Salinas, by contrast, led a direct assault on these privileges as part of an attempt to reconstruct the PRI's support coalition to match Mexico's increasingly heterogeneous social structure and neoliberal economic model. In the process, he came much closer to challenging the core interests of CTM leaders.

First, Salinas cultivated new interlocutors in the labor movement. Calling for a "new unionism" to meet the demands of a modernized and market-oriented economy, he began wooing the support of "modern" union leaders in the public sector and recently privatized sectors. With his implicit backing, several unions from the latter group formed the Federation of Goods and Services Unions (FESEBES) in April 1990 under the leadership of Francisco Hernández Juárez, the secretary general of the Telephone Workers' Union (STRM). Although the Labor Ministry did not grant the FESEBES's petition for registration until August 1992, Salinas appeared to be grooming Hernández Juárez and the FESEBES as an alternative to Velázquez and the CTM.

Second, Salinas enacted reforms to reduce union control over social programs. In 1989, he created a new National Solidarity Program (Pronasol) that bypassed traditional organizational and party channels to deliver benefits directly to poor consumers. This program received cabinet-level status with the creation of the Ministry of Social Development (SEDESOL) in March 1992. As part of Pronasol, Salinas formed the National Solidarity Institute (Insol), which organized training seminars for union cadres. Both agencies cultivated ties with the FESEBES, which participated in the Insol's creation and signed a Union Modernization Accord with the SEDESOL in February 1993 (*El Financier*, March 5, 1993). Although CTM members participated in Insol seminars, Velázquez became a vehement critic of the Institute as part of his crusade against FESEBES.[25]

Salinas also challenged the CTM's control over pensions and workers' housing. Although union opposition led government officials to withdraw an ambitious proposal to transform Mexico's entire social security system (IMSS) in early 1991, they went ahead with plans to create an individual pension fund (SAR) administered by private banks to complement the existing financial structure of the IMSS. They also engineered a reform of the workers' housing agency (Infonavit) to limit the role of the unions to "monitoring the global dynamic of the system, but without the power to intervene specifically in its regulation, administration, or direction" (Bertranou 1994, 256). Under the regulations approved for the Infonavit in September 1992, the unions lost their control over housing construction contracts and their capacity to assign housing credits to their members (*El Financiero*, February 17, 1993). Moreover, Salinas removed a close ally of Velázquez from the directorship of the Infonavit and replaced him with a financial technocrat committed to rationalizing the agency's administration.[26]

Finally, Salinas sought to reconstruct the popular bases of the PRI at the expense of organized labor. This initiative was prompted by the CTM's failure to get out the vote for the 1988 elections, in which the PRI suffered record losses. Some of the worst defeats came in districts with heavy concentrations of working-class voters (Alvarez Béjar 1991, 48).[27] In addition, union candidates fared badly. Of the 101 candidates for the Chamber of Deputies presented by the Labor Congress, 30 lost. The CTM was particularly hard hit, with only 34 of its 51 candidates winning seats (Reyes del Campillo 1990, 157–58). The CTM also failed to win a senate seat in the Federal District for the first time since 1940. Election losers included prominent members of the CTM's executive committee and secretary-generals of CTM-affiliated unions and federations.

In response to this debacle, Salinas set out to reorganize the PRI. In November 1989, the PRI's president, Luis Donaldo Colosio, announced an initiative to restructure the party along territorial rather than sectorial lines, with an emphasis on building new constituencies in poor, urban neighborhoods. In a document issued in mid-1990, Colosio stated that it was in the sectors that "the presence of the party has deteriorated most and, like it or not, political discontent has in great measure taken shape" (*El Financiero*, April 11, 1993). He suggested that the neighborhood, rather than the sectors, "is the natural place for the PRI to connect with the citizens" (Hernández Rodríguez 1991, 229). He also spoke of erasing the difference between workers and citizens and determining labor representation in the party on the basis of the real strength of the unions among workers (*La Jornada*, May 8, 1990).

Despite vehement opposition by the CTM, the XIV Assembly adopted several changes that undermined the CTM's influence. The new PRI statutes emphasized the importance of citizen activity and established equal representation for the sectors and the territorial structure in assemblies, councils, and conventions. They also restructured internal party organs at all levels to multiply the number of actors involved; eliminated the sectorial posts on the National Executive Committee (CEN); and added the category of "sympathizer" to the dual system of individual and collective affiliation (Hernández Rodríguez 1991, 242–42; Pereznieto Castro 1990, 297).

Keeping Fuel in the Old Jalopy

A decade after De la Madrid started Mexico down the path of neoliberal reform, the CTM found major facets of its socioeconomic, political, and organizational bargains with the PRI in disarray. Not only did CTM leaders have significantly less to offer their members, but their own leadership privileges were also under attack. At the same time, however, the PRI still relied on the CTM to carry out some crucial tasks. In the words of a Mexican labor expert, Raúl Trejo Delarbre, the CTM "is like an automobile built in the 1930s; it keeps functioning, even if badly."[28] Until the PRI could build a new, more efficient car to match Mexico's changing terrain, it needed to keep fuel in the old jalopy. Thus, even Salinas recognized limits to his assault on the leadership privileges of CTM leaders.

The CTM performed three functions that were particularly important to the PRI in the context of neoliberal reform: (1) endorsing and enforcing the anti-inflation pacts; (2) backing the PRI's policies of industrial restructuring and global integration, particularly negotiation of the North American Free Trade Agreement (NAFTA); and (3) exercising a stabilizing influence on the presidential succession. In exchange for these services, the PRI continued to respect some features of the old bargains and ultimately retreated from its attempts to undermine the CTM's organizational and political prerogatives.

Anti-Inflation Pacts

As discussed above, the CTM played a key role in the PRI's anti-inflation policy after 1987. Besides participating in periodic renegotiations of the *Pacto*, CTM officials were involved in weekly meetings of the Commission of Enforcement and Evaluation, which played "an extremely important" role in monitoring compliance.[29] Moreover, the CTM acted as "first among equals" within the labor delegation. According to Jaime Serra Puche, the Secretary of Commerce from 1988 to 1994, the Labor Congress was the formal representative of labor "but Fidel was the real leader."[30] Velázquez was the only union official to sign the original *Pacto* in 1987, and the Labor Congress extended his term as CT president until June 1988 to manage the sensitive negotiations regarding the *Pacto*'s renewal (Grayson 1989, 46).

As long as the *Pacto* remained a priority for the government, the PRI had strong incentives to ensure the CTM's ongoing participation by respecting some features of the old bargains. Well aware of its leverage, the CTM did not hesitate to threaten defection from the *Pacto* to win concessions on other issues. While these concessions tended to benefit leaders rather than workers, they played a role in keeping the CTM from moving beyond norm-based voice despite a permanent loss in its influence over wage levels.

Industrial Restructuring

Ratification of the PRI's anti-inflation policy was not the only means by which the CTM facilitated neoliberal reform in the 1980s and 1990s. Although with less fanfare, the confederation also provided essential support for industrial restructuring, which involved introducing new technologies, raising productivity, shedding excess labor, and flexibilizing the workforce through "the elimination of legal, political, and social restrictions to carrying out changes in the enterprise" (Pascual Moncayo and Trejo Delarbre 1993, 47). Although the government did not modify the Federal Labor Law, thousands of workers were affected by de facto flexibilization through the revision of collective contracts. Besides causing immediate layoffs and decreased benefits, these revisions permanently weakened some of Mexico's most important unions and shifted the balance of power between capital and labor within the workplace.

Despite congressional hearings on labor law reform and repeated threats by President Carlos Salinas to rewrite the LFT, the PRI took no real action to make formal changes in the rules governing industrial relations. First, Mexican unions were united in their virulent opposition to any devaluation of the legal rights of workers or unions. Thus, any serious attempt to reform the LFT was bound to elicit strong resistance by the labor movement. Second, the PRI discovered that the *threat* of labor law reform was a valuable bargaining chip for extracting other concessions from the CTM. Third, the PRI was not especially interested in jeopardizing those provisions of the LFT that enabled the regime to protect itself and its labor allies against workers' militance, particularly the exclusion clauses and the state's authority to determine the legality of strikes and intervene in disputes between groups of workers vying for control of a collective contract.

Paradoxically, these provisions ended up facilitating de facto flexibilization. Often with the collaboration of the CTM and the exclusion clauses, employers used the renegotiation of collective contracts to achieve significant changes, including fewer rules regarding the hiring and firing of permanent workers; more freedom to subcontract and hire temporary workers; greater control over labor mobility, task assignment, pay scales, and promotion criteria within the workplace; and the legal right to rescind the contract in the event of extreme economic necessity. Rather than resisting contract flexibilization as a threat to worker rights, the CTM saw it as an opportunity to maintain or expand its presence in key economic sectors.

The CTM pursued this strategy on two fronts. First, it capitalized on its reputation as an employer-friendly union to extend its influence in export-oriented growth sectors, particularly in transnational enterprises.[31] This trend was most pronounced in automobile manufacturing and the in-bond processing plants along the U.S.-Mexican border *(maquiladoras)* (Bensusán 1997, 15). Having lost its hegemony in the automobile industry to independent unions in the 1970s, the CTM seized the chance to gain title to contracts in new plants constructed by companies such as Ford, Nissan, and General Motors in the 1980s. In the process, the CTM regained its hegemony but at the expense of contracts that were more flexible than the norm (Von Bülow 1994, 28–30). Likewise, the CTM accepted flexible provisions in return for control over new contracts in the fast-growing *maquiladora* industry (De la Garza Toledo 1993, 155).[32]

Second, the CTM used contract disputes to seize or regain control in already-unionized plants undergoing industrial restructuring. In several conflicts in major firms (e.g., Ford-Cuahtitlán, Modelo Brewery, Tornel Rubber Company), the government sided with the CTM against rival unions because of the CTM's greater willingness to support the negotiation of "market-friendly" contracts. In a style reminiscent of the *charrazos* of previous decades, the labor authorities backed the CTM by declaring strikes illegal, refusing to recognize surveys granting a majority to a rival union, and/or turning a blind eye to coercion by union thugs. In most cases, the outcome was the reestablishment of CTM control and a much more flexible contract.

NAFTA

In the midst of this process of flexibilization, President Salinas proposed the negotiation of a free trade agreement with the United States in 1990.[33] Although the purpose of NAFTA was not so much to initiate neoliberal reforms as to deepen and formalize them, Salinas viewed the agreement as crucial to his project of transforming Mexico into a market-driven, globally integrated economy attractive to foreign investors. Particularly given the strong anti-NAFTA stance of U.S. unions, his administration made a concerted effort to win the support of Mexican unions, despite their longstanding nationalism and protectionist leanings.

According to one CTM official, a fierce debate took place within the CTM over whether or not to support NAFTA. In particular, the agreement's advocates had to work hard to convince Velázquez of its merits.[34] Ultimately, the nonagenarian leader decided in favor of the agreement, declaring in February 1991, "the CTM unconditionally supports the FTA between Mexico and the United States, because the federal government will respect the rights of workers" (Pascual Moncayo and Trejo Delarbre 1993, 20). The main price of the CTM's support was withdrawal by the government of its threat to modify existing labor laws.[35] More broadly, the PRI had strong incentives to invest in its alliance with the CTM as long as NAFTA's ratification was still pending, particularly given widespread opposition to the agreement in the United States.

Not surprisingly, the CTM's relations with the PRI improved in the months leading up to the NAFTA vote in the U.S. Congress in November 1993.

The CTM's support for NAFTA cannot entirely explain its improved relations with the PRI in the mid-1990s, however. With the approach of the *dedazo*, Salinas largely abandoned the project of alliance restructuring to refurbish the old but reliable CTM jalopy. Although the CTM could no longer deliver as many votes as before, it continued to play a crucial role in preserving the fragile equilibrium that enabled the PRI to renew its power while changing its leader. Moreover, the PRI needed every vote it could get in the face of increased electoral competition. Thus, as in previous *sexenios*, time ran out on the president's attempt to shift the bases of the PRI's support coalition.

Managing the Presidential Succession

The CTM's traditional role of mobilizing support within the PRI for the president's chosen successor may have become even more important in the 1980s and 1990s because of discontent among party leftists with the neoliberal turn of the PRI leadership. During the 1988 succession, a group of *priistas* led by Cuauhtémoc Cárdenas defected from the party to run against Salinas, with nearly disastrous results for the PRI. This split had its origins in the Democratic Current (CD) formed by PRI dissidents in 1986. At the PRI's Thirteenth National Assembly in March 1987, the CD challenged the party hierarchy in an attempt to loosen the hold of the neoliberal technocrats on the party through a reform of the candidate selection process and "an economic reactivation of nationalist and populist inspiration" (Corriente Democrática 1989, 213). The CD's rhetoric echoed the CTM's demand that "the PRI must change its course, renewing its principles and reviving the ideals that have sustained the revolutionary movement" (Durand Ponte 1991, 102).

Despite the close ideological affinity between the CD and the CTM, Velázquez and the CTM treated the *cardenistas* as their worst enemy. As in the 1940s, when Lombardo attempted to win CTM support for the Popular Party, the CTM now saw a progressive challenge by dissident members of *la familia revolucionaria* as a threat rather than an opportunity. While the CD lacked a clear position on the role of the sectors in the party, its members urged that unions maintain greater independence from the PRI (Garrido 1993, 112).[36] More importantly, making common cause with the *cardenistas* would have jeopardized the CTM's access to public office by antagonizing the party hierarchy. And Velázquez feared, quite presciently, that allowing the CD to gain a foothold in the PRI would lead to a debilitating division among party militants (*Proceso*, May 25, 1987).

Velázquez and the CTM spearheaded the campaign to discredit the CD and expel its members from the party. Following the PRI Assembly in 1987, Velázquez joined with the leaders of the CNC (peasants) and the CNOP (popular sector) to demand sanctions against Cárdenas, arguing that "he must leave the PRI, like any other person of the so-called Democratic Current who is not in agreement with the resolutions of the last party assembly" (*Proceso*, March 16, 1987). Although his threat that the PRI would expel the *cardenistas* in June 1987 was never carried out, the party resolved to "condemn, reject, and denounce" the activities of Cárdenas and his close ally, Porfirio Muñoz Ledo, in what was seen as an expulsion (*Proceso*, June 29, 1987).

Despite this unprecedented display of discontent within the PRI, De la Madrid broke with tradition to anoint a successor from the same wing of the party. Historically, outgoing presidents had used the *dedazo* to create a kind of "pendulum effect" in the policy orientations of successive administrations, thereby giving both the left and the right a continued stake in the party. But De la Madrid selected Salinas, who shared his profile as a Harvard-educated economist and was a key architect of the neoliberal reforms as Secretary of Planning and Budget. This choice was the last straw for Cárdenas, who defected from the PRI to run against Salinas in the July 1988 elections.

De la Madrid's selection of Salinas placed the CTM in a bind. On the one hand, Salinas personified the neoliberal turn within the party that the CTM so frequently criticized. Moreover, he had seriously antagonized the CTM-affiliated oilworkers' union by opening up the bidding process for contracts in the oil industry. On the other hand, the internal rebellion by the *cardenistas* made it more complicated for the CTM to confront the neoliberal technocrats. Besides threatening the CTM's political prerogatives, the *cardenistas* became the first opposition movement to succeed in appropriating the doctrine of revolutionary nationalism with which the CTM had long been associated.[37] As a result, appeals to revolutionary nationalism by the CTM risked playing into the hands of the PRI's enemies and thereby jeopardizing the foundations of the CTM's remaining power and influence.

Initially, it appeared that the CTM might be true to its principles and refuse to perform its traditional role of circling the wagons around the president's candidate. Although the CTM formally ratified Salinas's nomination, the Labor Sector was the last to proclaim him as its candidate. Moreover, Velázquez made no effort to hide his distaste for Salinas. Besides appearing less than enthusiastic during the traditional greetings (*abrazos*) with the candidate, he walked out in the middle of Salinas's acceptance speech (*Proceso*, October 12, 1987, November 9, 1987). But the CTM quickly conformed to the ritual of throwing its full organizational and ideological weight behind the president's choice. The day after the nomination, Velázquez praised Salinas as "a man born and raised in the bosom of the Revolution" (*Proceso*, November 9, 1987). In return, Salinas made conciliatory gestures toward Velázquez and the CTM, proclaiming, "I have learned to respect the quality of labor leaders in this country, most notably Don Fidel Velázquez, my friend and a leader I admire and respect" (*Proceso*, October 12, 1987). Two months later, the CTM emerged from intraparty negotiations with the same number of legislative candidacies as in the 1985 elections.

Although the CTM ultimately lived up to its end of the political bargain, the events surrounding the *dedazo* in 1987 suggested that its support for the president's choice could not be taken entirely for granted. Moreover, not all factions of the CTM followed Velázquez's lead in rallying behind Salinas. Of particular importance was the intransigence of the "leader emeritus" of the CTM-affiliated oilworkers' union, Joaquín Hernández Galicia, popularly known as La Quina. In a blatant act of disloyalty toward the PRI, La Quina reportedly informed Salinas, "we cannot say that you have been our candidate; you are so because Fidel Velázquez requested it" (Aguilar Camin 1988, 83). More importantly, he openly criticized Salinas's nomination and encouraged union members to vote for Cárdenas. Not surprisingly, some of the PRI's worst losses in July 1988 came in traditional PRI strongholds in oil-producing regions (Alvarez Béjar 1991, 48).

Salinas severely punished La Quina for his disloyalty by staging a dramatic raid on his house and jailing him on charges of corruption, which sent a clear signal to any other PRI-affiliated labor leaders contemplating disloyalty.[38] As discussed above, Salinas also attempted to reduce the PRI's dependence on the CTM to mobilize the working-class vote. However, time ran out on the latter strategy. Assuring a smooth transition to the next administration was too important to risk being caught between the old and the new. Thus, after four years of seeing its privileged status eroded, the CTM enjoyed a resurgence of its power and influence. To ensure the CTM's full cooperation with the *dedazo*, Salinas retreated from his assault on the CTM's political and organizational prerogatives toward the end of his *sexenio*.

The retreat began at the PRI's Sixteenth Assembly in March 1993.[39] Despite initial plans to "citizen-ize" (*ciudadanizar*) the party, the PRI ended up reaffirming the role of the sectors and restoring some of the privileges denied to them in 1990. The Assembly opened with the abrupt announcement by a CTM leader that the PRI's reformist president had been replaced. The CTM subsequently succeeded in defeating several proposals that would have diluted the Labor Sector's influence.[40] In addition, the PRI accepted a CTM proposal to reinstate the sectorial posts that had been eliminated from the CEN in 1990 (Mendez and Othón Quiroz 1993, 17). The CTM's secretary of social welfare, Abelardo Carrillo Zavala, concluded, "it is very heart-warming that when the time of the presidential succession approaches, the organic alliance between the sectors of the PRI and the government is reestablished" (*El Financiero*, May 7, 1993).

The CTM also enjoyed a revival of its privileges in the Infonavit. In April 1993, a close friend of Velázquez's, Francisco Ruiz Massieu, became president of the agency. After frequent meetings between the two leaders, the Infonavit's administrative council restored the old system of union intermediation in October 1993 (*El Financiero*, October 29, 1993).[41] Carrillo Zavala noted the benefits of the revised system: "Infonavit permits us to propose the construction of housing units, to present a list of those to whom we would like to provide housing and, in some way, to present a directory of builders who at the state, regional, and national level have the capacity to build where the unions would like, given the needs of their members" (*El Financiero*, October 29, 1993).

Finally, the CTM recovered its hegemonic position in the labor movement. Although the Labor Ministry finally granted the FESEBES's petition for registration in August 1992, the new federation lost influence with Salinas and the PRI in 1993, as indicated by the CTM's success in blocking the FESEBES's bid for legislative candidacies for the 1994 elections.[42] In the meantime, the CTM appropriated several of the "new unionist" reforms initially advocated by Hernández Juárez and his allies. In addition to approving several productivity accords, the CTM withdrew its opposition to the incorporation of productivity bonuses into contracted wage agreements during the renegotiation of the *Pacto* in October 1993 (*El Financiero*, October 7, 1993).[43] According to one CTM official, this version of the *Pacto* was the most generous to labor.[44]

By early 1994, the basic contours of the political and organizational bargains between the CTM and the PRI had been restored. In return, the CTM closed ranks with the PRI during a succession marred by the Zapatista uprising in January 1994 and the brutal assassination of Colosio, who had been named the PRI's presidential candidate, in March 1994. Velázquez spoke out against destabilizing forces in the country, and the CTM made an exaggerated but symbolically important promise to deliver 5.5 million working-class votes to the party in August 1994 (*El Financiero*, June 9, 1993). In the days leading up to the elections, the CTM and its affiliates offered financial incentives for workers to attend PRI rallies, threatened CTM members with sanctions if they failed to vote, and published an advertisement in the national media urging workers to support the PRI's replacement candidate, Ernesto Zedillo (*La Jornada*, August 12, 1994).[45] Although Zedillo did not receive an absolute majority, he won by a sizable margin in a relatively clean election. Soon thereafter, he appointed the CTM's secretary of education, Juan Millán, to the position of PRI secretary general, the highest PRI position ever held by a labor leader. Once again, the CTM's persistence with their traditional strategies of norm-based voice had paid off.

CHAPTER 6
The Socialist Divorce in Spain

The Spanish story takes a different turn than the Mexican one because of a crucial difference in the power of the party and workers to punish labor leaders for disloyal behavior. Prior to the reform period, Spain's alliance rested on the principles of democratic socialism and a set of norms generated by historic exchanges in the socioeconomic, political, and organizational arenas. As in Mexico, these principles and norms faced an unprecedented challenge in the 1980s and early 1990s. By adopting market reforms, the Socialist government of Felipe González violated the tenets of democratic socialism and placed UGT leaders in a loyalty dilemma.

Like the PRI, the PSOE lacked sufficient autonomy to join labor in resisting the reforms, which meant that labor leaders had to choose sides. But, unlike CTM leaders, UGT leaders sided with workers because they risked greater punishment by workers than by the party for disloyal behavior. Thus, as it became clear that the government would not reverse its reforms and the PSOE would not oppose the government, UGT leaders moved from norm-based voice to norm-breaking voice to exit.

Principles of Democratic Socialism

The vision of society that sustained the century-long alliance between the PSOE and the UGT grew out of their common origins as members of the Socialist Family *(familia socialista)*. The group of Madrid printers who founded the PSOE "occupied practically without exception the key posts in the party and the union" for several decades (Pérez Ledesma 1987, 232). Pablo Iglesias, who was popularly known as "the grandfather" *(el abuelo),* served as president of both the PSOE and the UGT until his death in 1925. Leadership overlap intensified during the Franco dictatorship, when the party formed a "PSOE in exile" in France (Gillespie 1989, 56–79). Even after undergoing a process of organizational differentiation in the 1970s, the PSOE and the UGT continued to share both leaders and ideals. At the PSOE's Twenty-ninth Congress in 1981, the UGT's secretary-general, Nicolás Redondo, declared, "[W]e are members of the same family" (Guindal and Serrano 1986, 261).

Although the *familia socialista* evolved over time from avowed Marxists to moderate social democrats, they retained a commitment to four principles that can be characterized as the tenets of "democratic socialism": (1) the use of state power to provide higher standards of living for workers; (2) a central role for unions in formulating social and economic policy; (3) opposition to "imperialist" wars or military alliances; and (4) support for democracy. At the UGT's Thirty-first Congress in 1978, Redondo proclaimed, "between the UGT and the PSOE there are nearly one hundred years of fraternal relations, characterized by the identification of both organizations with the same concepts of liberty, democracy, and socialism" (Guindal and Serrano 1986, 234).

Throughout most of its history, the *familia socialista* advocated a mix of revolutionary goals and reformist practices. The PSOE's first manifesto in 1879 included a maximum program and a minimum program. The maximum program called for the taking of power by the working class, the transformation of all private power into collective property, and the organization of society into an economic federation based on workers' collectives. The minimum program recognized the merits of choosing compromise over revolutionary adventurism and realizing more immediate goals such as democracy, civil liberties, and social welfare (Tezanos 1989, 462–63). Before entering into a brief phase of radicalism in the mid-1930s, the Socialists forged strategic alliances and promoted a reformist agenda emphasizing the collective rights of workers, social legislation, and a policy-making role for the unions.[1]

The Socialists returned to this mixed agenda during the transition to democracy in the 1970s. Even after abandoning their Marxist label in 1979, they retained their commitment to a radical, pro-worker vision. At the PSOE's Twenty-ninth Congress in October 1981, party delegates passed resolutions calling for "a drastic revision of the modes of production and consumption" (PSOE 1981, 8) and opposing Spain's membership in the North Atlantic Treaty Organization (NATO), which they viewed as an agent of U.S. imperialism.[2] Meanwhile, their concrete proposals gave priority to the consolidation of parliamentary democracy and supported policies that closely resembled the "postwar settlements" adopted by social democratic parties elsewhere in Europe. These settlements included Keynesian demand management with an emphasis on public spending, the establishment of tripartite institutions allowing unions to participate in the formulation and implementation of policy, and the construction of a welfare state (Pontusson 1992).

Norms of Exchange and Conflict Management

Although the PSOE had little opportunity to translate the principles of democratic socialism into concrete bargains because of its frequent exclusion from power, its long alliance with the UGT still generated norms of exchange and conflict management in the socioeconomic, political, and organizational arenas. The PSOE was expected to promote better living standards for workers, provide the UGT with a significant policymaking role in the government and party, and support the UGT's hegemony in the labor movement. In return, the UGT was expected to subordinate its mobilization strategies and demands to the interests of the *familia socialista*, support parliamentary democracy and the PSOE's quest for electoral victory, and contribute its moral, material and organizational resources to the party when its survival was at stake.

As in Mexico, the bargains in Spain were mutually reinforcing as long as the party could promote a development strategy based on extensive state intervention in the economy. At the same time, the underdeveloped nature of these bargains presented a special set of challenges to the PSOE that the PRI did not face. In concrete terms, the UGT did not have as far to fall when the party embraced market reform. The PSOE was not dismantling a development model it had previously constructed, nor were UGT leaders losing privileges to which they had become accustomed. In psychological terms, however, the blow was severe. First, the transition to democracy in the 1970s and the PSOE's landslide victory in 1982 generated high expectations among Spanish workers and unionists that they would finally reap the rewards that many of their European counterparts had enjoyed for decades.[3] Second, the bargains had not weathered previous episodes of stress, which meant that labor leaders had little on which to base their expectations of party behavior other than their solidarity ties with individual leaders. These factors created a situation in which high hopes and personal loyalties easily soured into disillusionment and feelings of betrayal when the PSOE failed to deliver on its promises.

Socioeconomic Bargain

Two norms of party behavior became established in the socioeconomic arena during the occasional periods of Socialist influence over policy. First, the PSOE would use state power, when available, to improve the living conditions of workers. Second, the PSOE would provide the UGT with opportunities to participate in policy making.

In the early years of the alliance, the PSOE supported direct exchanges between the UGT and the state to make up for the party's own lack of political representation. This strategy translated into several pro-labor measures and UGT representation on labor regulation and social welfare boards, particularly during the dictatorship of Miguel Primo de Rivera in the 1920s. With the establishment of the Second Republic in 1931, the PSOE finally gained sufficient access to state power to mediate the UGT's exchanges with the state.[4] Using its plurality in the parliament and three cabinet positions (including Minister of Labor), the PSOE pushed an agenda of social and economic reforms designed to raise the standard of living of workers and enhance the power of unions in the workplace. Although the results had an ambiguous effect on socioeconomic conditions, they brought major advances in social legislation (Brenan 1978; Redero San Román 1992).

The PSOE placed socioeconomic concerns on the back burner after the collapse of the Second Republic and its brutal replacement by the Franco regime, but these concerns regained their prominent place on the Socialist agenda with the restoration of political liberties in the mid-1970s. Like it had in the 1930s, the PSOE in the 1970s hoped to compensate workers for Spain's long isolation from the European mainstream by adopting pro-labor policies and giving unions a central role in policy making. During the 1982 electoral campaign, the party promised "the change" (el cambio), a program consisting of expansionary industrial and welfare policies. Even while preparing Spain for entry into the European Economic Community (EEC), the PSOE pledged to maintain workers' purchasing power, improve social welfare, and use public investment to create 800,000 new jobs to reverse an unemployment rate that had become the highest in western Europe.[5]

The PSOE also expressed its commitment to union power under a Socialist government. In the resolutions passed at its Twenty-ninth Congress in October 1981, the party promised "(a) permanent consultation and collaboration between the Party and the Union for the elaboration of the economic and social policies of the government; (b) a policy on the part of the government oriented toward considering the status of the union in society and fully guaranteeing the freedom of union action at all levels, firm, society, and public institutions; [and] (c) a government policy directed at an increase in union control in firms and institutions of economic planning" (PSOE 1981, 192).

The obstacles to realization of the PSOE's socioeconomic agenda finally appeared to crumble when the party won a landslide victory in the October 1982 elections. For the first time in its history, the PSOE had an overwhelming majority in parliament and therefore could govern as a hegemonic party. The day after the elections, the UGT triumphantly declared: "The immediate demands of the UGT, and we hope of the majority of Spanish workers, are captured in the project of change of the Socialist Party. The fight against unemployment and the crisis, the greater participation by workers in the firm and in the society, [and] the consolidation of a more modern, organized, and solidaristic society can be transformed from a demand into a reality" (UGT 1982). A few months later, the PSOE's secretary general and newly elected president of Spain, Felipe González, declared at a joint meeting of the PSOE and the UGT, "the electoral results place us in an ideal situation in which to reproduce in Spain . . . the social democratic model of northern and central Europe" (Díaz-Varela and Guindal 1990, 224).

In return for the PSOE's commitment to pro-worker policies, the UGT subordinated its mobilization strategies and socioeconomic demands to the general interest of the *familia socialista*. Except in moments of anti-dictatorial struggle, the UGT was expected to place limits on mobilization in order to avoid repressive backlash and allow for reformist measures. Reflecting the formative influence of Iglesias, the UGT emphasized negotiation, the prudent use of collective action, and opposition to violence (Pérez Ledesma 1987, 214–15). In the early years of the alliance, the UGT imposed internal controls on strike actions and used its presence on labor regulation boards to block strikes by its main rival, the anarchist National Labor Confederation (CNT). The UGT briefly radicalized in the mid-1930s, but the tragic consequences of this choice reinforced the norm of limited mobilization during the transition in the 1970s.[6] After leading strikes in support of the PSOE's strategy of rupture *(ruptura)* in the mid-1970s, the UGT quickly shifted from confrontation to negotiation when the PSOE pursued a strategy of pacted reform *(reforma pactada)* in response to changed circumstances in the late 1970s.

The UGT also made socioeconomic concessions on behalf of the *familia socialista*. In October 1977, the major political parties signed the Moncloa Pacts, which committed the PSOE to economic austerity and constraints on worker unrest in return for democratizing reforms. Although the UGT was very critical of the pacts, particularly the limits they placed on salary increases, it avoided opposing them outright so as not to embarrass the PSOE (UGT 1978, 192–93; Gillespie 1989, 334–35). When pact-making shifted from the parties to the social partners (unions and business) in 1979, the UGT signed several pacts that included concessions on labor market flexibilization. While the UGT's participation in these agreements strengthened the Socialists' reputation as the best choice for resolving the country's economic crisis, they imposed painful sacrifices on Spanish workers and, in the view of some analysts, accelerated the demobilization of the labor movement (Alonso 1991, 409).

As it did in Mexico for the CTM, the socioeconomic bargain in Spain allowed some room for voice by the UGT. In fact, the UGT had more liberty than the CTM to criticize the government's policies when the party was in power. The PSOE conceptualized the UGT as a formally autonomous union that would function as its ally in the labor movement. Consistent with this autonomy, the PSOE respected the UGT's right to stake out its own position on policy issues.

In the late 1970s, in anticipation of a PSOE victory in national elections, the *familia socialista* agreed on a norm of "critical support" (*apoyo crítico*) to govern the UGT's interaction with the PSOE. Redondo offered his interpretation of this norm in his opening remarks at the UGT's Thirty-first Congress in 1978: "Our support for a Socialist government will be critical and conditional support, because our confidence in the capacity for social transformation by a future PSOE government does not imply that the UGT is going to extend a blank check to the policies of our brother party" (Guindal and Serrano 1986, 233–34).

At a joint meeting in January 1983, the PSOE and UGT executives agreed that this norm should translate into a policy of "intelligent negotiation" by the UGT with the newly elected PSOE government (Santos and Sánchez 1990, 496). Although UGT leaders were free to take independent positions on policy issues, they were expected to lend their global support to the PSOE, which meant supporting the party's overall program and avoiding mobilizations that might jeopardize its electoral chances. As one high-ranking party leader expressed, "the UGT's role is to criticize the government on occasion, even if it is a Socialist government, but to support the PSOE" (Gunther, Sani, and Shabad 1986, 209).

Political Bargain

The party was expected to provide the UGT with representation in party organizations, input into the party's electoral platform, and access to public office through placement on party lists. Although the PSOE did not have access to many of these benefits during its long periods out of power, UGT leaders always held prominent positions within the party. Between 1899 and 1928, an average of 34.6 percent of UGT executive committee members simultaneously served on the PSOE executive. This figure rose to an average of 50.8 percent between 1944 and 1974, and, in the late 1950s, UGT executive committee members held nearly 90 percent of the positions on the PSOE's Federal Executive Commission.[7] In addition, the top two or three positions in each organization were distributed among the same people, leading to an "unwritten rule" whereby the highest office in one would be held by the second-in-command of the other.[8]

The PSOE and the UGT underwent a process of organizational differentiation during the democratic transition in the 1970s. The UGT's secretary general, Nicolás Redondo, declined an offer to become first secretary of the PSOE in 1974, and the UGT adopted a policy of "incompatibility of positions" with the PSOE as part of a fusion agreement with the Workers' Labor Union (USO) in 1977.[9] In conformity with this policy, Redondo and two other UGT leaders resigned from the PSOE's Executive Committee. Nonetheless, the UGT continued to take advantage of access to party posts. No UGT congress ever formalized the incompatibility of positions, and Redondo continued to attend meetings of the PSOE's Executive Committee on an informal basis.[10] Moreover, the UGT still accounted for over 50 percent of the members of the PSOE's Federal Committee, on which Redondo automatically received a seat as the UGT's secretary general.[11]

The PSOE also gave UGT leaders opportunities to express their opinions regarding party policy. Starting in the mid-1970s, Redondo was a keynote speaker at every PSOE congress (as was González at every UGT congress). The UGT also participated actively in preparing the PSOE's electoral platforms. In 1982, González met various times with Redondo and the UGT to negotiate the party's program, and UGT representatives sat on all of the PSOE commissions responsible for labor affairs (Guindal and Serrano 1986, 124).[12] In addition, the PSOE's Federal Committee urged the Socialist Parliamentary Group to meet periodically with the leaders of the UGT's industrial federations to discuss legislative matters (PSOE 1984, 17–18).

Finally, the PSOE placed UGT leaders on closed lists for elected office at the local, regional, and national levels. In the 1970s, the UGT proclaimed that its presence in the legislature "allows for the voice of the working class to be heard without intermediaries in the Parliament" (UGT 1977, 685). In the 1982 elections, UGT leaders won thirteen deputy seats and nine senate seats, which accounted for 21 percent of the PSOE's parliamentary group (*Cambio 16*, December 20, 1982; Tezanos 1983, 158). In the words of Redondo, "the UGT parliamentarians are the only trade unionists to occupy seats in the new [parliament], and this is very important for the labor movement, since now there is a guarantee that its voice will be heard where the laws that shape the destiny of the country are elaborated" (*Cambio 16*, December 20, 1982).

For its part, the UGT was expected to deliver two kinds of "goods" to the PSOE in the political arena: general support for parliamentary democracy and specific support for the party in its quest for political power. During periods of dictatorship, the UGT facilitated the transition to democracy by participating in mass mobilizations against the regime, including general strikes in 1930 and 1976. Once democracy was established, the UGT shifted from confrontation to demobilization. In the 1970s, this shift took the form of support for social pacts, which greatly eased Spain's transition to democracy. As discussed above, the UGT reluctantly accepted the Moncloa Pacts, which marked a crucial step toward the adoption of a democratic constitution in 1978. Several years later, the UGT and its main rival, the Workers' Commissions (CCOO), joined with the Spanish Confederation of Business Organizations (CEOE) and the government to express solidarity against an attempted military coup by signing the National Employment Accord (ANE), popularly known as "the pact of fear" *(pacto de miedo)*.

The UGT also lent specific support to the PSOE in elections. After several decades of claiming political neutrality, the UGT approved a recommendation in 1920 that its members vote for PSOE candidates. Through the end of the Second Republic, the PSOE relied heavily on the UGT to mobilize voters because of the party's low levels of formal affiliation (Puhle 1986, 331). While voter recruitment became less important after the PSOE reemerged as a political actor in the 1970s, the UGT continued to lend the party active support during election campaigns. The national UGT leadership disseminated propaganda in favor of the party, and most provincial and regional committees of the UGT endorsed the PSOE's list of candidates and urged members to vote for the party (Gunther, Sani, and Shabad 1986, 209).[13] In the general elections of 1979 and 1982, over 80 percent of UGT members cast their votes for the PSOE (Puhle 1986, 309).

Organizational Bargain

While the PSOE's frequent exclusion from power weakened the socioeconomic and political bargains, it reinforced the organizational bargain because the survival of the *familia socialista* was so often at stake. The key norm of party behavior for the PSOE, as for the PRI in Mexico, was support for the hegemony of its labor allies. Formally, the PSOE bolstered the UGT with a statutory requirement that its working-class members join the Socialist union. Informally, the PSOE used various policy instruments and party resources to bolster the UGT relative to its rivals.

Prior to the Civil War, the UGT's main rival was the CNT, an anarcho-syndicalist union formed in 1910. The PSOE played an important role in privileging the UGT over the CNT, particularly during the Second Republic. Aided by the Socialist presence in the government and control of the "mixed councils" (jurados mixtos) responsible for settling industrial disputes, the UGT spread to many districts where it had never had a presence (Brenan 1978, 259). In addition, the government used the Civil Guard and artillery against CNT workers (Blinkhorn 1990, 206).

The Franco regime decimated both the UGT and the CNT. Besides suffering harsh repression during the first two decades of the regime, the UGT adamantly refused to participate in any institutions established by Franco, even after he allowed collective bargaining by works committees (jurados de empresa) within the corporatist structure of vertical syndicates in the late 1950s.[14] Rather than attempting to infiltrate the corporatist structure, the UGT sought to establish works committees independent of the vertical unions.[15] This strategy had some success in the regions of Asturias and the País Vasco but was largely ineffective in the rest of Spain (Gillespie 1989, 180).

In the meantime, the CCOO began to win seats on the jurados de empresa. Initially more a movement than a union, the CCOO became a national organization in 1965 and adopted the express objective of infiltrating the vertical unions (Foweraker 1987, 63).[16] Franco initially tolerated the CCOO, which achieved major victories in the syndical elections of 1966. But as labor mobilization increased in the late 1960s, the regime reverted to repressive tactics, outlawing the CCOO in 1968, dismissing many workers from the jurados de empresa, and declaring states of emergency in 1969 and 1970.

Although weakened by repression, the CCOO was clearly the dominant force in the labor movement when the political system began to open in the 1970s. At this point, the UGT "was little more than historic initials, with a few thousand militants" (Santos and Sánchez 1990, 255). Not surprisingly, the UGT did poorly relative to the CCOO in the 1978 factory council elections.[17] The CCOO received 34.6 percent of the vote, compared to only 21.7 percent for the UGT (Führer 1996, 113). Moreover, the CCOO was the victor in twenty out of twenty-two sectors and ten out of fifteen regions (Pérez-Díaz 1979, 17, 19), and dominated major firms such as Renfe (transport), Astilleros (steel), Seat (automobiles), Telefónica (telecommunications), and Metro (public transport) (Santos and Sánchez 1990, 255).[18] While the UGT clearly outpaced other unions such as the CNT and the USO, it was a long way from being hegemonic in the labor movement.

As it had in the 1930s, the UGT relied on the PSOE for assistance in striving to overcome this deficit. First, the party devoted financial resources, technical assistance, and propaganda to improving the UGT's representation on the factory councils. Prior to the 1982 union elections, the two executive committees held joint meetings at the national and provincial levels to coordinate a "division of labor between the Party and the Union." The party also contributed ninety-two "electoral agents" with a budget of six million pesetas to conduct the UGT's campaign, particularly in firms where the UGT had little or no presence (PSOE 1983). Among the UGT's technical advisors were well-trained PSOE economists such as Carlos Solchaga, Miguel Boyer, and Alvaro Espina (Santos and Sánchez 1990, 291).

The party also mobilized its apparatus at the regional and local levels to assist the UGT. The Federal Executive Commission issued a circular to all party groupings at the subnational level requiring that a member of the PSOE executive participate in each electoral committee of the UGT. In addition, the party distributed ten thousand letters to its militants stating that "to fortify the UGT, to consolidate the socialist union as the hegemonic organization in the labor movement has become, today more than ever, our main objective assuring, in the first place, the attainment of the majority of personnel delegates and factory council members by the UGT." Finally, the party instructed PSOE mayors, city councilors, and other local officials to lend "support to the UGT in local firms" and "to carry out the parallel task of searching for candidates to stand in for or complement the candidates of the UGT" (PSOE 1983).

Combined with the PSOE's growing popularity in the political arena, these resources helped the UGT make a spectacular comeback in the union elections of 1980 and 1982 (see table 4.2).[19] In 1980, the UGT nearly caught up with the CCOO, winning 29.3 percent of the vote compared to 30.9 percent for its rival. In addition, the UGT began to reverse the trend of domination by the CCOO across sectors and regions, winning in eleven out of twenty-two sectors and nine out of fifteen regions (Führer 1996, 113, 124–25). It also prevailed in major firms such as Seat, Hunosa (mining), Altos Hornos (steel), and Telefónica (Santos and Sánchez 1990, 289; Köhler 1995, 148). Two years later, the UGT surpassed its rival altogether, winning 36.7 percent of the vote compared to 33.4 percent for the CCOO.[20]

Besides lending the UGT support in union elections, the PSOE contributed to the UGT's quest for hegemony by advocating a system of industrial relations that constrained the power of the factory councils in favor of union sections (internal unions). Although the 1978 Constitution and the 1980 Worker's Statute eliminated most features of the Franquist system of labor relations, the institution of shop-floor committees elected by all workers, regardless of their union status, survived. Against the CCOO, the UGT wanted to construct a system of labor relations that linked union power to dues-paying membership by giving union sections the right to bargain collectively and mobilize workers. This preference reflected not only the UGT's disadvantage relative to the CCOO in the factory councils, but also its historical tradition as a membership-based union with a centralized authority structure.

With the support of the PSOE, particularly its parliamentary delegation, the UGT succeeded in diluting the factor council model.[21] The Labor Ministry's first draft of a new labor law, presented to the Council of Ministers in April 1979, gave exclusive control over collective bargaining to the factory councils (Díaz-Varela and Guindal 1990, 184). But by the time the Worker's Statute passed in March 1980, the law had been amended to create a dual system of worker representation that granted bargaining rights to union sections as long as they achieved a minimum level of representation in factory council elections.[22] The UGT and the CEOE negotiated most of these changes prior to the parliamentary debate, resulting in the Basic Interconfederal Accord (ABI) of July 1979, but the Socialist Group introduced key amendments in the parliament (Führer 1996, 201–2).[23] After more than one thousand votes and the introduction of eight hundred amendments, the Worker's Statute passed almost exactly as it had been negotiated in the ABI (Santos and Sánchez 1990, 280).

The UGT's remarkable resurgence helped create an expectation that the UGT's alliance with the PSOE would produce the hegemony it had been seeking for nearly a century, particularly after the 1982 elections. Following the PSOE's victory, González pronounced, "[W]e are in real and objective conditions for the UGT to convert itself into the only union in Spain" (quoted in Díaz-Varela and Guindal 1990, 224). The UGT agreed, pronouncing in a document prepared for the union's Thirty-third Congress in 1983 that "the UGT must prepare itself organizationally and strategically to be in our country not only the majority union, which it already is, but the union that unifies the vast majority of the labor movement" (UGT 1983a, 205).

For its part, the UGT was expected to lend moral, material, and organizational support to the PSOE, especially when the party's survival was at stake. Historically, the UGT was the stronger organization within the *familia socialista*, in terms of both social base and leadership recruitment.[24] Even after the party and the union practically disappeared as mass-based organizations inside Spain after 1939, the UGT managed to preserve some of its organizing capacity in Asturias and the País Vasco, where the repression was less severe and leftist organizations were protected by the internal cohesion of the working class (Maravall 1978, 53–54).

The UGT contributed its greater organizational resources to the PSOE's revival in the 1970s. As in the 1930s, the UGT provided militants to serve as PSOE officials, particularly after the Socialists entered into a post-electoral pact with the PCE and other progressive forces in 1979 that extended left-wing control to over 70 percent of the municipalities in the country (Gillespie 1989, 340). According to one UGT leader, this process enriched the PSOE at the expense of the UGT, many of whose best militants shifted their priorities away from union affairs after being recruited to the PSOE's political machine.[25] The UGT also helped subsidize the party's activities with aid it received from the international trade movement, particularly the German Social Democrats (Gillespie 1990, 48). According to Redondo, "the money of the party was the UGT's, the instruments of propaganda were the UGT's, and they were put at the disposition of the party" (Guindal and Serrano 1986, 69).

Bargains in Crisis

Economic crisis convinced party leaders in Spain to adopt market reforms that seriously threatened the normative framework underlying their alliance with labor. Like the PRI, the PSOE found its bargains with the UGT to be a mixed blessing in this new context. On the one hand, the party had much less room to deliver on its promise to construct a postwar settlement in Spain, especially regarding public spending and job creation. Relatedly, the PSOE became much more hesitant to grant the UGT meaningful input into policy, since the union was likely to resist many of the party's reform initiatives.

On the other hand, the PSOE arguably became even more dependent on the UGT to validate the party's social democratic credentials during the implementation of painful reforms. In addition, the PSOE shared the UGT's interest in consolidating a system of industrial relations that guaranteed collective bargaining rights for unions and favored the PSOE-affiliated UGT over the PCE-affiliated CCOO. The PSOE also drew heavily on the working-class vote, although it soon discovered that winning this vote did not necessarily require maintaining good relations with the UGT.[26]

The party responded to this situation by devaluing some aspects of its bargains with the union while respecting others; the PSOE was far more generous to the UGT in the political and organizational arenas than the PRI was to the CTM. Although the PSOE reneged on many of its socioeconomic promises, the UGT enjoyed continued access to political posts as well as the consolidation of a favorable system of industrial relations. In contrast to what happened in Mexico, however, these concessions did not suffice to keep the UGT from defecting from the alliance. Because UGT leaders feared retaliation by workers, they could not afford to accept leadership privileges that did not translate into real improvements for workers.

When the government launched its reform program, UGT leaders remained patient because of the PSOE's promises of democratic socialism. As long as these promises remained feasible, UGT leaders had little reason to violate the norm of *apoyo crítico*, particularly given the culture of moderation among Spanish workers and the UGT's relative freedom to criticize the government. But as workers began to express their discontent and UGT leaders became convinced that these promises were not going to be realized, their calculations changed. At first, they experimented with norm-breaking voice to pressure the PSOE to respect its commitments to workers. When these tactics failed, they crossed the threshold from voice to exit, thereby ending their century-long alliance with the PSOE.

Norm-Based Voice, 1982–1984

Although UGT leaders criticized the PSOE's economic policies from the beginning, they limited their resistance to norm-based voice through the end of 1984. They negotiated social pacts in 1983 and 1984, participated in a Linkage Commission *(Comisión de Enlace)* set up by the UGT and PSOE executives to discuss issues of mutual concern, and opposed most of the strike actions against industrial reconversion organized by the CCOO and regional unions.[27] Moreover, they argued repeatedly that their criticisms of specific policies were consistent with an attitude of global support for the PSOE. In 1984, Redondo reiterated the UGT's commitment to *apoyo crítico*: "[W]e have criticized the Government and we will continue to do so when we believe it to be convenient. But we do not want to convert Spain into a battleground of strikes out of respect for the society in general and for the workers themselves" (UGT 1986a, 143). Acknowledging that the PSOE faced a difficult task in trying to accomplish "in one year what should have been done in forty," Redondo characterized the UGT's relations with the PSOE government as "fraternal regarding objectives and critical regarding the means" (Redondo 1984, 13).

UGT leaders had three reasons for choosing norm-based voice despite the harsh effect of the PSOE's policies on Spanish workers. First, they accepted the party's argument that its reforms were a necessary evil to overcome the economic crisis and prepare Spain for entry into the EEC, which the UGT and most Spaniards supported. The expectation of UGT leaders was that the PSOE would renew its commitment to constructing a postwar settlement in Spain once these short-term objectives were met.

Second, "there remained matters over which the UGT found it worth negotiating with the González administration" (Gillespie 1989, 430). Although the UGT declined positions in the PSOE cabinet, "there was a veritable race within the federations and [territorial] unions of the UGT to place their cadres in important posts in the administration."[28] More importantly, the UGT had not yet made the transition from "historic exchange" to "routine exchange" with the Socialist government (Prieto 1994, 381–82). Whereas routine exchange involved the daily administration of government, historic exchange involved the consolidation of a new system of industrial relations, including the passage of legislation affecting the collective rights of workers. As long as historic exchange had yet to be concluded, the UGT had strong incentives to win the PSOE's favor by making concessions regarding routine exchange.

Finally, the UGT perceived a willingness by the party to compromise on issues of importance to the union. This perception was reinforced by a "good cop, bad cop" routine. For example, the UGT received mixed signals regarding the PSOE's campaign promise to create eight hundred thousand new jobs. Several days after the minister of industry, Carlos Solchaga, announced that the promise was unrealistic, González's right-hand man in the party, Alfonso Guerra, told the delegates to the UGT's Thirty-third Congress that the government would keep its promise and that the success of the PSOE's project depended on the support of the workers. His words received a standing ovation (*Cambio 16*, June 13, 1984).

Norm-based voice led to compromise in several major disputes between the PSOE and the UGT. One such disagreement involved whether workers displaced by industrial reconversion would have their contracts terminated or suspended. Led by Solchaga, the government insisted on the termination of contracts, first in a report on reindustrialization in May 1983 and then in an executive decree proposing a Law of Reconversion and Reindustrialization in December 1983. The UGT quickly expressed its vehement opposition to the provision, and three UGT leaders—Redondo, José Corcuera, and Manuel Chaves—threatened to break party discipline in the parliament unless the provision were modified.

After several rounds of promising negotiations with the party followed by disheartening announcements by Solchaga that "the government continues to believe that the termination of contracts is absolutely necessary" (Santos and Sanchez 1990, 347), the government finally signed an accord with the UGT and the main union in the País Vasco, the ELA-STV (Basque Workers' Union), in February 1984 that explicitly rejected the termination of contracts (345–50). The PSOE then incorporated this compromise of "gentle reconversion" *(reconversión dulce)* into the Law of Reconversion and Reindustrialization passed in July 1984.

Another major dispute between the UGT and the PSOE early in the Socialist government involved flexibilization of the labor market. Under strong pressure by the private sector, the government indicated in September 1983 that it might consider allowing unrestricted layoffs *(despido libre)*. Faced with strong opposition by the UGT, the government negotiated a compromise that retained restrictions on layoffs while permitting temporary contracts for three years for all new investment, regardless of economic or employment conditions. Despite opposition by both the CCOO and CEOE, the PSOE incorporated this compromise into a law passed in December 1983.

The issue reemerged when the government met with the UGT, the CCOO, and the CEOE in July 1984 to discuss the negotiation of a new social pact. The CEOE pushed again for *despido libre*, which prompted the CCOO to abandon the table and forced the Labor Ministry to postpone the negotiations. Soon thereafter, the minister of labor sent Redondo a letter promising that the government would not modify the current labor legislation regarding layoffs (Tuñon de Lara 1992, 498; Guindal and Serrano 1986). As in 1983, however, the UGT extracted this promise at the price of further allowances for temporary contracts, which were included in the Economic and Social Accord (AES) in October 1984.

Experiments with Norm-Breaking Voice, 1985–1988

After two years of achieving small victories but failing to redirect the party's socioeconomic program, the conditions that had initially supported the UGT's use of norm-based voice began to deteriorate. To some extent, this deterioration resulted from the accumulating costs of supporting reforms that imposed painful sacrifices on workers. Serious concerns first emerged during the negotiation of the AES, which a faction of the UGT, led by José María Zufiaur, adamantly opposed. Unable to reach a decision by its normal procedure of consensus, the UGT executive took a vote on the union's participation in the pact. Although Zufiaur's faction lost, it laid the groundwork for a strategic shift away from norm-based voice beginning in 1985.[29]

This shift accelerated after the 1986 factory council elections. Although the UGT won with 40.9 percent of the vote, compared to 34.5 percent for the CCOO, the results debunked the UGT's expectation that the CCOO was on the verge of obscurity. Even worse, the aggregate figures "hid the fact that the loss of influence by UGT leaders was enormous in those factories and sectors where an organized labor movement existed" (Albarracín 1991, 418). In the five hundred largest enterprises, which employed over one million workers, the CCOO won 43.2 percent of the seats compared to 31.6 percent for the UGT. The CCOO also prevailed in public enterprises, with 46.4 percent of the vote compared to 32.9 percent for the UGT (Campos and Alvarez 1990, 74). Despite official pronouncements of victory, UGT leaders interpreted the

results "as an alarm bell: workers were requesting a stronger and more demanding union policy toward the government and employers" (Benegas 1990,
75). Redondo linked the UGT's poor showing to its cooperation with employers and the government: "We are primarily responsible. But there are other
factors that have taken away our votes: each time a minister speaks . . . we lose
votes; each time the 27 liberalizing measures are mentioned, we lose votes;[30]
when [the leader of the CEOE] meets with the president, we lose votes. . . .
Workers identify us with the actions of the government or with the actions of
public managers. And nothing could be further from the truth" (*El País*, December 18, 1986). Similarly, the UGT secretary general in the Metro argued
that "we have lost the elections because of a protest vote against the UGT. . . .
The undecided have voted for the CCOO not because they like this union but
because they reject us" (*Cambio 16*, January 5, 1987). According to this interpretation, workers were punishing the UGT for remaining loyal to the PSOE
at the expense of labor.

The threat of worker backlash was not the only factor that encouraged the
UGT to move from norm-based voice to norm-breaking voice, however. The
UGT also witnessed the evaporation of each of the three reasons for which it
had chosen norm-based voice in the first place. First, the PSOE persisted with
its policies of austerity and structural reform even after Spain signed the
Treaty of Adhesion to the EEC in 1985 and experienced a rapid economic recovery in 1986. Besides convincing many UGT leaders that the party had
abandoned its commitment to democratic socialism, this situation intensified
their loyalty dilemma. In the words of a UGT leader, "workers [will] not understand a discourse similar to that of the crisis when they live in a situation of
economic recuperation in which businesses are reaping significant profits"
(Saracíbar 1988, 182–83).[31]

Second, the PSOE adopted measures that consolidated Spain's new system
of industrial relations, thereby shifting the focus of party-union relations from
historic exchange to routine exchange. A 1985 Organic Law of Union Liberty
and a 1987 Organic Law of Representation in Public Administration guaranteed an array of institutional and financial privileges to "most representative"
unions and reinforced union sections and union delegates by enabling them to
operate more widely and with expanded rights on the shop floor. The Accord
on Union Participation in Public Enterprises of 1986 guaranteed union representation on the governing boards of public agencies. Finally, the Law on
Union Patrimony of the same year created mechanisms for returning property
confiscated by the Franco regime (Saracíbar 1986; Baylos 1991).[32]

Ironically, although these measures met several of the UGT's longstanding demands, they also increased the UGT's incentives to move along the continuum from voice to exit. First, the shift from historic to routine exchange highlighted policies that were much less favorable to unions and workers. Second, the balance of punishing power tipped even more in favor of workers. Because of its inability to revoke the UGT's new privileges once granted (see chapter 4), the PSOE lost much of its leverage over the union. At the same time, the new legislation increased the UGT's dependence on factory council elections, thereby reinforcing the leverage of workers. The result was a perverse cycle of concessions leading to radicalization, whereby the UGT became more able and willing to confront the PSOE when it persisted with its economic reforms. As a former PSOE labor minister complained, "We gave them the guns and the ammunition to wage their struggle effectively, and they turned around and used them against us."[33]

A third reason for norm-based voice that evaporated after 1986 was the PSOE's willingness to compromise on issues of importance to the UGT. In part, this change reflected a radicalization of the UGT's agenda. Whereas compromise was possible at the margins of the PSOE's reforms, it became much less likely when the UGT began demanding a fundamental reorientation in the government's economic policy. But the change also reflected shifting calculations on the part of the PSOE. Key players in the Socialist government, particularly the minister of finance, Miguel Boyer, became convinced that the costs of negotiating the reforms with the unions outweighed the benefits. Moreover, the PSOE won another absolute majority in the June 1986 elections despite an unemployment rate over 20 percent and increasingly acrimonious relations with the UGT, especially in 1985.[34]

As the margin for compromise between the government and the UGT narrowed, the "good cop, bad cop" routine broke down. As discussed in chapter 4, the PSOE lacked sufficient autonomy to challenge its own government. Thus, the party closed ranks with the government against the UGT, eliminating any remaining possibility that sympathizers in the party might be able to soften the government's policies. In this context, the UGT saw little choice but to move beyond norm-based voice to make its demands.

The UGT engaged in three major episodes of norm-breaking voice between 1985 and 1988. With each episode, UGT leaders committed more serious and more extensive violations of the norms governing their alliance with the PSOE. By the time the UGT concluded its third episode of norm-breaking voice in December 1988, the alliance was in tatters and could be repaired only by a radical policy change by the Socialist government. When that change did not occur, the UGT crossed the threshold into exit.

Pension Reform

The UGT's first foray into norm-breaking voice occurred in response to the government's proposal for pension reform. Initially, the conflict conformed to the pattern of norm-based voice followed by party concessions. When the minister of labor, Joaquín Almunia, presented a draft of the reform to the PSOE executive in June 1984, Redondo, with the support of Guerra, succeeded in blocking it until after the negotiation of the AES (Santos and Sánchez 1990, 381). Likewise, when Redondo threatened to suspend his attendance at meetings of PSOE committees to protest the reform, the PSOE reached an agreement with the UGT executive to intensify contacts at the highest level "with the goal of making more fluid the communication between the two organizations" (UGT 1985c). Meanwhile, Zufiaur succeeded in introducing several amendments to the reform as a member of the economic commission at the PSOE's Thirtieth Congress in December 1984 (Santos and Sánchez 1990, 382).

This time, however, the UGT was not satisfied with the concessions elicited by norm-based voice. In April 1985, the UGT's Confederal Committee voted to hold mobilizations unless the government made a substantial change in its latest proposal (*El País*, April 24, 1985).[35] At the closing of the committee's meeting, Redondo stated: "We have done too much. The government is seeking our support or our understanding and in this case we can give neither one" (*El País*, April 25, 1985). Although González responded with an offer that was much closer to the UGT's demands, it was insufficient to stop Redondo from engaging in norm-breaking voice. On May 30, 1985, Redondo violated party discipline in the parliament by voting to send the pension reform bill back to the government. Five days later, at least three UGT leaders with joint responsibilities in the party participated in demonstrations involving twenty thousand to sixty thousand people in Barcelona and around three hundred thousand people in Madrid (*El País*, June 5,1985). When the bill came up for a final vote on July 23, Redondo was again the only member of the Socialist Group not to vote in its favor, although he abstained rather than voting against it (*El País*, July 24, 1985).[36]

The UGT followed its norm-breaking response to the pension reform with other measures that strained the normative fabric of the alliance. In the spring of 1985, Redondo stopped attending meetings of the PSOE executive and terminated a joint PSOE-UGT commission to analyze government initiatives before they were approved by the Council of Ministers (Díaz-Varela and Guindal 1990, 285).[37] The following January, he sent a letter to the secretary general of the PSOE communicating his unilateral decision to abandon the *Comisión de Enlace* set up in 1983 (Santos and Sánchez 1990, 500). He also indicated a loosening of the political bargain at the UGT's Thirty-fourth Congress in April 1986 when he stated, "[O]ur objective is to open the organization to other workers who can have political options other than the socialist one" (*El País*, April 4, 1986).[38] Although several UGT leaders actively contributed to the formulation of the PSOE's electoral platform in 1986, the UGT decided not to participate as an organization.[39]

The UGT's first experiment with norm-breaking voice delivered a serious blow to its century-long alliance with the PSOE, but UGT leaders were careful to frame the experiment as an exception to the rule of norm-based voice. First, Redondo insisted on the personal nature of his decision to break party discipline in the parliament. In a letter distributed to UGT federations and unions prior to the final vote on the pension reform, he emphasized that no other UGT deputies were obligated to follow his lead (UGT 1985a). With the exception of Redondo and Ricardo Damborenea, who abandoned the chamber just before the vote, all other UGT deputies followed the party line.[40] Second, only two UGT leaders with responsibility in the PSOE responded to the contradictions of double militancy by choosing one organization over the other. Two weeks before the first vote on pension reform, José Corcuera resigned from the UGT executive out of frustration with trying to mediate between the PSOE and the more combative elements in the UGT. "To avoid being immersed in contradictions," he explained, "I abandoned the union and voted in favor of the law in the Congress" (Santos and Sánchez 1990, 381). Soon thereafter, Antonio Rosa, the secretary general of the UGT in Badajoz, resigned his seat in the Senate to retain coherence with the union (*El País*, June 4, 1985). Redondo, on the other hand, stated, "[I]t is more reasonable to vote 'no' than to resign my seat" (Santos and Sánchez 1990, 388).

Third, the UGT made a concerted effort to limit norm-breaking voice to the issue of pension reform. On May 21, Redondo assured the parliament that there were no problems of a personal nature between the UGT and the government, but rather a disagreement over certain measures (UGT 1985b). The UGT also refused to join a general strike organized by the CCOO and other unions on July 20, 1985.[41] Although the strike was billed as a protest against the pension reform, the UGT feared that the CCOO would take advantage of the strike to make broader demands and weaken the Socialist government (*El País*, May 14, 1985). Redondo indicated the UGT's awareness of the dangers of carrying norm-breaking voice too far: "We discussed the issue of the general strike, and at that moment I must confess there were sectors that were for it.

But we thought that if we begin with a general strike, we could end up with who knows what. If a general strike failed to produce results, we would have to resort to a revolutionary strike" (Guindal and Serrano 1986, 165). Even though their dissatisfaction with the pension reform pushed them to experiment with norm-breaking voice, UGT leaders were not yet prepared to risk an all-out break with the Socialist government.

The UGT's selective approach to norm-breaking voice was highlighted by its decision not to go beyond norm-based voice when the PSOE violated the principle of military neutrality by reversing its position on NATO. Despite strong support for Spain's withdrawal from NATO among members of the *familia socialista*, González rejected this position once it became clear that an anti-NATO policy could jeopardize Spain's entry into the EEC.[42] He won the party's support for Spain's continued NATO membership at the PSOE's Thirtieth Congress in December 1984 and achieved a surprise victory in a popular referendum on NATO membership on March 12, 1986.[43]

Although González's new policy flew in the face of the UGT's opposition to NATO, the union was careful to limit the scope of its resistance. Redondo decided against challenging González openly at the Thirtieth Congress even while UGT delegates voted against the pro-NATO resolution. In October 1985, one of Redondo's key allies on the UGT executive, Anton Saracíbar, voted in favor of the official position on NATO at a meeting of the PSOE's Federal Committee, just two months after the UGT executive had joined with the Socialist Youth and PSOE dissidents to sign an anti-NATO document (Santos and Sánchez 1990, 438–46). In addition, the UGT did not budget "one peseta" to the fight against NATO (Share 1989, 130) and refused an invitation by the CCOO to launch a unified anti-NATO campaign.[44]

The 1988 Budget

The UGT's second episode of norm-breaking voice occurred in response to the government's proposed 1988 budget, which maintained limits on spending despite two years of rapid economic growth. The budget produced "a huge rupture in expectations and the first rejection by the UGT of the social clauses of the [budget] since the end of 1982" (UGT 1989c, 7). Besides confirming the UGT's suspicions that the PSOE would never fulfill its promise to construct a Keynesian welfare state, this rupture occurred in the wake of the UGT's disappointing showing in the 1986 factory council elections and the shift from historic to routine exchange in party-union relations. At a meeting of the PSOE's Federal Committee on October 2, 1987, Saracíbar threatened that the UGT members of the Socialist Group would be obligated to "vote their conscience" unless the budget were revised to provide higher salary increases for public employees, a reduction in the minimum age for pensioners, and realization of the government's promise in the AES to provide unemployment insurance to 48 percent of jobless workers (Díaz-Varela and Guindal 1990, 268–69; Santos and Sánchez 1990, 523).

Initially, this threat of norm-breaking voice appeared to have the desired effect on the PSOE. Guerra, who was vice president of the government as well as leader of the party apparatus, engineered a budget compromise with the UGT on October 7. But Solchaga, with the support of González, torpedoed the compromise, and the Council of Ministers failed to get the UGT to agree to less favorable terms (Santos and Sánchez 1990, 523–33). In a last-ditch effort to prevent a confrontation in the parliament, the PSOE sent a letter to Redondo proposing a joint meeting of the two executives to try to resolve the budget conflict. As expected, however, the party defended the government's position. The message of the meeting was clear: the party would not stick up for the UGT against its own government.

Several UGT leaders expressed their frustration with the party's failure to challenge the Socialist government. Damborenea pointed to the consequences of the party's lack of autonomy: "The party has been suppressed in the government-party relationship, as has the parliamentary group. Since neither the party nor the parliamentary group exist, the differences with the government cannot be channeled through these two factors. They can only manifest themselves in the streets or through the UGT." Likewise, Saracíbar complained, "[T]he discrepancies between the UGT and the PSOE reside in the support that the party is giving to the Government" (*Cambio 16*, October 26,1987).

Unable to convince either the government or the party to revive the budget compromise, the UGT carried out its threat to resort to norm-breaking voice. Instead of merely voting against the party line, however, Redondo and Saracíbar resigned their seats altogether. They announced their decision to the presidents of the Congress and the Socialist Group on October 22 and sent letters of resignation to González on October 29. In his letter, Redondo stated, "[T]he motive of my resignation is the impossibility of continuing to maintain for any longer the existing contradiction between my responsibility on the executive commission of the UGT and my condition as a member of the socialist parliamentary group" (Díaz-Varela and Guindal 1990, 270). In a subsequent letter to UGT affiliates, he argued that the resignations, which signaled a rejection of the government's attempt to legitimate its economic policy, "became inevitable to salvage the autonomy of the union" (UGT 1987b).

As it had in 1985, the UGT insisted that its leaders were acting on the basis of personal decisions and that the conflict did not constitute a deeper crisis of the *familia socialista* (UGT 1987a). In practice, however, Redondo and his allies were far less careful about bracketing their use of norm-breaking voice. As suggested by Redondo's letter to UGT affiliates, the resignations reflected disagreements with the government's economic policy as a whole rather than with a specific program. In addition, Redondo asked all of the UGT members of the Socialist Group to resign with him, at both the national and regional levels. Many followed his lead, and those who remained in the parliament found themselves on an informal blacklist[45] As of February 1988, only one UGT leader remained in the Socialist Group in the parliament (*El País*, February 8, 1988).

In the view of Justo Zambrana, who chose to leave the UGT executive rather than give up his parliamentary seat, the resignations of Redondo and Saracíbar "were a crucial turning point in relations between the UGT and the PSOE."[46] Besides violating the norm of UGT support for the party in parliament, they accelerated the division of the PSOE and the UGT into distinct organizational camps. Only one region (Vizcaya) sent a pro-UGT delegation to the PSOE's Thirty-first Congress, and the delegates elected only two UGT leaders to positions of influence.[47] Meanwhile, the PSOE and the UGT vied for control of the UGT's industrial federations, particularly in the metal, chemical, and public service sectors (Gillespie 1990, 56). This battle erupted into open warfare in the metal federation, resulting in a purge of the pro-PSOE executive by the UGT's Confederal Committee (Santos and Sánchez 1990, 27–51; Wozniak 1991, 343).[48]

Even in the context of these strains, however, the PSOE and the UGT continued to invest in salvaging their alliance. In May 1988, they hammered out a "non-aggression pact" that essentially renegotiated the norm of *apoyo crítico* by the UGT. Under the new arrangement, the two organizations would maintain more independence from one another, and the UGT would have more room to criticize the government's policies (Share 1989, 131). Following an announcement by Redondo that "it is necessary to pact concrete issues, but without committing ourselves to anything" (Díaz-Varela and Guindal 1990, 286), the government agreed to establish a calendar of negotiations in separate "tables" concerning reform of the National Institute of Employment (INEM), unemployment insurance coverage, pensions, government salaries, employment, public enterprise and investment, and investment funds (Zaragoza 1989, 98).

The 1988 General Strike

The third and final episode of norm-breaking voice occurred in response to a Youth Employment Plan (PEJ) announced by the Labor Ministry in June 1988. In response to an unemployment rate of 41.3 percent among Spanish youth in 1987, the PEJ proposed to provide employment for eight hundred thousand youths over a three-year period by reducing employers' social security contributions and fixing wages at the statutory minimum (Rhodes 1997, 116). The UGT expressed its "radical opposition" to the plan, which it portrayed as a threat to job stability for young and old workers alike (UGT 1989c, 5). The CCOO was equally critical, proclaiming that the PEJ was "the most blatantly conservative proposal regarding employment policy that had been made explicit in the last decade" (Campos and Alvarez 1990, 51). Both unions characterized the proposed contracts as "garbage contracts" *(contratos de basura)* that "hired the son to fire the father."[49]

The UGT's Confederal Committee met in early November 1988 to denounce the government's proposal and to plan a series of mobilizations: "The Confederal Committee of the UGT . . . conscious that public denunciations have proven insufficient to modify the behavior of the Administration and business, has resolved to invite the working men and women of our country to express their opposition to the social insensitivity that the government has manifested" (UGT 1988b, 2). Among the UGT's demands were withdrawal of the PEJ and compliance with the AES, particularly the extension of unemployment insurance to 48 percent of the registered unemployed. Later that month, the UGT and the CCOO issued a joint document that reiterated the points in the Confederal Committee's resolutions (Campo and Alvarez 1990, 219–21). The centerpiece of the plan was a general strike scheduled for December 14, 1988.

The PSOE leadership responded aggressively to the UGT's strike plans and, in the process, consolidated a realignment of forces within the PSOE and the UGT that favored alliance breakdown. The UGT's former ally, Alfonso Guerra, led a campaign to discredit the general strike and foment divisions within the UGT.[50] At his bidding, the party sent a threatening letter to Redondo and conspired to take disciplinary action against UGT cadres in the PSOE.[51] Guerra's transformation from ally to opponent closed off the remaining possibilities for the UGT to rely on sympathizers in the party, at least at the national level, and increased the UGT's inclination to view the party as a coconspirator with the government rather than as a potential bulwark against the government's market-oriented reforms.[52]

Guerra's anti-strike campaign led to another round of departures by pro-PSOE elements in the UGT, particularly in the industrial federations. In late November, PSOE leaders met with important UGT leaders in an attempt to convince them to oppose the strike. When several federations came out publicly against the strike, Redondo and his allies imposed sanctions for indiscipline. On December 1, the UGT suspended 144 leaders, including the executive commissions of the Federation of Agricultural Workers and the Chemical Federation (UGT 1988a). According to Manuel Garnacho, other leaders were also critical of Redondo's combative policies but exercised self-censorship out of fear of being liquidated by the UGT executive.[53] Whether by attrition or control, the oppositionist faction clearly dominated the UGT by the time the general strike took place.[54]

Despite the PSOE's machinations, the general strike was a resounding success for the unions. The vast majority of workers did not report to work on December 14, and hundreds of thousands of people took to the streets the following week to protest against the government.[55] As only the fifth general strike in Spain's history—and the first in which the PSOE and the UGT were on opposite sides of the picket line—the strike clearly violated the norms that governed the party-union alliance.[56]

Moreover, in 1988, the UGT made even less effort than it had in 1987 to bracket its use of norm-breaking voice. First, the UGT planned the strike in close coordination with the CCOO, marking a clear shift toward unity of action with its former rival. The UGT's greater willingness to work with the CCOO reflected three factors: the results of the 1986 factory council elections, which indicated that PSOE hegemony in the political arena would not translate into UGT hegemony in the labor movement; a change of leadership in the CCOO; and the disappointing results of the UGT's alliance with the PSOE.[57] Zufiaur saw unity of action as part of a broader shift in strategy: "The strike of December 14 has re-unionized the unions by orienting them toward a greater connection with the workers, to a more elaborated capacity for proaction, and toward a relation of forces that arises from daily union action at the base; to seeking, in sum, a focus in their own action rather than in initiatives arising from political power" (1990, 8). Especially as relations with the PSOE worsened, key UGT leaders became convinced that unity of action within the labor movement would bring greater benefits than remaining loyal to the party.

Second, the UGT launched an all-out assault against the PSOE's economic program, demanding a "social turn-around" (*giro social*) that would entail "a distinct focus in employment policy, in social protection, in the redistribution of wealth and in the participation and advance of economic democracy"

(Zufiaur 1989, 7). Redondo argued that this shift necessitated a reevaluation of the PSOE's loyalties: "The *giro social* requires that the government rely on the unions, rely on the workers, rely on its social base. . . . Workers have been abandoned by the political class. They have not had the least attention from them. It is a working class that feels abandoned, without expectations, subject to a strict market economy" (1989, 52, 53). The message sent by the general strike was that the UGT was prepared to abandon the PSOE unless it demonstrated a renewed commitment to the principles on which the party-union alliance had been based.

From Norm-Breaking Voice to Exit

Although the 1988 general strike ended up clinching the UGT's exit from its century-long alliance with the PSOE, UGT leaders initially viewed the strike as an instrument of norm-breaking voice rather than an act of defection: "Our Union wants, with these mobilizations, to modify substantive aspects of the economic and social policy of the Socialist government. To ensure that nobody seeks other explanations beyond those that are strictly union-related, it is not the objective of the UGT to overthrow the Socialist government. . . . We do not want to change the government but rather to have the government change" (UGT 1988, 5). Similarly, Saracíbar suggested that the general strike "has as its principal objective to fortify the unions in order to be able to resume negotiations with the government with a little more seriousness" (1988, 90). In contrast with previous episodes of norm-breaking voice, however, UGT leaders were prepared to exit if the PSOE did not respond wholeheartedly to their call for a *giro social*. Moreover, the extremely high level of distrust between the two members of the *familia socialista* undermined any effort to negotiate a solution short of divorce.

The PSOE engaged in several last-ditch but unsuccessful efforts to salvage the party-union alliance. First, the government offered a relatively generous compensation package with funds for unemployment insurance, pension benefits, and remunerations for government employees. But rather than welcoming this package, Zufiaur and other UGT leaders viewed it as another attempt to outsmart the UGT: "The government . . . tried to prevent the union from winning. For this reason, it did not want a meaningful accord with the unions. It had absolutely no interest in a balanced agreement."[58] Second, the party extended several invitations to Redondo and the UGT to participate in joint meetings. Once again, Redondo interpreted the invitation as little more than a trick to repair the party's damaged credibility (UGT 1989d). In the absence of a clear commitment by the PSOE to undertake a major reformulation of its socioeconomic policy, the UGT viewed these overtures as manipulations to win the union's support for an agenda that violated the principles on which the *familia socialista* had always been based.

By early 1989, the UGT was taking clear steps to exit from its alliance with the PSOE. In March, the UGT executive decided to invite the CCOO but not the PSOE to participate in its May Day festivities (UGT 1989a). On April 18, Redondo sent a letter to the PSOE's president explaining that the UGT would no longer share organizational responsibilities with the PSOE because of its failure to live up to its commitments (UGT 1989b). Several days later, the UGT's Confederal Committee resolved for the first time since the 1920s not to solicit votes for the PSOE in the June 15 elections to the European Parliament (Santos and Sánchez 1990, 151). The UGT continued to withhold its support in subsequent elections.[59] With the approach of general elections in October 1989, the UGT spelled out its position in a special issue of *Unión*: "Our position in favor of a policy of progress has traditionally led us to give our electoral support to the Socialist option. Nonetheless, the Confederal Committee did not maintain such support in the recent elections to the European Parliament given the lack of a social policy of progress by the Socialist government . . . the current situation has not varied [and] under these circumstances, an equivalent exercise in reflection leads us to the identical decision" (*Union*, September 15, 1989). In addition, Redondo issued declarations that the PSOE was not the only representative of workers and insinuated his support for the leftist coalition, the United Left (IU).

Ironically, the PSOE's electoral victories in 1989 lowered the opportunity costs to the UGT of severing its remaining ties with the party. While linking the PSOE's losses to the government's inadequate social policies, the UGT noted after the June 1989 elections, "[T]he lesson of these elections is that social conflict does not necessarily benefit the right" (UGT 1989f). Despite the outpouring of support for the general strike in December 1988 and the UGT's refusal to endorse the PSOE, the Socialists continued to have success at the ballot box. They prevailed in the European Parliament elections in June and retained their legislative majority in October with 39.6 percent of the vote and 50 percent of the seats. Although they lost working-class votes to the IU (Gillespie 1990, 59), a striking 56.8 percent of UGT members cast their ballots for the PSOE in October 1989 (*El País*, May 24, 1992).

Over the next few years, the UGT terminated other aspects of its historic alliance with the PSOE. In 1990, the UGT rejected an offer of assistance by the PSOE in the factory council elections. Rather than viewing the offer as part of an organizational bargain with the party, the UGT saw it as part of a scheme to influence the outcome of the UGT's Thirty-fifth Congress later that month (*El País*, March 1, 1990). The UGT also asked political groupings other than the PSOE to attend the Thirty-fifth Congress, including the CCOO and the Popular Party. The UGT repeated this practice for the Thirty-sixth Congress in April 1994. Finally, the UGT repeated its policy of neutrality in the general elections of 1993 "in accordance with the plural character of the union's composition" (UGT 1994, 8).

The PSOE, for its part, took steps to extricate itself from links with the UGT. Following the general strike, Solchaga concluded: "The old model of party-union relations has been broken in Spain forever. This does not mean that we have to renounce our project, but simply that we must find other allies" (Díaz-Varela and Guindal 1990, 311). The PSOE adopted two strategies for achieving this goal. First, it reinforced its efforts to attract the urban middle classes, even though they constituted only a third of the party's votes.[60] Second, it launched a project to create a network of militants (*red de responsables*) in the factories to fulfill the UGT's earlier role of disseminating information and mobilizing support. According to sources within the party, "The action of the party in the factories has always rested on the UGT, since its representatives in the workplace were also PSOE members, and they took charge of transmitting the policies of the party. . . . Now we don't even know to whom to send materials, and we have a lot of trouble connecting with the workplace, which means we have to organize our own network" (*El País*, February 6, 1989). Although neither strategy met with much success, they both signaled the PSOE's recognition that its political bargain with the UGT was no longer in effect.

The PSOE formalized its separation from the UGT with a statutory reform in 1990 that eliminated the obligation for all working-class members of the party to belong to the UGT, requiring them instead "to participate in some social movement" (PSOE 1990, 159). According to one prominent Socialist, this reform was an "ad hoc clause" to allow CCOO members to fill leadership positions within the party.[61] Several CCOO leaders subsequently joined the PSOE executive, prompting a former secretary general of the UGT's Chemical Federation to complain that "there are leaders of *Comisiones* on the Executive Commission of the PSOE, but there is nobody from the UGT."[62] One of these leaders, Julián Ariza, attributed his presence on the executive to the previous rupture between the PSOE and the UGT: "The party recognized that the fall of the old model of relations between the party and the union was irreversible. It also expanded its thinking regarding the reality of union pluralism in Spain and the limitations of having an affiliation clause with only one union."[63] Although the PSOE continued to favor the UGT over other unions, the relationship was no longer exclusive, even in formal terms.

Voice after Exit

Exit does not necessarily lead to a termination of voice, especially when the deteriorating product or service is a public rather than a private good. Since many of the policies adopted by the Socialist government could not be avoided by workers and unions even after the UGT exited from the party-union alliance, UGT leaders continued to exercise "voice after exit."[64] In particular, they pursued two strategies that had begun to take shape prior to the breakdown of the alliance.

First, the UGT fully embraced the idea of partial rather than global agreements with the government. As explained by the UGT's secretary of union action at the time, "after the December 14 strike, the union could gain more through 'lay accords' that did not come from the 'spiritual father' and did not have any partisan sentiment."[65] This new approach took concrete form in a Priority Union Proposal (PSP) formulated by the UGT in the months after the general strike and released in conjunction with the CCOO in October 1989. The PSP contained twenty demands organized into four areas: employment, social protection, income redistribution, and worker participation (UGT 1989b). Although most of these demands were long-standing, the PSP established a distinct pattern of interaction: "The negotiation took place over an extended period of time, with diverse interlocutors, with autonomous negotiations regarding each issue, and based in general concepts, leaving economic quantification until the end" (Calvo 1990, 68).

At first, the approach outlined in the PSP met with significant success, prompting Zufiaur to comment that "the strike of December 14 had its victory a year later."[66] The unions achieved several important gains in 1990, including negotiating rights for public sector employees, improvements in pension benefits, and union participation in monitoring employment contracts (UGT 1994, 25). This success was short-lived, however. Economic recession and the impending formation of the European Monetary Union pushed the Socialists to adopt more restrictive policies. In June 1991, they released a Social Pact of Progress, which had the same initials as the PSP but called for global negotiations with the unions and emphasized inflation control and labor productivity.

The UGT and the CCOO roundly rejected the pact and countered with their own proposal, the Union Initiative of Progress, in November 1991. They reiterated their commitment to issue-specific accords: "The stage of global pacts has passed. Remedies do not exist that can bring solutions to complex problems in a short period of time nor that can ask of working men and women responsibilities that do not correspond to them. To achieve the objectives we seek, we believe in the necessity of a diversified process of negotiation of specific and concrete aspects" (UGT 1991, 2). Rather than responding favorably to the UGT's demands, the PSOE resorted to the tactics of using executive decrees and forging alliances with the conservative parties in Congress to pass legislation opposed by the unions. The UGT responded, in turn, by organizing general strikes with the CCOO in May 1992 and January 1994.

The second component of "voice after exit" was the UGT's unity of action with the CCOO. This strategy reflected the success of the general strike and a realization among UGT leaders that their previous goal of hegemony in the labor movement was unrealistic. Zufiaur expressed this attitudinal shift in no uncertain terms: "The bipolarity of the labor movement is not going to change. It is now a fact. Thus, the unions can stop their struggle for hegemony."[67] In accordance with the pattern established during the December 14 strike, the two unions continued to issue joint proposals and organize joint mobilizations, including the general strikes in 1992 and 1994. This strategy not only unified the vast majority of organized workers behind a single program but also conformed to the UGT's shift in preferences toward nonpartisan, union-based action.[68]

CHAPTER 7

Back from the Brink in Venezuela

The Venezuelan story offers yet another variation on the theme of choosing sides in a party-union alliance. Prior to the reform period, Venezuela's alliance rested on the principles of democratic petrostatism and a set of norms generated by exchanges in the socioeconomic, political, and organizational arenas. As in Mexico and Spain, these principles and norms faced an unprecedented challenge in the 1980s and early 1990s. The AD governments of Jaime Lusinchi and, especially, Carlos Andrés Pérez adopted economic reforms that imposed painful sacrifices on workers and violated the central tenets of democratic petrostatism, thereby creating a loyalty dilemma for CTV leaders.

Reflecting the institutional arrangements that shaped relations of power and autonomy in Venezuela, CTV leaders reacted differently to this loyalty dilemma than did their counterparts in Mexico or Spain. Workers posed enough of a threat to persuade them to experiment with norm-breaking voice, but the party used a combination of power and autonomy to get them to return quickly to norm-based voice. Initially, the party's resistance to its own government effectively "legalized" instruments of voice that ordinarily would have violated alliance norms under an AD administration. Thus, the CTV could resist the reforms without behaving disloyally toward the party. When AD reimposed limits on labor's demand making, however, CTV leaders retreated back to their traditional instruments of norm-based voice. Not only did they fear punishment for another foray into norm-breaking voice, but the party had also wrested some key concessions from the government that eased their loyalty dilemma.

Principles of Democratic Petrostatism

The vision of society behind the alliance between AD and the CTV can be characterized as "democratic petrostatism."[1] This vision incorporated three principles: the use of Venezuela's oil wealth to construct an interventionist and distributive state; guaranteed rights and privileges for organized labor; and support for democracy. Although the origins of democratic petrostatism can be traced to the early years of the alliance when AD militants *(adecos)* and the labor movement joined forces against authoritarian rule, its clearest statements can be found in documents issued after the transition to democracy in the late 1950s.

In August 1958, AD's National Convention issued a Labor Thesis that elaborated the first two principles of democratic petrostatism. Regarding AD's development strategy, the Labor Thesis declared: "The Venezuelan state, because of its financial power and the peculiarities of the country's economic evolution, should be the primary promoter and financier of production. . . . The industrialization of Venezuela should be fueled, fundamentally, by natural resources" (Godio 1985, 144–45). AD envisioned a privileged place for unions and workers in Venezuela's oil-based economy. The Labor Thesis identified unions as "the vanguard of the Revolution" and proclaimed, "*Acción Democrática* will only achieve its objectives—immediate or long-term—to the extent that it behaves as a Party that defends above all else the interests of the exploited of the factories, workshops, and farms" (Godio 1985, 162, 171).

In December 1958, AD joined with two other parties, COPEI and the URD, to sign a Declaration of Principles and Basic Program of Government that recognized labor as a fundamental element in economic progress and guaranteed the defense of workers and adequate protections for union liberty. These principles were later enshrined in the 1961 Constitution, which upheld the state as the "rector" of economic and social life and provided guarantees of social assistance, job security for union leaders *(fuero sindical),* and the collective rights of unions (López Maya and Werz 1981, 11–16).

The CTV, for its part, embraced the idea of a national project to achieve industrial development. It accepted AD's multiclass character and, instead of viewing domestic capitalists as the enemy, took a collaborative approach to industrial relations. In 1959, the CTV affirmed: "[W]e actively support national industrialists when they are under attack by international trusts and will form a common front with them when they resist foreign penetration" (CTV 1987a, 25). Like the CTM in Mexico, the CTV rejected class conflict as the primary means of improving the lives of workers and favored cooperation with domestic capitalists and the state to promote national development.

The *adecos* also eschewed the violent overthrow of existing power structures, preferring a democratic path to social change.[2] AD's statutes declare, "[T]he Party will act according to democratic methods and with respect for popular sovereignty in the national political arena in order to carry the Venezuelan people to the full realization of a social and economic structure based on liberty and justice" (AD 1977, 3; AD 1993, 9). Likewise, the CTV expressed its commitment to democracy in a 1959 Declaration of Principles: "[W]e reaffirm our disposition to fight for democratic norms of governance as the system in which the struggle and organization of workers can develop freely" (CTV 1987b, 171).

Norms of Exchange and Conflict Management

The principles of democratic petrostatism generated norms of exchange and conflict management in the socioeconomic, political, and organizational arenas. AD was expected to use state power to deliver material benefits to workers, provide CTV leaders with party posts and elected offices, and support the hegemony of its allies in the labor movement. In return, CTV leaders were expected to discourage workers' mobilization (except when AD was in the opposition), support democracy and AD's quest for electoral victories, and lend ideological and organizational backing to the party. These bargains were mutually reinforcing as long as AD could maintain its historic commitment to state-led development and distribution.

Socioeconomic Bargain

Under the socioeconomic bargain, the party was expected to use state power to deliver material benefits to workers. AD had its first opportunity to actualize this norm during its three-year tenure in government in the 1940s (the *trienio*). Flush with oil resources, AD promoted industrial expansion and raised the purchasing power of workers by subsidizing food prices, lowering rents and electricity rates, reducing the domestic prices of fuels, initiating worker housing projects, extending social security coverage to public employees, expanding health and education services, and launching school lunch programs and nurseries for working mothers (Bergquist 1986, 264). In addition, the AD Minister of Labor, Raúl Leoni, intervened in the process of collective bargaining to pressure employers to grant the higher wages and social benefits that had been mandated by the Labor Law but never implemented.[3]

AD renewed these policies after democracy was restored in 1958. Following a brief period of austerity in 1959–60, the government launched a strategy of state-led ISI fueled by vast oil revenues. In the process, the state became the main engine of growth in the economy. In the early 1960s, the AD administration of Rómulo Betancourt formed the Venezuelan Corporation of Guyana, a vast holding company for state-owned steel, aluminum, and hydroelectric projects. The government also created at least 79 other state-owned enterprises and became involved in at least 146 mixed enterprises, all of which were at least 25 percent state-owned (Karl 1982, 131). In the 1970s, another AD president, Carlos Andrés Pérez, nationalized the petroleum and iron industries. By the early 1980s, the state accounted for 43 percent of the gross national product, 32 percent of employment, 50 percent of gross domestic investment, and 20 percent of consumption (McCoy et al. 1995, 141).

From the 1950s through the early 1970s, this strategy helped the Venezuelan economy grow at an average annual rate of 6 percent while keeping annual inflation below 2 percent (McCoy and Smith 1995, 124). Even after inflation began to creep upward in the 1970s, state-led ISI generated positive externalities for workers. First, industries with relatively high rates of unionization experienced impressive job growth. The number of workers employed in the secondary sector of the economy (mining, petroleum, manufacturing, construction, and public utilities) grew from 390,513 in 1961 to 1.2 million in 1981.[4] Second, workers made substantial wage gains. Between 1968 and 1978, real wages increased by 93 percent in the nonagricultural private sector and 95 percent in the petroleum sector (Valecillos 1993, 2: 30–31).

Like their Mexican counterparts, Venezuelan workers also benefited from policies specifically designed to raise their living standards. The Labor Ministry pressured employers to negotiate collective contracts favorable to workers. The Finance Ministry also averted strikes by providing subsidies to companies to help meet the wage demands of the unions (Ellner 1993, xviii). In the event of a strike, the labor authorities often demanded that firms pay back wages *(salarios caídos)* as a condition for getting striking workers back on the job (Larrañaga V. n.d., 16).

When inflation began to undermine the effectiveness of collective bargaining in the 1970s, AD took unilateral actions to bolster the wages of workers. In 1974, Pérez established a minimum wage, a provision that had been authorized by the 1936 Labor Law but never implemented. He also imposed price regulations on a wide range of basic commodities and increased subsidies and training programs for workers. Finally, AD supported government-mandated salary increases, first by executive decree under Pérez in 1974 and then through a special law approved by the AD-dominated Congress under a COPEI government in 1979 (Larrañaga n.d., 16).

AD also provided non-wage benefits to workers. In 1966, the AD administration of Raúl Leoni extended Venezuela's social security system to provide service throughout the country, include previously uncovered workers (including public employees), and to add retirement and incapacitation benefits (Ellner 1993, 38). Social expenditure as a share of the central government budget expanded significantly in the 1960s and early 1970s (Márquez 1995, 408).[5] Upon regaining control of both the presidency and the Congress in 1974, AD passed legislation that designated a sizable share of Venezuela's booming oil revenues for social welfare programs (Ellner 1993, 50).

AD also adopted policies that enhanced job security. In 1970, AD's congressional delegation backed a law granting permanent job tenure *(estabilidad absoluta)* to public employees. Six years later, in the wake of the oil nationalization, Pérez made a similar concession to petroleum workers. In addition, he reformed the system of pension and severance benefits *(prestaciones sociales)* to make it very costly for an employer to dismiss or retire workers. He modified the Labor Law to make *prestaciones sociales* payable upon termination of a worker's contract regardless of the reason and supported a Law against Unjustified Dismissals that required any employer found to have laid off a worker without just cause to choose between rehiring the worker or paying double severance benefits (Ellner 1993, 51).[6]

Besides distributing benefits directly to workers, the party created institutional mechanisms whereby AD labor leaders could influence wage rates and social policies. Although most collective contracts did not extend beyond the firm, their terms tended to be set at the national level. During the 1960s and early 1970s, this process took the form of "programmed bargaining" (Fagan 1977), in which AD's Labor Bureau would draft an overall labor policy, send it to the party executive for approval, and then deliver the final document to the state and industrial federations for implementation (McCoy 1989, 46). This mechanism enabled AD labor leaders to play an important role in setting wage rates throughout the economy.

The CTV also enjoyed representation in government agencies responsible for economic and social policy. In 1966, AD promulgated a law granting unions the right to one representative and one alternate on the boards of state agencies (with the exception of the central bank and the armed forces) and companies with more than 50 percent state ownership. Between 1959 and 1989, labor representatives filled 30 percent of the 305 nongovernmental posts on the boards of the 68 public-law entities created, as well as 26 percent of the economic-based posts on the consultative commissions created to draft legislation, study issues, and advise policymakers (Crisp 1998, 39–42). The key agencies with labor representation included the Venezuelan Social Security Institute (IVSS) at both the national and regional levels (OIT 1991, 99) and the autonomous housing and economic planning institutes (Boeckh 1972, 254).

In the 1970s, Pérez broadened the CTV's input into economic policy making by establishing formal tripartite structures of decision making at the national level for the first time since the *trienio*, as well as social concertation among top leaders in the form of a High-Level Commission (McCoy 1989, 52). Once a month, top leaders in the CTV and the peak business organization, the Venezuelan Federation of Chambers and Associations of Commerce and Production (Fedecamaras), met with the president to discuss labor, social, and economic issues (OIT 1991, 96). In the opinion of an *adeco* member of the CTV executive, the tripartite commissions "gave the workers representation in high levels" (McCoy 1989, 52).

Like the PRI in Mexico, AD established a pattern of offering compensation to its labor allies during periods of high inflation. To some extent, this compensation took the form of new organizational privileges for the CTV, such as inclusion in tripartite structures of decision making. But, as indicated by its policies regarding wages, subsidies, and job protection in the 1970s, AD was much more willing than the PRI to deliver material compensation to workers. This willingness reflected not only a belief among *adecos* that Venezuela's oil wealth made such compensation affordable, but also the vulnerability of both AD and the CTV to punishment by workers if they failed to fulfill their promises. Whereas the PRI could satisfy the CTM with opportunities to distribute selective benefits to a few followers, AD was under pressure from the CTV to provide generalized benefits for workers suffering the negative consequences of inflation.

For its part, the CTV was expected to discourage workers' mobilization as a tactic of economic demand making, especially in times of austerity. In the early 1960s, Betancourt implemented an austerity package that included a 10 percent wage decrease for public employees and an indefinite freeze on collective contracts. Despite pressure from its leftist members, the CTV refrained from engaging in protest against the package, which became known as the "hunger law" *(ley de hambre)*.[7] The economic boom in the mid-1960s reinforced the CTV's inclination to postpone immediate demands in the interest of national development, particularly in state-owned enterprises where strikes were deemed unpatriotic (Boeckh 1972, 213). Preferring conciliation to confrontation, the CTV only rarely lent decisive support to workers for the purpose of winning a strike (Ellner 1993, 221). Combined with firm-level unionism, the near nonexistence of strike funds, and extensive state controls over workers' mobilization, the CTV's hands-off approach curtailed most labor unrest.[8]

There was one important exception, however, to the norm of demobilization. The CTV enjoyed significantly more autonomy to mobilize workers in response to economic hardship when AD did not control the presidency. As a result of this exception, strike activity—particularly the number of workers' hours lost in illegal strikes—increased during COPEI governments (see table 7.1). AD also condoned cooperation between the CTV and rival labor confederations when COPEI was in power. The CTV, the General Workers' Union (CGT), and the Unitary Central of Venezuelan Workers (CUTV) collaborated to an unprecedented degree during the COPEI government of Rafael Caldera (1969–1973). They proposed joint contracts for collective bargaining, cosponsored May Day parades, and organized a symbolic half-hour general strike in support of improved worker benefits in September 1973 (Ellner 1993, 47–48). After a brief hiatus during the Pérez administration, this collaboration was renewed under the COPEI administration of Luis Herrera Campins (1979–1983), including cooperation between the CTV and the CUTV in drafting a Law of Salary Increases with the strong support of the AD delegation in Congress.

Political Bargain

AD's side of the political bargain was to provide CTV leaders with party posts, input into party policy, and access to public office through placement on AD electoral lists. Most of these privileges were channeled through AD's Labor Bureau, which sat atop a pyramid of labor bureaus at the municipal, district, and regional levels. Assemblies of workers elected the labor bureaus, whose secretary generals automatically became members of the party's executive committee at the corresponding level (Collier and Collier 1991, 267–68). State and national labor secretaries served as delegates to AD's National Convention, which met each year to establish the party line and select the National Executive Committee (CEN) and the National Disciplinary Tribunal (Martz 1966, 151). Within the CEN, the Labor Secretary was a voting member of the Political Bureau, which ran the party on a daily basis. Although not all *adecos* in the CTV leadership sat on the Labor Bureau, all members of the Labor Bureau held important positions in the CTV.[9]

Reflecting its power to sway the outcome of party nominating conventions, the Labor Bureau became accustomed to receiving high-level party posts and meaningful input into party policies, particularly on labor issues, in return for

Table 7.1   Indicators of Strike Activity in Venezuela, 1962–1983
(years of COPEI administrations in italics)

Year	Illegal Strikes	Workers Involved	Worker Hours Lost	Ilegal Strikes	Workers Involved	Worker Hours Lost
1962	8	3,492	340,380	11	1,270	40,153
1963	5	483	105,928	4	1,535	117,602
1964	7	1,049	85,440	20	2,495	18,436
1965	4	2,255	73,912	20	2,435	68,493
1966	1	194	40,200	11	2,990	23,488
1967	5	1,154	54,638	29	2,973	41,327
1968	4	3,054	35,038	9	1,419	10,757
1969	*3*	*341*	*107,700*	*83*	*21,015*	*1,580,980*
1970	*2*	*902*	*265,502*	*64*	*23,934*	*1,874,782*
1971	*5*	*806*	*314,676*	*228*	*38,501*	*3,850,074*
1972	*7*	*2,609*	*328,068*	*172*	*24,654*	*1,169,486*
1973	*4*	*525*	*90,200*	*250*	*45,508*	*1,157,368*
1974	3	135	19,376	116	17,463	1,039,824
1975	3	164	62,928	100	25,752	804,336
1976	1	3,000	36,000	171	33,932	730,123
1977	0	0	0	214	63,923	687,976
1978	0	0	0	140	25,337	318,732
1979	*2*	*237*	*5,304*	*145*	*23,268*	*400,127*
1980	*4*	*494*	*52,592*	*185*	*63,644*	*2,431,754*
1981	*3*	*370*	*160,640*	*129*	*29,562*	*2,074,347*
1982	*2*	*253*	*31,264*	*102*	*14,869*	*2,605,560*
1983	*0*	*0*	*0*	*200*	*59,749*	*2,886,273*

Adapted from Valecillos 1993, vol. II, 137–38; McCoy 1989, 49.

its support in internal elections.[10] This trade-off reached its pinnacle in 1983, when Jaime Lusinchi appointed Manuel Peñalver, a member of the CTV executive, as secretary general of the party in return for the Bureau's backing for Lusinchi's nomination as AD's presidential candidate. After winning the elections in December 1983, Lusinchi proclaimed that he had been elected "on the shoulders of the workers" (Ellner 1993, 71).

Labor's organic links with AD also translated into candidacies for public office. During the *trienio*, AD labor leaders received more than twenty seats in Congress and were named to over fifty consultative agencies (Lucena 1982, 322). Although AD's overall share of elected offices declined after 1958, AD labor leaders continued to receive between fifteen and twenty congressional seats.[11] In addition, the Labor Secretary usually chaired a committee in the Chamber of Deputies (Martz 1966, 204). These results were tied to an unwritten pact whereby the Labor and Agrarian Bureaus had the right to name candidates for two well-placed positions on party slates in return for their commitment to party objectives (Ellner 1996, 97).[12]

The CTV's side of the political bargain was to deliver two kinds of "goods" to the party in the political arena: general support for democracy and specific support for the party in elections. The CTV closed ranks with AD against perceived threats to democracy from both the right and the left. At a mass rally a few months after the defeat of Pérez Jiménez in January 1958, the president of the construction workers' union, Juan Herrera, announced labor's willingness to take up arms to defend the country's nascent democracy. In July and September of that same year, the Unified National Labor Committee called general strikes to protest coup attempts against the provisional government. When the principal threat to democracy shifted from military coups to armed struggle by leftist guerrillas in the 1960s, the CTV leadership defended the government's anti-insurgency policies and placed additional constraints on worker mobilization.

CTV leaders also helped AD retain its electoral dominance by campaigning for the party, making union resources available to party militants, and encouraging union members to vote for AD candidates. The vital importance of this support became clear when several of AD's top unionists defected to form a rival party, the People's Electoral Movement (MEP), just before the 1968 elections. These defectors controlled the CTV presidency and dominated several key affiliates, including the Federation of Petroleum Workers (Fedepetrol) and the Federation of Metalworkers (Fetrametal). By splitting the AD vote, particularly among workers, they opened the door for COPEI's first presidential victory.[13] Aware of the importance of regaining working-class support, the AD launched a successful campaign to retake control of the CTV and lure key *mepistas* back to the *adeco* fold.[14] This campaign helped AD regain the presidency in the 1973 elections.

Organizational Bargain

Like the parties in Mexico and Spain, AD was expected to support the hegemony of its allies in the labor movement. This project presented a somewhat different challenge in Venezuela, however, as a result of the scope and composition of the CTV. On the one hand, AD did not have to worry too much about defending the CTV against other labor organizations. Even after rival confederations emerged in the 1960s and early 1970s, around 80 percent of Venezuela's labor unions belonged to the CTV.[15] Moreover, the CTV's reach extended to organized peasants and public employees. Although peasants and workers belonged to separate bureaus within AD, the CTV established an organic link between the peasant movement and the rest of organized labor.[16] In addition, 80 percent of all white-collar government workers belonged to the CTV (Ellner 1993, 88).

On the other hand, AD had to worry quite a lot about maintaining the hegemony of AD labor leaders within the CTV. In the early years of the alliance, these leaders faced their stiffest competition from the Venezuelan Communist Party (PCV).[17] During the *trienio*, the Labor Ministry played a key role in disadvantaging the PCV relative to AD. First, it tended to recognize AD-affiliated unions immediately while delaying decisions regarding unions founded by the Communists. Second, it encouraged the formation of parallel unions loyal to AD in workplaces already captured by the Communists (Ellner 1980, 96). Although AD failed to displace the PCV in strategic sectors, it controlled the vast majority of the country's unions by the time Pérez Jiménez staged his coup in November 1948 (Febres 1985, 295–96; Godio 1985, 39).[18]

After the return to democracy in 1958, the Labor Ministry approved the registration of thousands of new unions, many of which were parallel unions loyal to AD and/or in sectors traditionally dominated by AD. The party also used its access to state power to favor AD labor leaders in tripartite institutions and to seize control of labor organizations controlled by the left (López Maya and Werz 1981, 34–35). When the MEP threatened AD's hegemony in the late 1960s and early 1970s, AD's congressional majority negotiated the participation of Caldera's Labor Ministry in blocking the MEP's efforts to take control of key unions. AD and COPEI also joined forces to support maneuvers by their labor allies in Venezuela's largest union, the Single Union of Steel Industry Workers (SUTISS), to prevent a more radical party from taking control of the union despite having received the largest share of votes in union elections. Particularly as opposition parties gained strength in strategic sectors in the 1970s, "*adeco* domination of the CTV [came] to rest on its ability to use the Labor Ministry to manipulate elections and the collective bargaining process" (Hellinger 1991, 184).[19]

AD reinforced the hegemony of AD labor leaders in the CTV by enabling them to broker financial support from the state. Like the CTM and the UGT, the CTV relied on public subsidies to compensate for its failure to develop an effective system of self-financing. The CTV received funds from the national legislature, nearly every ministry of the federal government, governors, state legislatures, and municipal councils.[20] Even after losing its monopoly in the labor movement in the early 1960s, the CTV retained its lock on parliamentary subsidies, as well as labor positions on tripartite boards (Boeckh 1972, 202).[21] Although the subsidized share of the CTV's total revenues fell from its peak of 90 percent in 1961, it ranged between 45 and 50 percent from 1964 to 1980 (Boeckh 1972, 202; McCoy 1989, 59).[22]

AD also granted the CTV a tremendous fiefdom when President Leoni created the Venezuelan Workers' Bank (BTV) in July 1966. In conjunction with a holding company formed by the CTV in 1965 (Coracrevi), the CTV used the BTV to build an economic empire that consisted of forty-two enterprises worth over one hundred million dollars in 1980. This made the CTV the fifth-richest labor organization in the world (McCoy 1989, 59; López Maya and Werz 1981, 76). Access to these benefits became even more closely associated with AD's control of the state when the COPEI government of Luis Herrera Campins seized the BTV and terminated its operations for failure to pay its debts (Ellner 1993, 185).[23] Not surprisingly, one of Lusinchi's campaign promises during the 1983 elections was that he would restore the BTV if elected president.

Like the CTM and the UGT, the CTV was expected to lend ideological and organizational backing to the party. As in Spain, this backing often overlapped with the defense of parliamentary democracy, which, in Venezuela, extended to support for AD's counterinsurgency policies in the 1960s. The CTV also provided critical human resources in the form of labor militants who served as AD officials and ran AD's political machine. Finally, the CTV helped AD retain its legitimacy as a social democratic party committed to the working people of Venezuela. Besides reinforcing AD's progressive image in speeches and political propaganda, the CTV cultivated strong ties with social democratic labor organizations in Europe.[24]

Bargains in Crisis

The party-union alliance suffered when the party responded to a serious economic crisis with market reforms that undercut its bargains with its labor allies. As explained by a CTV advisor, Hector Valecillos, AD's reforms "made it increasingly difficult for the CTV majority to justify before its bases its support for a policy decided by the party but objectively counterproductive for the working population" (1990, 510). In other words, AD labor leaders in the CTV faced a loyalty dilemma as a result of the government's policies. In some respects, their dilemma was more vexing than that in Mexico or Spain because of the power of both the party and workers to punish them for disloyalty. Regardless of which ally they betrayed, they were likely to suffer serious consequences. In response, they vacillated between collaboration and confrontation, including an experiment with norm-breaking voice in early 1989.

Norm-Based Voice, 1983–1989

Like the UGT at the outset of the Socialist government in Spain, the CTV was initially willing to tolerate austerity policies as a necessary evil to overcome the country's economic crisis. In March 1984, the president of the CTV, Juan José Delpino, stated: "To neutralize the effects of [the economic crisis], it has been necessary to take a set of economic measures that involve a series of sacrifices by sectors of Venezuelan society. In this sense, the CTV has stated that the measures are necessary and indispensable, and that we are disposed to contribute with the quota of sacrifices asked of us" (*El Nacional*, March 7, 1984). In 1983 and 1984, the CTV backed policies designed to promote investment and productivity in the private sector while seeking to protect employment. On the wage front, the CTV abstained from requesting a general salary increase in favor of collective bargaining to achieve increases in sectors in recuperation (McCoy 1988).[25] The CTV also discouraged strikes during this period, resulting in relative labor peace despite a significant increase in the cost of living. In mid-1984, a Venezuelan labor expert drew an explicit parallel between the CTV's response to Lusinchi's policies and its submissive behavior during the austere years of the early 1960s (Arrieta 1984a, 301).

Norm-based voice included rhetorical attacks on neoliberal members of the president's cabinet. The Labor Bureau and the CTV harshly criticized several of Lusinchi's economic ministers, even demanding their resignations. But AD labor leaders were careful to place these attacks in the context of overall support for the government. In July 1984, the president of the Labor Bureau, Antonio Ríos, insisted that his criticisms of the government's program "do not signify in any way that the Labor Bureau withdraws its support for and solidarity with the President of the Republic and his governance" (*El Nacional*, July 11, 1984). AD labor leaders also lambasted non-*adeco* members of the CTV executive for participating in a joint meeting with leaders from the CUTV, the CGT, and the Confederation of Autonomous Unions (Codesa) and the subsequent mobilization of a protest march against the government's reforms (Paralelismo 1984; Arrieta 1984b).[26]

In return for their forbearance, AD labor leaders expected compensatory programs for workers, along with opportunities to influence policies concerning labor. Lusinchi responded quite favorably to their demands. First, he offered substantial concessions to workers in the form of subsidies, job creation, and minimum wage increases. Not coincidentally, he promised an ambitious package of pro-worker programs during union elections in 1985. Second, he gave CTV leaders input into policy making. Besides backing Peñalver as secretary general of AD, he appointed a CTV advisor, Luis Raúl Matos Azócar, to head the critical Ministry of Development and Planning (Cordiplan). He also oversaw passage in October 1984 of the Law of Costs, Prices, and Salaries, which fulfilled a campaign promise to create the Commission of Costs, Prices, and Salaries (Conacopresa), a tripartite commission to negotiate wage and price increases.

These measures elicited a positive response by CTV leaders, but they had only a short-lived impact on the CTV's loyalty dilemma because of the government's inability or unwillingness to maintain its commitments. Venezuela's main business organization, Fedecamaras, withdrew from the Conacopresa in November 1984, and a tripartite commission established by Lusinchi to take its place failed to produce any meaningful results (McCoy 1988). To make matters worse, Matos Azócar resigned from his position as Minister of Cordiplan in January 1985 out of frustration with resistance within the cabinet to his ambitious development plan (Guevara 1989, 230–33). Finally, Lusinchi kept delaying the promised return of the BTV, and, in September 1985, the cabinet postponed implementation of the pro-worker programs announced earlier in the year because of a funding shortage (*Veneconomía*, September 1985).

These disappointments contributed to an escalation of tensions between AD and the CTV. At the CTV's Ninth Congress in May 1985, Delpino engaged in a war of words with Lusinchi over the government's economic policy, its weak commitment to social concertation, and the bureaucracy's intransigence (CTV 1987c, 208).[27] The CTV subsequently radicalized its position regarding the promotion of a general wage increase and heightened its criticism of the government for making unilateral decisions.[28] These tensions persisted even after Lusinchi abandoned his austerity policies in late 1985. Although persistent inflation dampened the impact of the recovery on real wages, the rate of open unemployment fell from 13 percent in 1984 to 7.3 percent in 1988 (see table 3.7). In addition, large increases in public spending enabled Lusinchi to deliver a new and more extensive round of compensations to workers and their families.

Lusinchi's concessions to labor did not lessen the CTV's attacks against his government because these attacks were part of a regularized pattern of intraparty struggle over AD's presidential nomination. As in previous successions, the Labor Bureau opposed the candidate favored by the incumbent president. Despite reservations stemming from his personalistic style of governance during the 1970s, the Labor Bureau voted to support the charismatic Pérez over Lusinchi's ally, Octavio Lepage. In return, Pérez promised the Labor Bureau that he would appoint a pro-labor finance minister, reopen the BTV, and entertain the possibility of naming a labor leader to a ministerial post (Ellner 1993, 79). As part of their internal campaign, AD labor leaders lambasted government policies and accused Lusinchi and his allies of corruption. In November 1987, Pérez won the nomination with 65 percent of the vote, and the Labor Bureau imposed sanctions on AD labor leaders who openly supported Lepage.[29] AD labor leaders did not overstep the boundaries of norm-based voice, however. Once Pérez prevailed over Lepage, the warring parties put aside their differences to focus on the elections in December 1988.

Aided by Lusinchi's generous spending policies, Pérez and his labor allies engineered another AD victory at the ballot box in December 1988. Pérez won 52.9 percent of the vote in the presidential elections, compared to 40.4 percent for the COPEI candidate, Eduardo Fernández.[30] In the Chamber of Deputies, AD won ninety-seven seats, compared to sixty-seven seats for COPEI (Lazcano 1989, 4; España 1989, 15). As a result of a deal worked out between Lusinchi and Pérez regarding the composition of AD's electoral lists, AD trade unionists also did well, winning seventeen deputy seats and two Senate seats.[31]

The 1989 General Strike

Many working-class Venezuelans expected that Pérez would bring back the heady days of oil-led prosperity that had characterized his first administration in the 1970s. To their shock and dismay, he opted instead for "the great turn-around" *(el gran viraje),* an orthodox program of market-oriented reform.[32] Besides imposing austerity measures that caused a dramatic decline in wages and employment, he violated AD's core principles by attempting to dismantle much of Venezuela's interventionist state (see chapter 3).

At first, CTV leaders resorted to their usual strategy of norm-based voice aimed at persuading the president to soften his reforms. In a meeting with Pérez in December, the Labor Bureau received the program submitted by Pérez's economic team with surprise and disappointment. Bureau members also objected to Pérez's violation of the traditional practice whereby the president would defer to the Labor Bureau regarding selection of the Labor Minister and the director of the IVSS.[33] But despite their failure to negotiate major changes in either the economic program or Pérez's cabinet, both AD and the CTV tentatively supported *el gran viraje* after the presidential inauguration in early February, conceding that the crisis demanded difficult measures.[34]

The CTV's public ratification of the government's program coexisted, however, with growing internal pressures to take a more confrontational stance.[35] Not surprisingly, the minority factions of the CTV demanded a frontal attack against the reforms. This time, they received support from some of their AD colleagues. In mid-February, the CTV's economic advisors, who included prominent *adecos* such as Matos Azócar and Valecillos, sparked a conflict within the AD faction by drafting a document that harshly criticized Pérez's economic program. According to one of the advisors who contributed to the document, the conflict pitted Ríos, who defended AD's position as secretary of the Labor Bureau, against Delpino, who supported a more combative posture (*El Nacional*, February 15, 1989). Although the party hierarchy successfully pressured AD labor leaders to reject the draft in favor of an alternative version supporting Pérez's program and denouncing mobilizations (*El Nacional*, February 12, 1989, February 14, 1989), the conflict suggested that the minority factions could find allies among AD labor leaders in their struggle to reorient the CTV's strategy.

The fragile dominance of the pro-government faction unraveled entirely when thousands of Venezuelans took to the streets on February 27, 1989 to protest a sudden increase in bus fares. The riots, which erupted in four major cities and lasted for three days, were spontaneous, violent, and unprecedented in democratic times. Although set off by anger against bus drivers for raising their fares without warning, they reflected social tensions that had been building over years of economic hardship and governmental inefficacy. They also delivered a harsh wake-up call to the CTV, which had clearly failed to channel the demands of working people. One of Delpino's allies in the CTV executive, Pedro Brito, concluded, "We are the natural leaders of the workers, and it appears that until now we have not known how to lead them, for which we are paying the consequences" (*El Nacional*, March 8, 1989).

Delpino moved almost immediately to reorient the CTV's strategy.[36] In early March, he called for concertation among all fractions in the CTV (*El Nacional*, 7 March 1989). Breaking with tradition, he also encouraged CTV affiliates to defend the jobs of their members and, if necessary, to engage in local mobilizations against employers. It took longer for Ríos and other members of the Labor Bureau to move toward norm-breaking voice, but the continued refusal by both the government and the party to revise the reforms convinced them to support a demonstration of the CTV's solidarity with the workers.[37] According to Delpino, his fellow *adecos* finally realized that "if we do not maintain conduct that is autonomous, independent, critical, rebellious toward the parties and the government, then this labor movement will escape our control" (*El Nacional*, April 6, 1989).

In late March 1989, the Labor Bureau voted to organize a special congress of the CTV to discuss a program of action against the reform package. Inspired by the Spanish strike in December 1988, Ríos even suggested the possibility of holding a general strike (*El Nacional*, March 29, 1989). The bureau's decision elicited a very negative reaction by the AD leadership. The president of AD, Gonzalo Barrios, lambasted the bureau for failing to consult with the party and warned that convocation of a special congress "would signify pulling the rug out from under the government politically" (*El Nacional*,

April 1, 1989).[38] When it became clear that the special congress would take place, Pérez tried to prevent a vote in favor of a general strike, which he called "insanity" that "would run the risk of discrediting the labor movement" (*El Nacional*, April 21, 1989). The secretary general of AD, Humberto Celli, stated that all *adecos* should support the Pérez government and that Delpino would be called more frequently before the AD executive to justify the CTV's actions (*El Nacional*, April 28, 1989, May 2, 1989).

Although these pressures led Ríos to retreat temporarily from his call for a general strike, Delpino continued to advocate confrontation. In response to Pérez's threat, he stated, "[T]he insanity would be to fail to respond to this [economic] package that has caused grave harm to the working class and to all the popular sectors" (*El Nacional*, April 22, 1989). He also defied Celli's challenge by stating, "[T]he AD has the obligation to support its government, but this government is not a government of *Acción Democrática*" (*El Nacional*, May 2, 1989).

Delpino's defiance continued at the special congress. He demanded a new direction in the government's economic policy and an end to its treatment of the CTV "as a simple receptor of information—often partial regarding policies already decided and negotiated" (CTV 1990, 130). He also spoke of a crisis of representation, arguing that "when a collectivity decides to carry out its demands in a direct form, it is because the institutions that represent or defend it are not adequately fulfilling their function of channeling these demands" (CTV 1990, 123). To combat this crisis, he advocated the use of strikes and mobilizations as instruments of pressure. Responding to his appeal, the delegates to the special congress unanimously approved a twelve-hour general strike for May 18, 1989 and ordered the CTV executive to establish a plan of action with the country's other labor confederations. On the day of the strike, an estimated 98 percent of the labor force did not report to work (*Veneconomía*, May 1989).

Both the special congress and the general strike violated the norms of conflict management in the party-union alliance. The only other special congress ever organized by the CTV (in the early 1960s) had received the active endorsement of the AD leadership because it sought to expel critics of an AD administration. The 1989 special congress, by contrast, united competing factions within the CTV against the policies of an AD government and defied the wishes of the party and its president. The general strike dealt an even greater blow to the normative framework of the alliance. As in Spain, the strike was of tremendous symbolic importance. Venezuela had not experienced a general strike since 1958, when AD and its labor allies joined other pro-democracy forces to protest an attempted military coup. Nor had the CTV ever taken such a combative posture when AD was in power. Moreover, the CTV invited other labor organizations to participate, a tactic usually reserved for periods of opposition government. Like the UGT, the CTV continued to issue joint statements and to organize joint actions with other confederations after the strike.

The Venezuelan general strike, however, differed in fundamental ways from its Spanish counterpart. Rather than being a final expression of norm-breaking voice before crossing the threshold into exit, the Venezuelan strike was a relatively isolated and tentative abandonment of norm-based voice. In this respect, it more closely resembled the UGT's resistance to the PSOE's pension reform in 1985. First, AD labor leaders took precautions to safeguard their relationship with the party. Just four days before the strike, the Labor Bureau issued a document that declared conditional support for Pérez and his economic policies (Documentos 1990, 119–20).[39] In addition, no CTV leader resigned from the Labor Bureau (or the Congress) to resolve the contradictions of double militancy. Although Delpino left the CTV presidency prematurely, he did so out of frustration rather than defiance. According to the secretary general of the CTV, he resigned "because he knew he would be constantly confronting Carlos Andrés Pérez."[40] In the end, he chose to retreat from this confrontation rather than suffer its consequences.

Second, CTV leaders continued to rely on norm-based voice in their other dealings with AD. One example is the CTV's response to privatization. The CTV took a relatively neutral position and refrained from mobilizing protest in return for selective benefits for its members. The extent to which these benefits came at the expense of workers' rights varied from one industry to another. At one extreme was the case of the ports, where laid-off unionists received double their *prestaciones sociales*—and some union leaders walked away with over two hundred thousand dollars—in return for acceptance of a complete liquidation of the unionized workforce (Hernández Alvarez 1993, 85). At the other extreme was the case of the National Telephone Company of Venezuela (CANTV), where workers received job guarantees and an opportunity to buy shares in the company after it was privatized.

Third, the Venezuelan strike did not represent as blatant an act of disloyalty toward the party as the Spanish strike because of the pluralist composition of the CTV. AD labor leaders repeatedly used this pluralism to justify their actions. Delpino, for example, insisted, "I have to respect the ideas of the comrades who are not *adecos* on the executive committee of the CTV" (*El Nacional*, April 6, 1989). Likewise, a prominent member of the Labor Bureau, César

Gil, emphasized that "the CTV is a pluralist and autonomous institution to which all the political forces belong . . . neither the executive committee of AD nor Doctor Barrios has jurisdiction over the decisions of the CTV" (*El Nacional*, April 4, 1989).

While remaining firmly opposed to the strike, AD ultimately accepted these justifications. A week before the strike, Celli conceded, "We are tolerant of the criticisms of an entity such as the CTV because we know that Delpino speaks as a representative of the CTV and not as an AD leader" (*El Nacional*, May 9, 1989). A few days later, the AD executive reiterated its solidarity with Pérez and the reforms but authorized AD labor leaders to participate in the strike in recognition of the multiparty nature of the CTV leadership (*El Nacional*, May 13, 1989). Thus, in contrast to either Spain or Mexico, the plurality of voices within the CTV allowed AD labor leaders to engage in norm-breaking voice without taking full responsibility for their actions.

Finally, the Venezuelan general strike turned out to be an isolated act of disloyalty rather than the first of several experiments with norm-breaking voice. Like the Spanish government, the Venezuelan government granted minor concessions to labor but refused to reverse the reforms or to reduce the influence of the neoliberal technocrats on government policy. Yet the CTV did not keep moving along the continuum from voice to exit. Like Redondo in 1985, Delpino feared an escalation of the conflict with the government. Some years later, he reflected, "[W]e would have had to hold successive strikes, not only of twelve hours, but to have decreed strikes for months, that is to say, an open war against the government."[41] But whereas UGT leaders eventually became convinced that the benefits of such a war outweighed the costs, CTV leaders reached the limits of their resistance with the 1989 general strike and subsequently retreated back to norm-based voice.

To some extent, their retreat can be explained by their incentives to avoid punishment by the party. Having demonstrated their solidarity with workers by organizing the general strike, they had strong incentives to repair relations with the party by returning to norm-based voice. But their retreat is unlikely to have been so dramatic had the party not offered them relief from the loyalty dilemma. By challenging its own government, AD effectively "legalized" tactics that would ordinarily qualify as norm-breaking voice. Thus, rather than having to defy the party to demonstrate their loyalty to workers, as in May 1989, CTV leaders could do so with the party's blessing and support. Although this window of opportunity eventually closed, it proved sufficient to swing the pendulum back toward norm-based voice for the duration of the Pérez administration.

AD Against Its Own Government, 1990–1991

AD's bitter differences with the Pérez government broke out into the open after its disappointing showing in state and local elections of December 1989.[42] After publicly blaming the results on the economic reforms and AD's lack of representation in the cabinet, AD began behaving like an opposition party (Corrales 2002).[43] The battle between AD and the government became increasingly open and vitriolic during 1990 and 1991, culminating in a landslide victory by an anti-Pérez faction *(ortodoxos),* led by Luis Alfaro Ucero, at AD's national convention in October 1991.[44]

This feud had two salutary effects on the CTV's loyalty dilemma. First, it effectively freed the CTV to treat the Pérez administration like a non-AD government, thereby transforming actions that would normally constitute norm-breaking voice into norm-based voice. As in the years when COPEI controlled the presidency, the CTV was granted greater leeway to support antigovernment initiatives in Congress, carry out joint actions with other labor confederations, and mobilize workers. Second, AD's congressional delegation took the CTV's side against the government on several important issues, resulting in policy outcomes that eased the strain on the CTV's relations with workers.

These effects played out most clearly in three issue areas: labor law reform, rationalization of *prestaciones sociales,* and wage policy. Following the general strike, the CTV resurrected a labor law reform that had been proposed by Rafael Caldera, the founder of COPEI, back in 1985. Contrary to prevailing trends in other countries, the so-called Caldera Law enhanced worker entitlements and job stability. Aware that the law went against their market reforms, Pérez and his economic cabinet adamantly opposed it. But rather than defending the government's position, AD legislators cooperated with Caldera and the CTV. Celli declared that AD should follow the wishes of the CTV and promote the bill in Congress. With the help of the AD delegation, the Chamber of Deputies passed the new law in August 1989. AD was similarly cooperative in the Senate; David Morales Bello, the AD president of the Senate, gave the bill top priority and authorized its approval with only one debate (Corrales 2002). Although Pérez unsuccessfully called for a delay in passage of the law, he was unwilling to pay the political costs of exercising a veto.[45] He signed the law in November 1990, handing the CTV a significant victory in its antireform crusade. Moreover, this victory did not require AD labor leaders to behave disloyally toward the party because the party was willing to oppose its own government.

The debate over *prestaciones sociales* generated more ambiguous support by AD but involved greater use of combative tactics by the CTV. In November

1990, the government introduced a proposed reform of the existing system in Congress. The reform aimed to ease the burden on employers by forcing workers to liquidate their *prestaciones* each year and to encourage investment of these funds in private institutions. Arguing that the reform was both reactionary and unconstitutional, the CTV launched a campaign to defeat the law in Congress. Led by AD labor leaders such as José Beltran Vallejo and Federico Ramírez León, the campaign utilized instruments of voice that would have qualified as norm-breaking had the usual collaboration between AD and its own government been in effect.

In June 1991, the CTV joined with the CUTV, Codesa, and the CGT to issue a proclamation to the two houses of Congress arguing that the government's proposed reform violated the rights and guarantees of workers (Urquijo and Bonilla 1992, 85). These unions also held a joint assembly with the presidents of state labor federations from the four confederations to ratify a national program of mobilization. As part of this initiative, they formed a "commando of union action" to carry out joint protests in various states (OIT 1991, 58) and organized a protest in front of Congress on June 18 that was attended by a large and diverse group of labor organizations. A few days later, when Pérez refused to suspend discussions of the proposed reform in a meeting with the Labor Bureau and leaders from the four confederations, the secretary general of the CTV, César Olarte, announced that unionists would continue to picket Congress and threatened a national strike in early July (*El Nacional*, June 21, 1991).

At first, the AD leadership complied with Pérez's wishes to push the reform through Congress. In late May, the AD delegation backed a report that included a recommendation of support for the proposed law.[46] But this vote revealed serious divisions within AD, which were exacerbated by Luis Alfaro Ucero's crusade to seize control of the party for the *ortodoxos* at the national convention a few months later. As the CTV's resistance to the proposed law escalated, the *ortodoxos* began to cultivate the Labor Bureau's support by expressing their sympathy for the CTV's position against the government (*El Nacional*, June 26, 1991). Given the bureau's control over a large bloc of votes in internal elections, this move created incentives for the incumbent leadership to compete with the *ortodoxos* for labor's backing. In late June, the AD executive announced its rejection of the new regime of *prestaciones sociales* proposed by the president (*Diario de Caracas*, June 26, 1991). At AD's urging, the Congress voted on July 9 to defer the debate over the proposed law until the next parliamentary session in October, which effectively halted all action on the reform for the rest of the Pérez administration.[47]

The debate over wage policy brought labor leaders another small victory. In response to growing pressures by the CTV on wage policy, the president issued two decrees in April 1991 granting a higher minimum wage (Decree 1585) and a wage increase of 15 percent for workers in the private sector not covered by collective contract (Decree 1590). Rather than welcoming these measures, the CTV rejected Decree 1590 as inadequate and sent Congress a proposed Law of Wage and Salary Increases that would provide a general increase of 45 percent (Urquijo and Bonilla 1992, 82–83).

AD refused to support the Law of Wage and Salary Increases but sided with the CTV on the wage decree. The AD president of Congress, Pedro París Montesinos, announced, "[T]here is a growing inclination to reject [Decree 1590], in which case the Congress will formulate some criticisms and propose some modifications with the goal of having the president present a new project that is more compatible with existing expectations regarding wage increases" (*El Nacional*, May 16, 1991). Citing the need "to leave a margin of maneuver for both the chief executive and the Confederation of Venezuelan Workers" (*El Nacional*, May 23, 1991), AD voted with the opposition to send Decree 1590 back to the president for reconsideration.[48] Pérez responded with a revised decree mandating a 20 percent increase for workers in the private sector not covered by collective bargaining, which Congress approved.

But AD was not willing to support the CTV's more radical demands. The proposed Law of Wage and Salary Increases languished in committee because of a lack of support from either COPEI or AD. Several days before the vote on Decree 1590, Gaston Vera asked that AD labor deputies be excused from party discipline so that they could continue defending the legislation. The president of AD, David Morales Bello, responded that the party could not grant special dispensations to some members and not others (*El Nacional*, May 21, 1991). Although AD labor leaders did join their non-*adeco* comrades in a failed attempt to draft alternative language for sending Decree 1590 back to the president, the Law of Wage and Salary Increases never came up for a vote.[49]

Return to Traditional Instruments of Norm-Based Voice, 1992–1994

The window of opportunity in which CTV leaders could remain loyal to AD while using instruments of voice normally reserved for opposition governments closed soon after Alfaro and the *ortodoxos* took control of the party in October 1991. The CTV's last act of legalized norm-breaking voice occurred the following month, in the form of a twelve-hour general strike in several states that the CTV organized with the CUTV, Codesa, and the CGT. Although the party officially opposed the strike, CTV leaders received thinly veiled signals of support by the *ortodoxos*.[50] At the same time, however, they were pressured to limit the scope of their resistance. Soon after the top leadership of the four confederations issued a document threatening to paralyze the entire country unless the government met their demands (Urquijo and Bonilla 1992, 103), the CTV cancelled its plans to extend the protests to other states in return for an agreement by the government, under pressure by the *ortodoxos,* to hold regular consultations with labor leaders (*Veneconomía,* November 1991).

The CTV's margin for combative action diminished even further when an attempted coup in February 1992 altered the balance of power between the government and the party. Following the coup, Pérez sought to mend relations with AD, particularly the *ortodoxos,* by agreeing to remove some of neoliberal technocrats from the cabinet, decelerate or reverse key reforms, and provide AD with greater policy input (Corrales 2002; Navarro 1994, 25). This deal narrowed the chasm between AD and its own government, which implied a "recriminalization" of tactics the CTV had been using since 1990. The CTV responded by returning to its traditional instruments of norm-based voice.

AD labor leaders clearly signaled their strategic retreat during a congressional debate over a motion of censure against Pérez's pro-reform cabinet in March 1992. Introduced by a dissident AD legislator, Matos Azócar, the motion received unanimous support from the opposition deputies.[51] Yet, despite the motion's coherence with the CTV's official position, AD labor leaders followed the party line by voting against it. César Gil tried to rationalize the contradictory behavior of AD's labor delegation: "There is a double discourse, there is a discourse as a labor leader and a discourse as a political leader. I have an *adeco* discourse in the Congress, and I am a labor leader, and I am against the economic policy of Pérez" (*El Nacional,* March 27, 1992). Similarly, the president of the CTV, Federico Ramírez León, insisted that "here we are not acting as unionists but as AD leaders against a political manipulation" (*El Nacional,* March 27, 1992).[52] Not surprisingly, CTV leaders from other parties harshly criticized this response. Expressing a widespread sentiment, the labor secretary of Movement Toward Socialism (MAS), Rafael Colina, complained, "this ambiguity before the government is what has weakened the credibility of the CTV" (*El Nacional,* March 27, 1992).

The chasm between AD and Pérez reopened after a second attempted coup in November 1992. Responding to a dramatic escalation in social protest and a decision by the Supreme Court to indict Pérez for misuse of funds, AD senators voted with the opposition in May 1993 to suspend Pérez from office.[53] He was later expelled from AD and spent several years under house arrest after being found guilty by the Supreme Court. In June 1993, Congress chose Ramón Velásquez to serve as interim president until a new president could be elected in December 1993 and inaugurated in February 1994.

Although the vote against Pérez was AD's most extreme expression of autonomy against its own government, it did not prompt another round of combative actions by the CTV. The confederation's moderation reflected a dramatic change in circumstances since 1991. First, the deal between Pérez and AD after the February 1992 coup had derailed several of the government's unpopular reforms, including price hikes on goods and services provided by state-owned firms, a restructuring of the IVSS, and another round of privatizations (Corrales 2002). These victories alleviated the CTV's loyalty dilemma and thereby lowered its incentives to engage in more combative tactics. Even after AD voted to grant Velásquez emergency powers to enact two other stalled reforms (a value-added tax and a new banking law), CTV leaders could take some refuge in the government's inability to implement these reforms because of widespread civic unrest (Corrales 2002).[54]

Second, the two attempted coups and ensuing social upheaval raised the specter of a collapse of Venezuela's thirty-five-year-old democracy. In contrast to the UGT, whose initial concerns with democratic consolidation receded over the course of the reform period, the CTV suddenly had to worry about the stability of established democratic institutions. Particularly after November 1992, instruments of voice that fueled unrest and weakened the government carried a new set of risks that CTV leaders were reluctant to take. While they shared many of the complaints of the anti-Pérez protesters, they also depended on the existing political system for their influence and resources. Thus, they preferred to keep a low profile and hope for a return to order once Pérez was gone.[55] They were soon to discover, however, that the conflicts of the Pérez years had unleashed forces that would ultimately threaten the old system almost as profoundly as a military coup.

CHAPTER 8

Party-Union Relations in a Liberalizing World

Not long after Venezuela's general strike in May 1989, the International Labour Organization (ILO) concluded that "the CTV is evolving from a posture similar to the organic links between the Mexican labor movement and the PRI toward a position of greater independence similar to what the Spanish UGT has with the Socialist Workers' Party" (OIT 1991, 67). Although the CTV's evolution stalled in the 1990s, the ILO's statement captures a global trend in relations between parties and unions. Alliances built on strong collective identities, iterated exchanges between clearly delineated groups, and relatively stable expectations about outcomes and behavior are being loosened or superceded in the context of economic and political uncertainty, social heterogeneity, weak loyalties, and broken promises. Spain represents the extreme of alliance breakdown, but other countries have also experienced a relaxation of party-union ties. In Britain and Argentina, reformist factions in the Labour Party and the Peronist Party, respectively, engineered rule changes that reduced the power of the unions and thereby freed party leaders to respond more flexibly to volatile economic and political environments.[1] In Sweden, both the party and the union have taken steps to enhance their strategic autonomy and flexibility, including the termination of collective party affiliation by union members (Arter 1994; Jenson and Mahon 1993; Pontusson 1994). Similar developments can be observed in party-union alliances elsewhere in the world.

At first glance, Mexico and Venezuela appear to be exceptions to this trend. While the less captive labor leaders in Spain jumped ship in response to the party's adoption of market reform, their counterparts in Mexico and Venezuela remained on board despite similarly stormy seas. They held on even tighter when the political regimes that had long sustained them began to crumble.

The potential cost of behaving disloyally toward the party now included the collapse of institutions on which they had come to depend for their political survival. Moreover, as long as these institutions continued to function, even if badly, labor leaders had incentives to remain loyal toward the party. Rather than cutting their losses and shifting allegiances to the opposition, they dug in their heels even deeper, closing ranks with their party allies.

By 2002, however, the institutional foundations of both alliances were in serious jeopardy. In Mexico, the PRI had suffered a steep decline, culminating in the loss of the presidency in July 2000. One consequence was the emergence of more autonomous labor organizations and the beginnings of a new system of labor relations with fewer leadership protections. Even if the CTM survives, it is likely to face growing competition from less partisan rivals. In Venezuela, AD has experienced even more deterioration in the context of widespread disaffection with traditional parties and the rise of independent candidates, particularly Hugo Chávez. These events resulted in a change in the rules governing union elections and a reshuffling of the CTV's authorities at all levels. Although the CTV seems likely to remain hegemonic in the labor movement, its leaders must now be elected under non-party labels and share their power with less partisan rivals. As a result of these changes, the prevailing model of party-union relations in both countries may end up looking more like the one emerging elsewhere: looser and more contingent exchanges between relatively autonomous organizations.

There are two features that distinguish Mexico and Venezuela from most other cases, however. First, alliance loosening in other countries has taken place within relatively stable institutional contexts. Even the radical break between the UGT and the PSOE occurred in a consolidated democracy and did not threaten the survival of either organization. By contrast, the transformation of party-union relations in Mexico and Venezuela is integrally linked to regime transitions. Not only have these transitions been necessary to alter the institutional foundations of alliance survival, but they are also partly a result of the same variable that contributed to such survival: the unresponsiveness of political elites to their bases. The danger of this more tumultuous path to change is that workers may be left without any effective organizations to represent them.

Second, the change in the prevailing model of party-union relations in other countries has occurred largely through adaptations by the historically dominant parties and unions that have helped them preserve their central roles in society. In Mexico and Venezuela, by contrast, CTM and CTV leaders have resisted adaptation, leaving them unwilling and/or unable to take the lead in transforming party-union relations. Instead, emerging labor leaders and organizations are taking advantage of new opportunities provided by regime transitions to challenge the old hegemonies. If they succeed, they are likely to construct an alternative model of party-union relations in which unions are less tied to political parties and more jealous of their strategic autonomy and flexibility. Whether the parties and unions featured in this book can survive in this new institutional context remains to be seen.

As this book has shown, party-affiliated leaders in Mexico, Spain, and Venezuela responded very differently to similar challenges in the 1980s and 1990s. Moreover, their divergent responses did not change fundamentally over the next decade. In Mexico, not even the collapse of the economy in 1995 and major electoral losses for the PRI in 1997 and 2000 convinced CTM leaders to abandon the alliance. Their autonomy from workers, which had been to their advantage when the PRI was firmly in control, left them with few alternatives. They lacked sufficient legitimacy to place their fate in the hands of workers, and the PRI's rivals in the party system dismissed them as vestiges of the old, authoritarian regime. Their best hope was to fight to the death for the PRI as the only party willing to offer them leadership privileges and protections.

In Spain, UGT leaders continued to preserve the union's autonomy from all parties and to pursue unity of action with their main rival in the labor movement, the Workers' Commissions (CCOO). They maintained this strategy even after the PSOE lost to the conservative Popular Party (PP) in 1996. Notwithstanding their preference for a Socialist government, they had little incentive to reconstruct their institutionalized ties with the party. The factory council system and integration into the European Union continued to place a premium on union flexibility, and the UGT's strategy of "voice after exit" had proven quite effective.[2] Although party-union relations became less acrimonious in the mid-1990s, especially after Nicolás Redondo stepped down as secretary-general, the two organizations remained independent.

In Venezuela, the CTV continued to muddle through after AD lost control of the presidency in 1994. While remaining loyal to the party, AD labor leaders took steps to distance the CTV from all political parties, especially after Chávez won the presidential elections in 1998 and attempted to dismantle or weaken the traditional parties and their affiliated organizations. Although CTV leaders maintained their close ties with AD, they also experimented with statutory reforms to loosen the confederation's dependence on the parties.

These remarkably durable patterns in Mexico and Venezuela may not last much longer, however. Because of the political transformations that have occurred in these countries over the last few years, the institutional foundations of their party-union alliances are coming unraveled. Even if the leaders of the CTM and the CTV remain loyal to their party allies, their hegemony is being challenged, either from the outside by rival labor organizations or from the inside by rival leaders not affiliated with the party. These rivals tend to place greater emphasis on autonomy from parties and representing workers in the workplace. If successful, they are likely to replace the prevailing model of party-union relations with one that is more informal, contingent, and heterogeneous.

From Divergence to Convergence?

Several factors favor looser relations between parties and unions in Mexico and Venezuela. As discussed in chapter 1, conditions of economic and political volatility are encouraging organizational flexibility. Meanwhile, political decentralization and the proliferation of potential allies in the party system, the labor movement, and civil society are giving unions in these countries greater opportunities to switch allegiances in response to changing conditions.

In addition, constructing new institutions is more difficult than maintaining old ones, particularly today. The regularized exchanges and established expectations that produced the party-union alliances in this book took years to develop and required substantial initial investments by the participants. Replicating this process would be difficult under any circumstances. As Norbert Lechner argues, it faces additional obstacles under the time pressures created by technological advances: "One of the functions of institutions is to assure the continuity and calculability of social processes, neutralizing subjective considerations and transitory political forces. Institutionalization thus serves to create a temporal horizon reaching beyond the present. To generate this time horizon, however, institutions require time; only by persisting through time can institutions generate confidence in 'investing in the future.' The credibility of institutions requires time for the development of ties of reciprocal trust. Time, nevertheless, is nowadays among the scarcest of resources" (Lechner 1998, 31). In a world where information and resources travel at lightning speeds, quick reactions and short-term results tend to prevail over long-term investments and stable relationships. As a result, new institutions are difficult to construct, and old institutions often move too slowly to match the accelerated pace of change, undermining their legitimacy relative to more mobile forms of political representation and authority.

All three of these factors conspire against the reconstruction of the old alliance between the UGT and the PSOE in Spain and the creation of new alliances between emergent parties and unions in Mexico and Venezuela. This is not to say that unions will abandon all partisan preferences or prohibit their members from being politically active. Nor will all unions pursue the same organizational strategies. Recent trends suggest, for example, that union partisanship is likely to remain stronger in Mexico and Venezuela than in Spain. Nonetheless, the days of formal alliances based on dense networks of principles and norms are likely to be over. Instead, party-union relations in Mexico and Venezuela appear to be moving closer to the model pioneered by the Spanish UGT.

Party Competition and Emergent Alternatives in Mexico

By 2002, nearly all of the institutional arrangements that had determined the fate of the CTM-PRI alliance in the 1980s and early 1990s were falling apart. First, punishing power was shifting away from the PRI and toward workers as a result of changes in the legal framework governing industrial relations, the structure of the labor movement, the party system, and the party's mechanisms for filling party posts. Second, the PRI's capacity to act autonomously from its own government was increasing as a result of new spaces for intraparty dissent and a potential relocation of supreme authority away from the chief executive when the party is in government. These changes have had two effects on party-union relations: a slow but undeniable shift in the incentives of CTM leaders regarding their relations with the PRI; and the emergence of rival organizations that favor informal, heterogeneous, and issue-oriented strategies of organizational linkage.

When Ernesto Zedillo took office in December 1994, he held out the hope of better times for working Mexicans. Campaigning with the slogan, "For the welfare of your family," he argued that the hard years of transition to a market economy were over and that his administration could now turn to improving the living conditions of the majority of Mexicans. His promises quickly proved illusory, however. Less than two weeks after his inauguration, the Mexican peso crashed, and the economy went into a deep recession. His immediate response was to reimpose austerity and accelerate structural reform. He agreed to the terms of an emergency bailout package by the United States, imposed harsh austerity measures, and sought to extend privatization into sectors such as petrochemicals, social security, and electrical power. During 1995, economic output declined by more than 6 percent, nearly one million workers lost their jobs in the formal sector, and real manufacturing wages fell by 13.5 percent (Lustig 1998, 190, 211). In addition, Mexico City experienced a crime wave that affected all income groups.

Especially after so many promises by Salinas of a neoliberal Mexican miracle, the economic collapse fueled a wave of anti-PRI sentiment that translated into major gains for the opposition. In July 1997, the PRI suffered two defeats that significantly shifted the balance of power in the political system. First, Cuauhtémoc Cárdenas, the candidate for the PRD, won the first election for administrator *(regente)* of the Federal District. Second, and more importantly, the PRI lost its majority in the Chamber of Deputies for the first time since 1929. This defeat transformed Congress from a rubber stamp into a real check on executive power.

These losses set the stage for the most deadly blow of all to the PRI. Despite Zedillo's attempt to enhance the PRI's chances by replacing the *dedazo* with an open primary to choose the most electable candidate, the PRI finally lost its hold on the presidency in July 2000. In the cleanest elections in Mexican history, the National Action Party (PAN) candidate, Vicente Fox, won with 42.7 percent of the vote, compared to 35.7 percent for the PRI candidate, Francisco Labastida. The PAN also did very well in legislative races. Although the PRI retained a plurality in both houses of Congress, it lost its majority in the Senate for the first time.[3]

The emergence of a genuinely competitive party system in Mexico has major implications for party-union relations.[4] First, the PRI no longer possesses the vast array of instruments it once had available to punish CTM leaders for disloyal behavior. Even before it lost control of the presidency, its ability to offer (and withdraw) inducements to labor leaders shrank as a result of the unprecedented checks and balances imposed by an opposition majority in the legislature. Relatedly, the party leadership lost its ability to dole out (or withhold) candidacies for public office with a guarantee of victory. These constraints tightened with the PRI's defeat in July 2000. Once in the opposition, the PRI no longer controlled the state resources it had historically used to manipulate the labor movement, particularly labor policy and the power to intervene in unions and industrial disputes.

Second, party competition and the transformation of the legislature into a real policymaking body opened spaces for internal dissent within the PRI. Because PRI candidates must be electorally competitive to win, the party leadership has less control over who carries the PRI banner into public office. Moreover, a pluralist legislature offers the possibility of interparty alliances and the defeat of presidential initiatives, thereby giving PRI legislators more autonomy. Combined with Zedillo's hands-off approach to party affairs, these conditions prompted dissidents within the PRI to break the old rules regarding party discipline. At the party's national congress in September 1996, the delegates rejected Zedillo's proposal for privatizing the secondary petrochemical industry and dashed the presidential hopes of most members of Zedillo's cabinet by requiring that the nominee be a PRI member and have held elective office. A few PRI legislators dared to violate the party line in Congress, and a reformist faction of the PRI joined a campaign in 1999 against Zedillo's plans to privatize the electrical power industry.[5]

Third, and relatedly, the unprecedented separation between the PRI and the state that occurred when Fox took office in December 2000 profoundly altered the location of supreme authority within the party. As long as the PRI is in the opposition, it must look to someone other than the chief executive for leadership. The struggle to determine who this will be and what powers he or she will have is part of a larger project to construct an institutional infrastructure and identity that is distinct from the Mexican state. During the PRI's first year out of power, this struggle revolved around the party's selection of a new president. After an acrimonious campaign and frequent delays, a leader from the party's traditionalist wing, Roberto Madrazo, prevailed over his more technocratic rival. It remains to be seen how much authority he can actually exercise and whether control of the party will shift back to the chief executive if and when the PRI retakes the presidency. The most likely outcome is that supreme authority will be less absolute than in the past but more firmly rooted in the party's internal machinery.

These changes in the political system have produced mixed incentives for CTM leaders regarding their relationship with the PRI. The PRI now has less power to punish them for disloyalty, and they stand to benefit from deals with the Fox administration that help to preserve their remaining privileges. Not surprisingly, CTM leaders changed their attitude toward Fox after he took office in December 2000. Despite their vitriolic rhetoric against him before and immediately after the elections, they soon fell into their traditional pattern of collaboration with the state, particularly the chief executive. They invited Fox to speak at their National Council meeting in February 2001 and appeared to be moving toward an accommodation similar to the one they had with Salinas: support for Fox's privatization plans in return for their continued presence on tripartite bodies and the freedom to repress independent unionism within CTM-controlled plants.[6] The Fox administration responded favorably to their overtures by reserving a seat for the CTM on the new Council for Dialogue among the Productive Sectors, refusing to intervene in several conflicts on behalf of anti-CTM dissidents, and promising to retain CTM representation on the JCA (Fox 2001a).[7]

At the same time, changes within the PRI and its continued presence in Mexican politics suggest that maintaining the party-union alliance might still be in the CTM's interest. The new openings for internal dissent and the potential autonomy of the party from its own government create new possibilities for cultivating sympathetic allies and resisting painful reforms without behaving disloyally toward the party. The inclination of CTM leaders to remain within the PRI fold received an additional boost from the PRI's victory in several state races and the election of labor's longtime ally, Roberto Madrazo, to the party presidency.[8] Ultimately, their loyalty to the PRI will depend on the PRI's electoral fortunes, Fox's willingness to perpetuate the historic exchange of leadership privileges for cooperation, and the ability of CTM leaders to avoid dissent and defection by their members.

The PRI's loss of hegemony in the context of renewed worker hardship has unleashed significant changes in the structure of the labor movement and the legal framework governing industrial relations. The labor movement is being reconstituted by the emergence of new organizations with a preference for greater autonomy and more flexible relations with political parties. The legal framework has experienced slower but potentially more profound changes as a result of proposals for labor law reform and court decisions declaring exclusion clauses and other forms of representational monopoly unconstitutional. Both changes promise to alter the prevailing model of party-union relations in Mexico.

As noted in chapter 4, independent unions have always existed in Mexico, but the PRI always co-opted, repressed, or marginalized them when they threatened the CTM's hegemony. This pattern began to break down in the late 1990s, however. Not only did the PRI face unprecedented political competition, but the CTM's longtime leader, Fidel Velázquez, died in June 1997, removing a critical source of the confederation's power. Another member of the old guard, Leonardo Rodríguez Alcaine, took the helm of both the CTM and the Labor Congress (CT), but he lacked Velázquez's personal authority and connections. Although Zedillo and the PRI continued to pay homage to the CTM as a valiant defender of Mexican workers, the confederation faced serious challenges to its hegemony that the PRI was less able and willing to block.

After several years of mobilization against Zedillo's austerity and privatization policies, independent labor leaders emboldened by Velázquez's death and the PRI's loss of its majority in the Chamber of Deputies formed a new umbrella organization to rival the CTM-dominated CT. In August 1997, more than 300 delegates from 132 unions claiming to represent over one million workers agreed to create the National Union of Workers (UNT).[9] The UNT was formally established at a convention in November 1997 with an estimated membership of 1.5 million workers (*La Jornada*, November 28, 1997).[10] In addition to mobilizing workers, the UNT planned to use the newly independent Congress as an avenue for demand-making. Soon after the organization's creation, the UNT executive expressed the expectation that the legislature "will be a new arena of action for independent unionism" (*La Jornada*, November 28, 1997).

In contrast to the Labor Congress and the CTM, the UNT made an explicit commitment to union autonomy and political pluralism. The objectives established at its founding convention included: to reform the relationship between the state, parties, and unions to guarantee the political independence of the labor movement; and to institute a new labor law to end corporatist control mechanisms and permit new forms of labor relations more appropriate to a global economy (La Botz and Smucker 1997).[11] In addition, the UNT's statutes guaranteed freedom of association for its members. According to Francisco Hernández Juárez, one of the UNT's three presidents, "[T]he workers are going to have absolutely the most complete freedom to join or sympathize with the party that best represents their interest" (Progressive 1997).

The UNT also welcomed partisan diversity into its leadership. One of its three presidents, Agustín Rodríguez Fuentes, openly sympathized with the PRD. Hernández Juárez was a longstanding member of the PRI, but he increasingly distanced himself from the party's policies, particularly after 1995. In August 1999, he was dropped from the PRI's National Political Council, perhaps for stating in a newspaper interview that "only if the PRI loses the next election will there be real change within the labor movement" (National 1999). He finally resigned his PRI membership in 2002 and said he had no plans to join any other party (Hérnandez Juarez 2002).

The UNT was not the only new organization to challenge the CTM and the CT during this period. Zedillo sparked another organizing drive when he announced that he would seek a constitutional amendment to allow privatization of the electrical power industry. His proposal met with fierce resistance by the Mexican Electrical Workers' Union (SME). In response, the SME, along with thirty other labor organizations, PRD legislators, a reform faction of the PRI, dissident members of the Sole Union of Electrical Workers of the Mexican Republic (SUTERM), and leaders of the Union of Mexican Petroleum Workers (STPRM), created the National Front of Resistance against Privatization of Electrical Industry (FNRCPIE) in February 1999 (*La Jornada*, February 12, 1999). In March, the FNRCPIE organized a demonstration attended by an estimated one hundred thousand workers, and, by April, it had established a presence in over half of Mexico's states (*La Jornada*, April 6, 1999, April 27, 1999).

The FNRCPIE's anti-privatization crusade crystallized a wider opposition to the CT and the government's economic program. In April, the SME announced that it was withdrawing from the CT because "we have not been treated with dignity by [Rodríguez Alcaine], who has shown a lack of interest in taking an urgent stand regarding the privatization of the electrical power industry" (*La Jornada*, April 6, 1999). The following month, the most important independent unions, including the FNRCPIE, the SME, the UNT, FES-EBES, the Mexican Union Front (FSM), and the May First Inter-Union Group, marched together on May Day for the first time in many years to protest neoliberal reform, antidemocratic labor structures, and privatization. According to one labor historian, "[T]his is the first time that an independent demonstration has been larger than the official one" (*La Jornada*, May 2, 1999).[12] Later that year, the UNT, the SME, and the FSM signed a Unity Pact pledging to work together to meet the challenges of globalization and modernization, fight for union autonomy and democracy, improve collective bargaining and the minimum wage, and inculcate class consciousness in workers (UNT 1999).

This groundswell of unified opposition by independent unions threatened the CTM on several levels. First, it represented a clear and viable alternative to the CTM's strategy of currying favor with the PRI government. Besides winning the support of thousands of workers, the movement enjoyed uncharacteristic freedom to form a broad front against government policy. Although clearly irked by the direct challenge to his agenda, Zedillo no longer possessed a highly disciplined, hegemonic machine that could easily restore the primacy of the CTM and its collaborationist policies. Thus, he did not subject the movement's instigators to the *charrazos* of the past, despite the proximity of the presidential elections, and he retreated when the privatization plan was blocked in Congress (Electrical 1999). This sequence of events reinforced the impression that new spaces had opened up for independent action in the Mexican labor movement.[13]

Second, the movement sparked dissidence within the CTM's own ranks. As noted above, the FNRCPIE included factions of the STPRM (oil) and the SUTERM (electrical power), both of which were affiliated with the CTM and officially supported Zedillo's privatization policies.[14] In fact, Rodríguez Alcaine was secretary-general of the SUTERM as well as being secretary-general of the CTM and president of the CT. Thus, internal opposition to the SUTERM's support for the reform translated into a direct challenge to the leadership of the CTM and the CT. In May 1999, more than three thousand workers from forty SUTERM locals marched to oppose privatization and to demand the resignation of Rodríguez Alcaine as head of both the SUTERM and the CTM (Thousands 1999). In late 2000, one of the SUTERM's dissident factions called for broader change in a document demanding an end to forced affiliation with the PRI and government control of labor unions (SUTERM 2001)

Besides challenging the hegemony of the CTM, the growth of independent unionism promises to modify the prevailing model of party-union relations in Mexico. Although the CTM's rivals have cultivated ties with parties, particularly the PRD, they continue to emphasize autonomy and pluralism in their organizational structures and statutes. Several prominent leaders have assumed partisan positions with the PRD and/or become involved in internal PRD politics, but these personal linkages have not translated into organizational or statutory commitments to the PRD or any other party.[15] For example, the UNT and the PRD signed an agreement in January 2001 to work together to defend workers' rights but without any commitment by the UNT to pressure its members to vote for the PRD (Party 2001).

These developments suggest that Mexican unions and parties will continue to cooperate in pursuit of shared interests but on a relatively contingent and informal basis. Although the unions are likely to be more partisan than the post-1988 UGT, at least while they have a sympathetic ally on the left, there is little chance that they will construct the kind of institutionalized alliance that the CTM had with the PRI. In addition to the general obstacles cited above, no party is likely to regain the overwhelming dominance enjoyed by the PRI, which means that unions will have fewer temptations to sacrifice autonomy in return for privileged access to inducements, as the CTM did in the 1930s.

The fragility of the CTM's hegemony and the disincentives for unions to make binding commitments to parties have been reinforced by several changes or proposed changes in the legal framework governing industrial relations. First, there have been calls for a reform of the Federal Labor Law (LFT) that would remove the buffers against dissent that protected CTM leaders for so long. As discussed in chapter 5, Salinas kept reform of the LFT on the back burner in return for the CTM's cooperation with NAFTA and industrial restructuring. The PAN and the PRD reignited the debate during the Zedillo *sexenio* by introducing proposals for labor law reform in the Mexican Congress. While differing in important ways, both proposals called for changes that would enhance union autonomy, encourage union democracy, and transfer control of labor justice from the executive to the judiciary (Cook 1998, 17).

The PAN proposal, presented to the Congress in 1995, was the most far-reaching of the two. Besides calling for a prohibition against exclusion clauses, the elimination of all registration requirements, the inclusion of transparent electoral procedures within unions, and the creation of special judges to re-place the tripartite JCA, the PAN proposal drew explicitly on the Spanish Workers' Statute to advocate the creation of "factory councils" to represent workers on the shop floor (Cook 1998, 15; PAN 1995). Although unions could still have a presence in the workplace, they would no longer have the right to bargain collectively except insofar as workers elected their activists to serve on the factory councils. As illustrated in the Spanish case, this system would radically diminish the protections from worker dissent presently en-joyed by the CTM and other official unions.

The PRD proposal, presented to Congress in 1998, stopped short of pro-hibiting exclusion clauses and preserved a central role for unions in represent-ing workers.[16] Nonetheless, the proposal called for an end to government in-tervention in union affairs (e.g., registration, strikes, wage bargaining), the removal of labor justice from the hands of the tripartite JCA, and a prohibi-tion against the collective affiliation of unions to parties (Cook 1998, 17). All three reforms would prevent "business as usual" by the CTM. Besides requir-ing its members to belong to the PRI, the CTM continues to depend heavily on its dominance of the labor seats on the JCA to squelch dissent from within and outside the CTM. Without these protections, the CTM would be highly vulnerable to backlash for its collaboration with policies that have brought far more pain than prosperity to organized workers.

Neither of these proposals was put to a vote in Congress during the Zedillo administration, not even after the PRI lost its majority in the Chamber of Deputies in 1997. Nor are the most radical elements—such as the PAN's call for a factory council system—likely to be adopted. But several features of the two proposals have been kept alive. Just before taking office, Fox indicated his support for controls on union corruption as well as measures to enhance em-ployment, training, productivity, and competitiveness (*La Jornada*, November 2, 2000). He reopened the debate over labor law reform in August 2001, when the Labor Ministry began talks with unions, employers, and government officials.[17] In addition, the Fox administration expressed support for legisla-tion proposed by the PRD in April 2002 that would amend the Federal Code of Electoral Institutions and Procedures to empower the Federal Electoral In-stitute (IFE) to oversee union elections. Particularly given the IFE's nonparti-sanship and technical competence, this change would radically reduce the ca-pacity of either CTM leaders or the labor authorities to manipulate electoral outcomes.

In the meantime, several features of the PAN and PRD proposals have been enacted elsewhere with the same result of weakening the corporatist protec-tions long enjoyed by the CTM and other official unions. One initiative came out of the PRD-controlled Mexico City government. In 1999, the city's labor department created a public registry of unions in cooperation with the Local Board of Conciliation and Arbitration (JLCA) (STDF 1999). Reflecting a generalized demand for greater transparency in government, this decision put a dent in a longstanding policy by labor authorities of guarding union data like a state secret.[18] In the process, it threatened to expose the thousands of protection contracts that existed in the Federal District, often under the control of the CTM.[19]

The most far-reaching initiatives, however, came not from the legislature or local governments but from the Mexican Supreme Court (SCJM). In early 1996, the SCJM ruled that public employees have the right to affiliate freely with unions of their choice or to create new unions. This ruling overturned a provision of the LFT that required public employees to belong to the FSTSE (Supreme 1996). A subsequent ruling by the SCJM in May 1999 made its decision regarding union freedom for public employees binding on all lower courts (Mexican 1999). These rulings prompted the defection of dozens of public employee unions from the FSTSE, which had been closely affiliated with the PRI since its foundation in 1937.[20] Although the rulings did not directly threaten the CTM—and even enabled the CTM to recruit public employees—they signaled a new willingness by the court to challenge the protections upon which CTM leaders have always depended.

This trend accelerated after the PRI lost the presidential elections in July 2000. The following September, the SCJM issued an unprecedented decision in favor of four hundred members of the SUTERM who claimed that Rodríguez Alcaine had embezzled their savings and ordered the labor leader to return the equivalent of twenty million dollars to the union's mutual fund (Mexican 2000). Seven months later, the SCJM took aim at the LFT's exclusion clauses. In response to a petition filed by a group of sugar workers who had been fired because they lost their union membership for trying to organize an independent union, the court declared the exclusion clauses unconstitutional. Although the court must rule similarly in four more cases before its decision becomes binding on the lower courts, the ruling is likely to end one of the key mechanisms by which CTM leaders have protected themselves from dissent from below.

Party Decline and Forced Restructuring in Venezuela

As in Mexico, a regime transition has significantly altered the landscape of party-union relations in Venezuela. By 2002, the CTV-AD alliance was operating in a radically different context than it had in the 1980s and early 1990s.

In particular, three of the four variables determining the distribution of punishing power had changed: the party system, the legal framework, and the structure of the labor movement. The party system was no longer dominated by AD and COPEI, both of which had lost tremendous ground to independent candidates backed by loose coalitions, particularly Hugo Chávez. Relatedly, new leaders and organizations had gained representation in the CTV, partly as a result of changes in union statutes and the rules determining leadership selection in the labor movement. Although AD-affiliated labor leaders continued to dominate the CTV even after union elections in 2001, they were elected under nonpartisan labels, had fewer incentives to remain loyal to AD, and were sharing power with labor leaders who had weaker, if any, party ties.

Three related changes in the political arena contributed to the collapse of Venezuelan's old party system. The first two changes, implemented during the Pérez administration, were political decentralization and personalized voting.[21] In December 1989, Venezuelans directly elected their mayors and governors for the first time. This reform undermined the control and resources of centralized party machineries and created opportunities for new challengers (Grindle 2000, 81–84). Rather than depending on the incumbent parties for nominations to state and local office, candidates had to win votes. This new dynamic placed a premium on local reputation, encouraged policy independence, and enabled small parties to build a following at the local level. It also enabled mayors and governors to develop relatively autonomous bases of support that they could mobilize in negotiations with the party leaders and use as launching pads for higher offices. In addition, organizations in civil society gained new interlocutors at the state and local levels that were not beholden to party dictates.

The second change was an electoral reform that allowed open and un-blocked lists of candidates for legislative offices (Grindle 2000, 37; Buxton 2000, 6). This reform gave the electorate a choice between voting for individuals listed by name or voting for a party list, which had previously been the only option. The result was that "the vote became personalized, in the sense that citizens would be able to identify their votes with particular individuals" (Grindle 2000, 38). The reform provided additional opportunities for new parties and independent candidates to win public office.

Political decentralization and personalized voting contributed to a third change: the dominance of independent and/or coalition-backed candidates, particularly in presidential elections. As AD and COPEI lost control over political offices and proved vulnerable in subnational and legislative elections, renegade candidates gained a chance to present themselves as viable options, particularly to an electorate deeply disillusioned with the traditional parties. Ironically, one of the founders of Venezuela's old party system, Rafael Caldera, first broke the hold of these parties on the presidency by winning as an independent in 1993. Five years later, not a single party in existence before the 1980s ran its own candidate, preferring to join coalitions backing independent candidates. This pattern repeated itself in the elections of July 2000.

These three changes dramatically reduced the power and influence of AD. The first sign of this shift was the rise of a new leftist party, Causa R, which had very close ties to independent unionism. In 1989, a prominent independent unionist, Andrés Velásquez, was elected as governor of the state of Bolívar. Velásquez had engaged in a bitter fight with AD and COPEI for control of Venezuela's largest union, SUTISS, in the 1970s and 1980s (see chapter 4).[22] Another Causa R candidate with ties to labor, Aristóbal Istúriz, became mayor of Caracas three years later. Causa R extended its challenge to the national level in the December 1993 elections. In the presidential elections, AD rallied around the candidacy of Claudio Fermín, a popular former mayor of Caracas. Although Fermín performed remarkably well given the upheaval of the Pérez years, he came in second and received only 1.6 percent more of the vote than Causa R's candidate, Andrés Velásquez. In addition, Causa R gained only fifteen fewer seats than AD in the Chamber of Deputies (forty compared to fifty-five) and seven fewer in the Senate (nine compared to sixteen).

The greatest threat to AD, however, was not Causa R but the capture of the presidency by independent candidates. Rafael Caldera started the trend in 1993 when he abandoned COPEI and won as an independent candidate with 30.5 percent of the vote (Political Database of the Americas 2001).[23] At the time, his victory did not raise major alarm bells for AD. The party still controlled the largest share of seats in both houses of Congress and therefore had significant influence over policy outcomes. AD also recovered from a significant drop in its share of governors and mayors in 1992 with an impressive comeback in 1995, when it gained control of 54.5 percent of the governors and 59.1 percent of the mayors (Grindle 2000, 88).[24] Meanwhile, Caldera proved incapable of solving Venezuela's economic crisis, which resulted in another IMF austerity package in 1996, and Causa R succumbed to the pressures of its rapid growth as a political force and split into two parties in April 1997, with a majority of its congressional representatives forming Country for All (PPT) (Buxton 2000, 10).

Rather than providing an opportunity for AD to stage a comeback in the next elections, however, these developments merely encouraged the voters to search for more alternatives to the traditional parties. They found one in Hugo

Chávez, a former lieutenant colonel who had spearheaded the attempted coup in February 1992. After being pardoned by Caldera and released from jail in 1994, Chávez put together a loose coalition of anti-system parties and organizations, the Movement of the Fifth Republic (MVR), and began laying the groundwork for a run on the presidency. He struck a deep chord with the electorate, particularly the growing ranks of the poor. In December 1998, he won in a landslide with 56 percent of the vote.

Chávez's success marked a critical turning point for AD. First, the party showed new signs of electoral weakness. Already disappointed by losses in the gubernatorial elections in November 1998, AD abandoned its presidential candidate, Luis Alfaro Ucero, when public opinion polls indicated that he would receive less than 10 percent of the vote.[25] Instead, the party joined a coalition backing another independent candidate, Henrique Salas Romer. Alfaro competed in the elections without AD's endorsement and received only 0.4 percent of the vote.[26] Salas Romer won 40 percent of the vote but failed to defeat Chávez.

AD's Labor Bureau inadvertently contributed to this debacle. In 1997, the Labor Bureau began lobbying for procedures that would enable the party hierarchy to control the outcome of the presidential nomination. Besides hoping for a candidate who would support pro-labor policies, bureau members opposed attempts to rejuvenate the party with more participatory processes of leadership selection. The open primary that had allowed Fermín to win the party's presidential nomination in 1993 had also resulted in the fewest legislative seats for AD labor leaders since 1958 (Ellner 1996, 97).

In March 1998, the secretaries-general of twenty-five sections of AD voted to support the Labor Bureau's proposal to select the party's presidential candidate by "consensus" rather than by a vote of the rank and file (*El Nacional*, March 15, 1998). This procedure led to the nomination of Alfaro, who controlled the party apparatus but had almost no popular appeal. For individual labor leaders, this strategy paid off. They more than doubled their representation in Congress from four to nine seats. Sources inside AD indicated that this positive outcome was a result of Alfaro's backing during the drafting of the electoral lists (*El Nacional*, December 24, 1998). For the party, however, the strategy proved disastrous. Besides leading to the nomination of a candidate who had no chance of winning, it reinforced AD's reputation as a closed, undemocratic party.

The second, and more devastating, effect of Chávez's victory on AD was his crusade against the "partyarchy" *(partidocracia),* which included formal changes in the rules of the political game. In July 1999, he held elections for a Constituent Assembly in which his coalition gained 122 of the 131 seats (Corrales 2000, 41), with only one of those remaining going to the traditional parties (Lowenthal 2000, 43).[27] The assembly seized legislative and judicial powers during its deliberations and submitted a new constitution to the electorate in December 1999. Approved by 71 percent of the voters, the constitution extended the president's term from five to six years, allowed for reelection, created a unicameral legislature by eliminating the Senate, established "citizen power" *(poder ciudadano)* to monitor public affairs, retained the state's extensive powers to intervene in the economy, and expanded the rights of Venezuelan citizens (Corrales 2000, 44–45).[28]

A week after the constitutional referendum, the Constituent Assembly appointed Chávez's associates as the new attorney general, comptroller general, and president of the Supreme Tribunal. It also selected an interim legislature after dissolving the Congress, the Supreme Court, the National Electoral Council (CNE), the Justice Council, and the state legislatures (Corrales 2000, 46). The voters then elected new authorities at all levels of the political system in the so-called "mega-elections" of July 2000. Backed by a large coalition of parties, Chávez won reelection with 60.3 percent of the vote.

Chávez's constitutional reforms destroyed one of the few arenas in which AD had continued to perform well: the Chamber of Deputies and the Senate. AD increased its share of seats in both houses of Congress in 1998 only to have them dissolved by the Constituent Assembly in 1999. Wracked by defections and a serious internal division, AD was unable to repeat its legislative performance in the July 2000 elections. Besides abstaining entirely from the presidential race, AD won only 29 out of 165 seats in the National Assembly, compared to 76 seats for the MVR.[29] Ironically, the only arena in which AD maintained a plurality was local government, where the old party system had first begun to break down in the late 1980s. In 2000, AD won 92 of 335 municipalities, compared to 79 for the MVR (*El Nacional*, August 2, 2000).

The decline of AD and the proliferation of new alternatives has profound implications for party-union relations. The most obvious is that AD no longer controls the inducements with which it maintained the loyalty of CTV leaders. In contrast to the 1980s and early 1990s, these leaders no longer depend on AD (or the other traditional parties) to gain access to state resources or public office. In fact, too close an association with AD has become a liability in the context of public disenchantment with parties and Chávez's concentration of power.

There are signs that AD has been rejuvenated by its role in the growing anti-Chávez movement, but the party is unlikely to regain its prior dominance. In fact, no single party is likely to offer labor leaders consistent access to inducements. Although the Venezuelan political system is still in transition (as witnessed by the short-lived coup against Chávez in April 2002), a pattern appears to be emerging whereby candidates win office and politicians govern with the support of temporary coalitions constructed around short-term interests. In this context, labor leaders will need to keep their political options open to maintain access to resources and influence.

As in Mexico, changes in Venezuela's political system have prompted a restructuring of the labor movement. In particular, the composition of the CTV has begun to change, largely as a result of new rules governing union elections. Although AD labor leaders remained hegemonic even after direct elections in late 2001, the minority factions now include unionists linked to new parties, such as Causa R and the MVR, or without party ties at all. In addition, the trend of opportunistic electoral coalitions that has already become dominant in the political arena appears to be spreading to the CTV.

Unlike the CTM, the CTV tried to preempt external attacks on its hegemony through unilateral restructuring. Following the creation of the Constituent Workers' Front (FCT) by Chávez in January 1998, the CTV changed its electoral rules in March to require direct election of the leaders of its national, regional, and industrial federations. Six direct elections were held at these levels in 1998 (*El Nacional*, January 18, 1999). CTV leaders also publicly admitted that the CTV's petroleum, education, and construction affiliates were in drastic need of reform. They subsequently disincorporated one of the CTV's oilworkers' federations for failing to hold internal elections and demanded an accounting of its finances (*El Nacional*, December 23, 1998).

The CTV's scramble to save itself accelerated after Chávez won the elections and called for "demolition" of the CTV (*El Nacional*, December 23, 1998). Citing "the new political reality and the era of change in which the country is living" (*El Nacional*, January 23, 1999), the CTV executive organized a special congress in April 1999 to carry out a fundamental reform of the CTV's statutes.[30] The new statutes mandated the direct election of all CTV authorities (including the president and secretary-general) by the membership, ballots without party labels, impeachment mechanisms, limits on reelection, obligatory referenda to consider issues of fundamental importance to workers, and elimination of political secretariats and party representation on electoral commissions (*El Nacional*, March 4, 1999, April 7, 1999). Hailing the changes, Ramírez León proclaimed that the CTV "is declaring the departidization of labor organizations and the recovery of total autonomy before the State, the parties, and employers" (*El Nacional*, April 9, 1999).

These last-minute adjustments proved too little and too late, however, to prevent an externally imposed reshuffling of the CTV's leadership. Upon taking office, Chávez launched a multitrack campaign to disempower the CTV. First, he refused to recognize the CTV as a valid interlocutor for representing the interests of workers, which translated into an unwillingness to accept the CTV's participation in tripartite institutions or to negotiate policies such as the national minimum wage (*El Nacional*, January 8, 1999). Second, he continued his efforts to construct a pro-government alternative to the CTV. When a faction of the FCT became critical of the government, Chávez loyalists left to form the Bolivarian Workers' Force (FBT) in September 2000, which became Chávez's main pillar of support in the labor movement (*El Nacional*, November 17, 2000). In January 2002, the FBT announced the creation of a National Union Confederation (*Coordinadora Sindical Nacional*) to rival the CTV.

Finally, Chávez made several attempts to unseat the CTV leadership.[31] In 1999, he tried to use his majority in the Constituent Assembly to dissolve the CTV and other labor organizations as part of a massive reorganization of public institutions. Ultimately, fears of a backlash at home and abroad convinced the delegates to modify the decree to declare a "national reorganization" and to limit their powers of intervention to the three branches of government. He then threw his support behind the proposed Law for the Protection of Union Guarantees and Freedom, which called for the election of new authorities at all levels of the labor movement. As in the past, however, the bill languished in the legislature.

Chávez finally prevailed in his third attempt to reshuffle authority within the CTV. On December 3, 2000, he held a referendum requiring that workers replace their entire union leadership within 180 days. The referendum, which he bluntly called "a missile against the CTV" (Díaz 2002), survived a constitutional challenge and won by a two-thirds majority.[32] Soon thereafter, the CNE drafted the Special Statute for the Renovation of Union Leadership and ordered each organization within the CTV to create an electoral commission to implement the provisions of the statute (CNE 2001).[33] In preparation for the elections, the CTV replaced its executive committee with a temporary Board of Union Management (*Junta de Conducción Sindical*), which included representatives from currents never previously incorporated into the CTV.

As in the past, candidates were placed on closed lists for seats to be allocated by proportional representation. The key change was the absence of party labels. The six contenders for CTV president were Carlos Ortega of the United Workers' Front (FUT), Aristóbulo Istúriz of the Autonomous Labor Alliance (AAS), Alfredo Ramos of New Unionism (NS), Carlos Navarro of the Independent Union Alliance (ASI), Froilán Barrios of the FCT, and Reina Sequera of the Bolivarian-200 Workers' Force (FBT-200).

Of these candidates, only Ortega was clearly associated with Venezuela's traditional parties. The bulk of his support came from the FUT, which was composed of AD unionists. He also received support from the labor wing of COPEI and labor organizations associated with the Red Flag party *(Bandera Roja)* and Union for Progress. The latter was a new party with ties to Francisco Arias Cárdenas, Chávez's main challenger in the 2000 elections. Ramos and Istúriz drew their primary support from organizations linked to new parties. Although Ramos was allied with MAS labor leaders, the bulk of his support came from NS, which was associated with Causa R but had a relatively autonomous identity and history of struggle. Istúriz was considered the "official" candidate because his supporters had ties with two new parties in the Chávez coalition, the PPT and the MVR. The other three candidates did not have party ties. A former *copeyano* who had been president of the CTV in the 1990s, Navarro founded the ASI as a non-partisan organization after leaving COPEI. Barrios and Sequeros both led organizations that had been former supporters of Chávez but became dissidents because of disagreements with the FBT leadership.

The elections took place in August and September 2001 for firm-level unions and national federations and October 2001 for regional federations and the confederation. To the dismay of those who had hoped for a radical change, the FUT coalition—and therefore AD—won in a landslide. According to the CTV's electoral commission, Ortega prevailed in the elections for the executive committee with 57.5 percent of the vote, compared to 15.8 percent for Istúriz, 11 percent for Ramos, 6.4 percent for Navarro, 5 percent for Barrios, and 4.3 percent for Sequera. These votes translated into ten out of the seventeen seats on the CTV executive committee for the FUT list, two each for the FBT and New Unionism lists, and one each for the three remaining lists *(El Nacional*, November 19, 2001). According to the former president of the *Junta de Conducción Sindical*, the FUT also won forty-five of the CTV's fifty-four federations and twenty-four of its twenty-five regional federations *(El Nacional*, January 8, 2002).

The FUT's impressive showing in the CTV elections defied predictions that workers would use their votes to remove unionists closely associated with Venezuela's traditional parties. In addition to fraud, one probable reason for this outcome is that AD's networks and organizational resources remained far more developed on a national scale than those of its competitors. Moreover, Chávez's popularity had declined dramatically since the July 2000 elections, as illustrated by the demonstrations and nearly successful coup against him in April 2002.

Nevertheless, the FUT's victory may only be a transition to a more heterogeneous and non-partisan CTV. First, the FUT's mandate is weakened by an abstention rate of over 50 percent, the arrival of only 49 percent of the ballots to the CTV's electoral commission,[34] and petitions before the CNE to annul the results. Although the government toned down its assault on the CTV immediately following the attempted coup, the CTV continues to have serious legitimacy problems.[35] Second, the CTV is no longer the exclusive domain of the political parties. Although AD labor leaders are accustomed to negotiating with minority factions, they have never been forced to interact (or compete) with labor leaders who are not similarly subject to party dictates.

Combined with AD's greatly reduced capacity to grant and withdraw inducements, this new dynamic is likely to encourage more independence by AD labor leaders, particularly if AD cannot recover its electoral strength. Moreover, a regular cycle of direct elections for leadership positions at every level promises to give workers more power to punish labor leaders for disloyal behavior. Meanwhile, the new spaces that now exist for nonpartisan—or contingently partisan—participation in the CTV may encourage young unionists with leadership ambitions to bypass party channels altogether, particularly if such a decision enables them to be more responsive to workers. As in the political arena, elections and governance in the CTV may become a game of shifting, contingent coalitions rather than competitive but stable party loyalties.

Implications for Interest Representation

Despite their many differences, Mexico, Spain, and Venezuela have all moved toward more contingent, nonpartisan, and informal ties between parties and unions. They are joined by other countries with histories of institutionalized alliances between parties and unions. In a world of capital mobility, just-in-time production, fluid and multiple identities, and immediate access to information, organizations are finding themselves handicapped by overly rigid ties and commitments. As a result, partners in established alliances are loosening their mutual obligations, and organizations without prior commitments are guarding their autonomy and flexibility. Among the latter we find not only emergent labor unions but also "new social movements" (Offe 1987; Escobar and Alvarez 1992; Foweraker 1995; Alvarez, Dagnino, and Escobar 1998), "associative networks" (Chalmers, Martin, and Piester 1997), and "left-libertarian parties" (Kitschelt 1990), all of which tend to privilege flexibility and informality over long-term commitments and institutionalization.

These changes have both positive and negative implications for the nature and quality of interest representation in Mexico, Spain, and Venezuela. The implications are clearest in the Spanish case, where party-union delinking occurred more than a decade ago. The UGT's reorientation toward representing workers on the shop floor after its divorce from the PSOE has produced several positive results. First, the breakdown of centralized wage pacts has given sectorial and firm-level leaders more control over collective bargaining and greater flexibility to adapt to local circumstances (Jordana 1996, 219). Second, the UGT has improved and expanded the services it offers to its members, including the monitoring of employment contracts, pensions, life insurance, housing, and legal assistance. Third, the UGT has enjoyed some success in reaching out to underrepresented collectivities, particularly temporary and self-employed workers.

In addition, the UGT continues to influence policies directly affecting the labor movement. A good example is the Accord for Employment Stability (AIEE) negotiated by the UGT, the CCOO, and the Spanish Confederation of Business Organizations (CEOE) in 1997.[36] After years of refusing to make any concessions on protections for permanent workers, the UGT moderated its position in response to three factors: the continued preference among employers for temporary rather than permanent contracts; a consequent decline in the number of factory council seats in firms with fewer than fifty workers, which contributed to the UGT's first loss in factory council elections since 1980; and the election of a conservative government that was likely to proceed with labor market reform with or without the unions.

Rather than being left out in the cold, the UGT and the CCOO participated in negotiations that produced the AIEE, whereby employers agreed to improve conditions for temporary and part-time workers in return for concessions by the unions on dismissal procedures for permanent workers. The reform provided an immediate impetus to the growth of permanent contracts and contributed to a major decline in the unemployment rate, which fell from 22.2 percent in 1996 to 10.5 percent in 2001 (MTAS 2002). In addition, the AIEE mandated a minimum-wage floor for workers on training contracts and social security benefits for part-time workers, as well as the creation of a tripartite commission to monitor the temporary employment sector.

Nonetheless, while the UGT's autonomy from the PSOE did not harm its ability to deliver favorable policies to its members, it did not significantly enhance it either. The UGT still lacks the capacity to change the overall direction of economic and social policies. After cooperating with the unions for a few years after the 1988 general strike, the Socialist government hardened its stance in response to economic recession and the impending formation of the

European Monetary Union. The general strikes held by the UGT and the CCOO in 1992 and 1994 had very little impact on policy, and the PSOE forged ahead with a labor market reform in 1994 over the unions' vehement objections. Similarly, the PP government became less responsive to the unions after the AIEE and proceeded with controversial reforms despite mobilizations by the unions, including a general strike in June 2002. Meanwhile, temporary contracts continued to represent nearly a third of all contracts and accounted for 91.3 percent of the contracts signed in 2001 (Eguiagaray Ucelay 2002).

It remains to be seen how much influence the UGT will have under another PSOE government, but it is unlikely the situation will improve dramatically. Meanwhile, the collapse of the alliance has only exacerbated the weak ties between political parties and civil society in Spain. The PSOE continues to have a very low ratio of affiliates to members and has failed to develop close ties to intermediary organizations outside the labor movement. Relatedly, Spanish civil society is notoriously weak. Only one-third of Spanish adults belong to any voluntary association, and Spain has experienced much less growth in new social movements than most other EU members (Encarnación 2001, 63–65). Although these conditions facilitated the PSOE's adaptation to the pressures of globalization in the 1980s and 1990s (Kitschelt 1994; Koelble 1991), they have also contributed to concerns about the quality of Spanish democracy.

The implications of changes in party-union relations for interest representation in Mexico and Venezuela are far more ambiguous. Not only are these implications still unfolding, but they are occurring in the context of political transformations that are having their own profound impact on interest representation. Nonetheless, we can draw three tentative conclusions from current trends. First, unions are likely to become more responsive to workers and more concerned with local and workplace issues as a result of workers' greater access to voice and exit and the growing salience of subnational politics. Increased autonomy from parties and the state may also enable them to form broader alliances and mobilize more effectively against unfavorable government policies, as in the campaign against electric utility privatization in Mexico in the late 1990s.

These effects will be gradual and uneven, however, as demonstrated by AD's capacity to maintain its hegemony in the CTV despite direct elections at every level. Moreover, the Venezuelan labor movement is likely to remain highly centralized and politicized, at least as long as Chávez is in office. In Mexico, obstacles to internal democracy are likely to persist, even in more independent unions, unless unions are required to follow democratic procedures in their leadership selection.[37]

A second conclusion is that unions are becoming one of many interlocutors between working people and policymakers. In contrast to Spain, Mexico and Venezuela have experienced significant increases in new civil society organizations since the 1980s. In Mexico, particularly along the United States border, there are growing signs of "social movement unionism" whereby labor unions work closely with other civil society organizations, such as neighborhood associations, nongovernmental organizations (NGOs), and women's groups. Venezuelan unions have shown less of a propensity to engage in social movement unionism, perhaps because the CTV continues to represent 80 percent of organized labor. Nonetheless, Venezuelan NGOs and neighborhood associations are increasingly occupying the representational space previously monopolized by unions.

The emergence of alternative channels of demand making promises to increase and diversify working people's participation in political life, particularly since new civil society organizations are often more responsive, horizontal, and grassroots-based than traditional institutions. But, as Frances Hagopian points out, greater participation does not necessarily lead to more effective representation: "New social movements may have *mobilized* broader segments of the citizenry than parties did in the past (and in so doing they have broadened the bases for political association), but they have not necessarily *represented* them as effectively. . . . When citizens are represented largely by social movements or NGOs, they are detached from the political institutions whose function it is to aggregate interests in a democratic society. This divorce may leave citizens unrepresented on such salient issues as monetary and trade policy, social security reform, and consumer protection" (1998, 125–26). Kenneth Roberts makes a similar argument that Latin America suffers from "a form of segmented collectivism that keeps popular actors self-contained in their democratizing potential so as to preclude a cumulative process of popular empowerment" (1998, 71). Like Hagopian, he highlights the "challenge of social and political coordination, or the horizontal linkage of decentralized forms of organization" (1998, 70). This challenge is especially daunting in Venezuela, which has experienced a profound delegitimation of mass-based organizations and fragmentation of civil society.[38]

A third, related conclusion is that unions (and their leaders) are increasingly likely to enter into informal, issue-based, and contingent alliances with other political and social actors. In Mexico, where the party system is relatively stable but the labor movement has become much more fluid and heterogeneous, we see these alliances mostly among labor organizations and, in some cases, other civil society groups.[39] In Venezuela, where most of the labor movement is still within the CTV but the party system is highly unstable and characterized by shifting coalitions, we see these alliances mostly among labor leaders from different political currents, particularly during union elections.

The positive implication of this development is that it enables unions and their leaders to be more responsive and flexible in a context of economic and political volatility. But shifting coalitions organized around short-term goals may lack the coherence and staying power to resist clever strategies of divide-and-conquer or to promote the formulation and adoption of policies favorable to working people in the long run. Moreover, leaders who can change allegiances too easily are difficult to hold accountable and may become more concerned with forming winning coalitions than with representing workers.

On balance, the loosening ties between parties and unions promise to have more positive than negative effects on interest representation in Mexico, Spain, and Venezuela, particularly given the realities of economic and political liberalization. Since unions have little chance of reviving the days of stable, privileged, party-based access to resources and influence, they must devise new organizational strategies to survive and remain relevant. Their greatest challenge is to find a workable balance between autonomy and influence in a world of market uncertainty. Spanish unions have done a respectable job of meeting this challenge within existing institutional arrangements. Unions in Mexico and Venezuela face a more daunting task because the institutional arrangements themselves are in transition. The hope is that the collapse of the old arrangements will prompt the emergence of more representative organizations and give working people a stronger voice in their own future. The fear is that it will leave them even more marginalized and underrepresented than before.

Acronyms

AAS — Autonomous Labor Alliance
ABI — Basic Interconfederal Accord
AD — Democratic Action Party
AES — Economic and Social Accord
AIEE — Accord for Employment Stability
ANE — National Employment Accord
ANSD — National Alliance for Democratic Unionism
APRA — American Popular Revolutionary Alliance
ASI — Independent Union Alliance
BTV — Venezuelan Workers' Bank
BUO — Labor Unity Bloc
CANTV — National Telephone Company of Venezuela
CCOO — Workers' Commissions
COR — Revolutionary Workers' Confederation
CD — Democratic Current
CEC — Confederal Executive Commission
CEN — National Executive Committee
CEOE — Spanish Confederation of Business Organizations
CGT — General Workers' Union
CNC — National Peasants' Confederation
CNE — National Electoral Council

CNOP — National Confederation of Popular Organizations
CNSM — National Minimum Wage Commission
CNT — National Labor Confederation
Codesa — Confederation of Autonomous Unions
Conacopresa — Commission of Costs, Prices, and Salaries
COPEI — Social Christian Party of Venezuela
COPRE — Presidential Commission for Reform of the State
COR — Revolutionary Labor Confederation
Cordiplan — Ministry of Development and Planning
CROC — Revolutionary Confederation of Workers and Peasants
CROM — Regional Confederation of Mexican Workers
CSE — Commission for Monitoring and Evaluation
CSIF — Independent Union Confederation of Public Employees
CSUN — National Unified Labor Committee
CT — Labor Congress
CTM — Confederation of Mexican Workers

CTV	Confederation of Venezuelan Workers
CUTV	Unitary Central of Venezuelan Workers
EAP	economically active population
EEC	European Economic Community
ELA-STV	Basque Workers' Union
FAT	Authentic Labor Front
FBT	Bolivarian Workers' Force
FBT-200	Bolivarian Workers' Front-200
FCT	Constituent Workers' Front
FCV	Venezuelan Peasant Federation
Fedecamaras	Venezuelan Federation of Chambers and Associations of Commerce and Production
Fedepetrol	Federation of Petroleum Workers
FEDEUNEP	Federation of Public Employees
FESEBES	Federation of Goods and Services Unions
Fetrabolívar	Federation of the State of Bolívar
Fetrametal	Federation of Metalworkers
FNRCPIE	National Front of Resistance against Privatization of Electrical Industry
FPE	Fund for the Promotion of Employment
FSM	Mexican Union Front
FSTSE	Federation of Public Service Workers' Unions
FUT	United Workers' Front
GATT	General Agreement on Tariffs and Trade
GDP	gross domestic product
IDB	Inter-American Development Bank
IFE	Federal Electoral Institute
ILO	International Labour Organization
IMF	International Monetary Fund
IMSS	Mexican Social Security Institute

INEGI	National Institute of Geographic and Statistical Information
INEM	National Institute of Employment
Infonavit	National Worker Housing Institute
INI	National Institute of Industry
Insol	National Solidarity Institute
INTG	Trade Union Confederation of Galicia
ISI	import substitution industrialization
IU	United Left
IVSS	Venezuelan Social Security Institute
JCA	Boards of Conciliation and Arbitration
JLCA	Local Board of Conciliation and Arbitration
LFT	Federal Labor Law
MAS	Movement Toward Socialism
MEP	People's Electoral Movement
MIR	Movement of the Revolutionary Left
MTAS	Ministry of Labor and Social Affairs
MTSS	Ministry of Labor and Social Security
MVR	Movement of the Fifth Republic
NAFTA	North American Free Trade Agreement
NATO	North Atlantic Treaty Organization
NGOs	nongovernmental organizations
NS	New Unionism
OIT	International Labor Office
PAN	National Action Party
PCE	Spanish Communist Party
PCV	Venezuelan Communist Party
PDN	National Democratic Party
PEJ	Youth Employment Plan

PIRE Program of Immediate Economic Reorganization

PNR National Revolutionary Party

PP Popular Party

PPT Country for All

PRD Party of the Democratic Revolution

PRI Institutional Revolutionary Party

PRM Party of the Mexican Revolution

Pronasol National Solidarity Program

PSOE Spanish Socialist Workers' Party

PSP Priority Union Proposal

SAR System of Retirement Savings

SCJM Mexican Supreme Court

SEDESOL Ministry of Social Development

SME Mexican Electrical Workers' Union

SNA national autonomous unions

SNTE National Teachers' Union

SNTSS National Social Security Workers' Union

STDF Subsecretaría del Trabajo del Distrito Federal

STFRM Union of Mexican Railroad Workers

STPRM Union of Mexican Petroleum Workers

STPS Ministry of Labor and Social Welfare

STRM Telephone Workers' Union

STUNAM Union of National Autonomous University of Mexico Workers

SUTERM Sole Union of Electrical Workers of the Mexican Republic

SUTISS Single Union of Steel Industry Workers

UCD Union of the Democratic Center

UDP Democratic Union of Pensioners

UGT General Workers' Union

UNT National Union of Workers

URD Democratic Republican Union

USAID United States Agency for International Development

USO Workers' Labor Union

ZURs Zones of Urgent Reindustrialization

Notes

Notes to Chapter 1

1. In Spanish, the unions called these contracts *"contratos de basura."* Unless otherwise indicated, all translations in this book are by the author.

2. Some labor-backed governments took a lesson from the disastrous attempts to increase state intervention by the Socialist government of Francois Mitterand in France in the early 1980s and the American Popular Revolutionary Alliance (APRA) government of Alan García in Peru in the mid-1980s.

3. I am focusing on this limited universe of cases because some of the variation across the larger set can be explained by the differential capacity of the unions to influence policy outcomes. In Sweden and Germany, for example, the parties adopted far less draconian reforms, and the unions retained much of their political and organizational power. It is therefore not surprising that they remained in alliances with their parties, although even these unions took steps to distance themselves from government policies.

4. Because Pérez left office under charges of corruption in May 1993, his term was completed by Ramón Velásquez, also of AD.

5. It should be noted that union density figures are notoriously unreliable in all three cases.

Notes to Chapter 2

1. Although rules and procedures are also important, I argue that they can be subsumed under norms.

2. My original inspiration for this idea was the argument by Gourevitch et al. that a "hostage dilemma" is created when labor leaders are pulled in strategically contradictory directions (1984, 11).

3. In theory, a fourth strategic option would be no demand making *(silence)*. But since disaffected labor leaders are highly unlikely to remain silent in a party-union alliance that provides channels for negotiation and exchange, I do not include it.

4. In their influential work on Latin American corporatism, Ruth Berins Collier and David Collier define inducements as the application of advantages "through which the elite attempts to motivate organized labor to support the state, to cooperate with its goals, and to accept the constraints it imposes" (1979, 969).

5. I am using the concept of party system broadly to cover all the possible options, including a no-party state in an authoritarian regime. For a narrower definition, see Mainwaring and Scully 1995, 4.

Notes to Chapter 3

1. Charles Sabel defines Fordist mass production as "the manufacture of standard products with specialized resources" (1987, 35). This production process is especially amenable to long-term plan-

ning because inputs and outputs tend to be stable, clearly defined, and predictable. For an extensive analysis of the contours and historical origins of Fordism, see Piore and Sabel 1984.

2. Even the newly industrializing countries in Latin America had much more heterogeneous and geographically dispersed working classes than many countries in Europe, due in part to the weak penetration of Fordism and the large size of their informal sectors. Nonetheless, the workers who were employed in the formal sector were numerous enough and shared enough of these features to provide a strong and stable constituency for labor-backed parties in several countries.

3. These leaders came to be called the "Generation of '28" because of their emergence as opposition leaders during student protests against the Gómez dictatorship in 1928.

4. The relative scores for Mexico and Venezuela correspond roughly to other measures of reform progress in Latin America. For example, indexes created by the Inter-American Development Bank (IDB 1997) and Vittorio Corbo (2000, 77) measure the change in economic openness between 1985 and 1995 and find Mexico above the regional average and Venezuela below the regional average.

5. Open unemployment is calculated as the difference between the economically active population (EAP) and those who were unemployed for at least one hour during the week of reference. Particularly given the lack of unemployment insurance in Mexico, this figure is not very helpful because it includes people in conditions of very precarious employment, including those who worked for no pay. Implicit unemployment is based on the ratio of total employment to the EAP (Lustig 1998, 78, 244, n. 37).

6. Notably exempt from this policy were a large holding company expropriated in 1983 and the sectors in reconversion.

7. Between 1987 and 1994, collective agreements fixed the pay for just under 90 percent of all workers in the formal economy (Rigby and Lawlor 1994, 266).

8. For example, workers in the FPE were entitled to receive 80 percent of their salary for three years. By the end of 1986, 22,763 workers had been incorporated into the FPE (Navarro 1990, 68).

9. In 1989, inflation mushroomed to 80 percent, interest rates hit 40 percent, and the economy shrank by nearly 10 percent (Naím 1993, 50, 59).

10. Venezuela's spectacular growth rates were fueled by increased oil revenues linked to the Iraqi invasion of Kuwait in early 1991.

11. Top officials in the administration argued that these reforms, particularly a tax overhaul delivered to Congress in 1990, would enable them to finance higher levels of public spending (Navarro 1994, 20).

12. The figures in this paragraph are the result of calculations based on Valecillos 1993, Volume 2, 152, 246.

13. Moreover, we might expect this particular kind of hardship to dampen union combativeness, since workers in fear of losing their jobs are often more reluctant to engage in collective action.

14. The Mexican government began collecting data on underemployment in 1987 and found that more than one-fifth of the economically active population worked fewer than thirty-five hours per week between 1987 and 1995 (Zedillo 1997). The Venezuelan government did not report underemployment figures, but according to an Index of Labor Precariousness constructed by two Venezuelan scholars—based on wage levels, weekly hours worked, job stability, social security, and severance benefits—the share of the employed Venezuelans working in precarious conditions increased from 62 percent in 1987 to 67 percent in 1992 (Fajardo Cortez and Lacabana 1993, 134).

15. The Pérez administration introduced unemployment insurance in Venezuela in 1989, but rates of coverage fell from 26.9 percent in 1990 to 20 percent in 1992, and the program was plagued by administrative and coordination problems (Rodríguez, Betancourt, and Márquez 1995, 224–25).

16. In an indication of the misleading nature of unemployment numbers, from 1983 to 1992 the number of new entrants in the labor force was much greater in Mexico than in Spain, yet industrial employment grew slightly more in Spain (7.8 percent) than in Mexico (6.9 percent).

17. For an overview of the likely intensity of labor resistance to different kinds of market reforms, see Madrid 2003.

18. Although the PRD garnered less than 20 percent of the votes in national elections in 1994 and 2000, it became an important minority player in Congress and won control of Mexico City in 1997.

Notes to Chapter 4

1. The constitution also empowered the state to intervene generally in the economy. The most important articles were Article 27, which made natural resources the inalienable property of the nation and allowed for the expropriation of private property in the public interest, and Article 28, which prohibited the formation of monopolies (Hamilton 1982, 61).

2. Moreover, workers had no formal means of appealing these decisions once they had been made (Middlebrook 1995, 173).

3. Upon approval of such a request, striking employees were required to return to work within twenty-four hours, and the employer was legally permitted to replace them if they failed to do so (*Ley Federal del Trabajo* 1931, 119). Unions could seek an injunction against a decision to declare a strike nonexistent, but the long delay in resolving the dispute was likely to render the strike action irrelevant (Franco and Fernando 1991, 18).

4. Cárdenas initially supported a unified labor organization in 1936 as a key ally in his struggle to establish control over the Mexican political system. Once his conservative rivals had been defeated, however, he had incentives to divide the popular classes into separate organizations so that they would be less able to turn against him.

5. This division gained constitutional status in 1960, when Congress reformed Article 123 to create a separate set of regulations *(Apartado B)* for federal employees (La Botz 1992, 51).

6. The party found the Popular Sector to be a more reliable ally than the Labor Sector primarily because its members were much more dispersed and unorganized and therefore less likely to mount a unified challenge to the party leadership.

7. During the 1930s, national autonomous unions (SNA) were formed by workers in the following industries: railroads, mining and metalworking, electric utilities, telecommunications, petroleum, transport, sugar, textiles, and printing. Although some of these unions were affiliated with the CTM, they retained their organizational autonomy.

8. Dan La Botz estimates that protection contracts accounted for nearly 75 percent of the labor contracts in the Federal District (1992, 54). They were also common in the *maquiladora* plants along the U.S.–Mexican border.

9. Despite the opposition of many of Lombardo's supporters, he weighed in on the side of Velázquez to preserve unity within the confederation.

10. Presidents Avila Camacho and Lázaro Cárdenas endorsed Velázquez's reelection by attending the closing ceremony of the CTM Congress (Medina 1978, 184).

11. They also changed the CTM's slogan from "For a society without classes" to "For the emancipation of Mexico" and eliminated the general strike as a union tactic.

12. As one prominent PRI member explained, "Fidel is a leaders' leader." He illustrated his point with an anecdote about Velázquez's use of loyal subordinates to mobilize actions in favor of a construction project on the resort island of Cozumel, which local merchants from the other side of the island were resisting out of fear of losing business. Pedro Jiménez [pseud.], interview by author, June 19, 1996, Mexico City.

13. Police arrested seven PSOE executives inside Spain between 1939 and 1954 (Maravall 1978, 24).

14. Matilde Fernández, interview by author. Madrid, June 23, 1995.

15. Although the right to strike was guaranteed by the 1978 Constitution, a law to regulate these strikes was not passed until 1992.

16. In the 1980s, the PCE merged with several other leftist parties to form the United Left *(Izquierda Unida),* which became Spain's third electoral force at the national level.

17. For example, the secretary general decides the composition of the CEC, which is then ratified by the Confederal Congress (Führer 1996, 159–60).

18. The resolutions of the Confederal Executive Commission won by margins of 76.6 percent in 1983, 99.9 percent in 1986, and 100 percent in 1990 (UGT 1983b, 1986a, 1990).

19. Closed shops are illegal under the 1978 Constitution, which prohibits any requirement that a worker join a union to gain employment (Fundación FIES 1985, 236).

20. Many small and medium-sized firms did not have a sufficiently organized workforce to hold factory council elections.

21. In the event that the national-level unions signed a wage pact with business and/or the state, the factory councils were responsible for imposing the conditions of the pact within the firm (Escobar 1993, 30).

22. In workplaces with more than 250 workers, union sections were entitled to have at least one delegate on the factory council with a voice but no right to vote (Escobar 1993, 37).

23. According to one survey, 40 percent of the UGT delegates elected in 1986 did not even belong to the union at the time of their election (Bouza et al. 1989, 18).

24. As mentioned above, the state also lacked the authority to regulate strikes.

25. In the December 1947 elections, the AD candidate won 74.4 percent of the presidential vote, and AD won 70.8 percent of the legislative vote. As a result, AD controlled 38 out of 42 seats (90.5 percent) in the Senate and 83 out of 111 seats (74.8 percent) in the Chamber of Deputies (Blank 1984, 26).

26. Betancourt won the presidency in 1958 with 49.2 percent of the vote (Blank 1984, 30). Under the power-sharing arrangement, his government included two cabinet positions for AD, three for the URD, two for COPEI, and five for independents. Until the URD withdrew from the pact in 1960, the three major parties also shared governorships and leadership positions in Congress (Ewell 1984, 127).

27. This system of negotiated two-party dominance came to be known as "*guanábana* politics." Besides being a pear-shaped fruit, symbolizing AD's larger influence relative to COPEI (Hellinger 1991, 117), the *guanábana* is green on the outside (COPEI's color) and white on the inside (AD's color). Francisco Iturraspe (professor, Universidad Central de Venezuela), interview by author, Caracas, March 7, 1995.

28. Under this pact, the party in the executive would name the president of the Senate while the other party would name the president of the Chamber of Deputies. The two parties also agreed to cooperate in the nomination of supreme court justices and key officials such as the comptroller of the nation (McCoy 1989, 65, n. 19).

29. More generally, no statute existed to determine the rights and obligations of the labor inspectors (OIT 1991, 24).

30. The conciliation process could legally be extended for another thirty days and, in practice, often lasted even longer.

31. In 1983, collective bargaining in the public sector covered some 250,000 employees, more than in the private sector (OIT 1991, 122).

32. The 1936 Labor Law "prohibited the existence of unions of a national or even regional character" (Lucena 1982, 217).

33. As of 1983, only unions in the construction industry negotiated contracts on an industry-wide basis (McCoy 1989, 57).

34. AD did adopt a dual structure whereby the party was organized along both sectorial and territorial lines. As in Mexico, the inclusion of multiple social groups enhanced the independent power of party leaders, who "were able to play off one group against the other in the name of the party as a whole" (Kornblith and Levine 1993, 5).

35. The CSUN was composed of members proposed by AD, COPEI, the URD, and the Venezuelan Communist Party (PCV) and ratified by the union directives.

36. AD suffered an earlier split when *adecos* sympathetic to the Cuban Revolution, some of whom were labor leaders, defected to form the aforementioned MIR in 1960. This split was traumatic for AD, but it did not have nearly as dramatic consequences for AD's power in the political system and the labor movement as the 1968 formation of the MEP.

37. They also continued to enjoy access to elected office as MEP members *(mepistas)* because of the system of proportional representation in the political arena.

38. UGT members constituted a sizable share of the delegates to PSOE Congresses, but the UGT did not act as an organized faction within the party.

39. This imbalance was exacerbated by "networks" of mini-unions in which real elections never took place (Arismendi and Iturraspe 1990, 249).

40. In some unions, such deals preempted the convocation of assemblies altogether. For example, the large Federation of Public Employees (FEDEUNEP) did not hold a national assembly for the first twenty-six years of its existence (Coppedge 1994, 272, n. 35).

41. At the CTV's Eighth Congress in 1980, for example, no voting occurred because the parties had previously agreed to the resolutions and the composition of the new executive (Larrañaga n.d., 11).

42. The employer was only obligated to negotiate a collective contract with the union that represented the absolute majority of workers. This contract was then applied to all workers (*erga omnes*) regardless of whether or not they belonged to a union. Thus, "there could be more than one union in the same labor arena, but no more than one negotiating agent" (OIT 1991, 61).

43. Mexican presidents (along with all other elected officials) are constitutionally prohibited from running for reelection.

44. From the 1940s to the early 1970s, the president personally picked around 20 percent of the deputies and 60 percent of the senators in the Mexican Congress (Smith 1979).

45. The president's powers of appointment created a system whereby moving up the political hierarchy required joining a network (*camarilla*) based on crosscutting, fluid, patron-client relationships aimed ultimately at winning the presidency. This system was reinforced by Mexico's no-re-election rule, since political survival depended on capturing a series of different governmental posts (Smith 1979, 166).

46. From the 1940s to the early 1970s, the Chamber of Deputies passed about 95 percent of the legislative proposals delivered by the executive (Smith 1979). In addition, the president could rewrite the Mexican Constitution nearly at will. Between 1917 and 1992, there were approximately 250 constitutional reforms and substantive additions (Bolivar Espinoza and Bonifaz Moreno 1992, 37).

47. The Spanish executive was also protected by a requirement that the parliament pass a "constructive" motion of censure, which required unanimous agreement on a replacement for the prime minister, to defeat a government (Bonime 1985, 23).

48. Because of the filtering effects of these provisions, a critical faction within the PSOE (the *críticos*) received only 10 percent of the delegates to the Twenty-ninth Congress (and no seats on the party executive), despite having the support of as much as 40 percent of the party membership (Gillespie 1989, 356).

49. Party members also had to defend congressional resolutions and decisions taken by the party leadership and needed permission to attend demonstrations or political meetings organized by associations independent of the PSOE (Gillespie 1989, 346–47).

50. In 1983, the PSOE legalized "currents of opinion" (but not organized tendencies) and tempered the majority vote principle by reserving 25 percent of the seats for a minority that received at least 20 percent of the votes cast. The 20 percent barrier was so high, however, that it effectively blocked the consolidation of minority currents (Satrústegui 1992, 43).

51. The ratio of the PSOE's affiliates to its electorate, already the lowest among European Socialist parties in Europe in 1979, plummeted to 1:90 in 1982 (Puhle 1986, 331). This low level of membership left PSOE deputies with little room for autonomous initiative and heightened the importance of González's electoral appeal (Heywood 1991, 104).

52. Formally, the CEN was beholden to two higher authorities: the National Convention and the National Directive Committee. But these bodies met only occasionally, whereas the CEN operated continuously and had the authority to manage the daily affairs of the party (Martz 1966, 148–61).

53. According to Michael Coppedge (1994), party control over candidate nominations was far more centralized than in most other democracies. State-level executive committees could send unranked draft lists for senate and deputy positions to the CEN, but the CEN had the right to eliminate five candidates for every one selected, to replace up to half of the proposed candidates, and to rank the candidates. The CEN had similar powers at the state and municipal levels. In 1985, the CEN designated 100 of the 202 candidates for city council president (20–22).

54. As in Mexico, the Venezuelan president was constitutionally prohibited from succeeding himself, although he could run for reelection after being out of office for at least ten years.

55. Coppedge (1994) characterizes these factions as the "Ins" and the "Outs." The Ins revolved around the incumbent president, and the Outs revolved around a party leader who was excluded from the inner circle of government (104).

Notes to Chapter 5

1. The CTM received seven out of the ten labor positions in the first IMSS General Assembly, created in 1945 (Wilson 1981, 208–26).

2. The participation of unionized workers in external promotions increased from 32 percent in 1975 to 60 percent in 1976, and the share of housing assignments made on the basis of external promotions increased from 27 percent in 1976 to 100 percent in 1980 (Aldrete-Haas 1991, 93–94 n. 9, 109 n. 36).

3. In 1979, the CTM controlled the presidency of the bank's administrative council, along with 75 percent of its members (Zazueta and de la Peña 1984, 384). When López Portillo nationalized Mexico's banking system in September 1982, he spared the *Banco Obrero*, which remained in the hands of the unions.

4. In 1979, the CTM controlled 78 percent of the labor representatives on the special boards (Zazueta and De la Peña 1984, 379–380).

5. Figures on labor representation in the Congress vary, partly because not all labor candidates are part of the Labor Sector. I chose Grayson's data because he refers specifically to the Labor Sector.

6. One of these eight seats was controlled by the petroleum workers' union, which was affiliated with the CTM. An additional two seats were held by the FSTSE, which was part of the Popular Sector rather than the Labor Sector (Zazueta and de la Peña 1984, 371).

7. The only other labor organization to do so was the teachers' union, which belonged to the Popular Sector.

8. The pact declared that each internal election within the party "will be dictated by the principle of the right of the majorities who participate in each of the Peasant, Worker, and Popular Sectors of the Party. And that said organisms and their members are the depositories of the will of these majorities and the executors of their resolutions" (PRI 1982a, 225).

9. The reformed statutes also added an article stating, "the members of the Party will be grouped into the Peasant Sector, the Labor Sector, and the Popular Sector" (PRI 1982b, 650).

10. For a more detailed discussion of this episode, see Burgess 1998, 101–3.

11. The PRI did not hesitate to encourage the elimination of political options within the CTM. Just a week before the CTM's Assembly in March 1947, the PRI president proclaimed that the PRI would no longer accept members who also had loyalties to another party, which had previously been tolerated. Soon thereafter, the party expelled CTM leaders who lent their support to the PP, including a deputy and two senators (Medina 1979, 177, 138–39).

12. Although this sanction was rarely enforced, workers understood that "the possibility always existed that it would be" (Bizberg 1990, 125).

13. In the late 1970s, the SNA's average size was 35,823 workers, compared to only 412 workers for unions organized by the CTM (Zazueta and de la Peña 1984, 451). Despite being periodically affiliated with the CTM, the SNA maintained autonomous leadership structures.

14. These boards were responsible for legally registering unions organized in local jurisdiction activities, granting legal standing to collective contracts in both local and federal jurisdictions, approving requests by firms for contracts modifications, resolving individual and collective labor disputes, and ruling on the legality of strike petitions (Middlebrook 1995, 61).

15. *Charrazos* refers to actions taken by the government that involve the same machinations and outcomes as in the case of *el charro* in 1948.

16. Fidel Velázquez once proclaimed, "[W]e the revolutionaries arrived here with bullets. He who wants to remove us will not be able to do so with votes, but will have to do so with bullets as well" (Aguilar Camin 1988, 72).

17. In June 1983, for example, the government refused to grant a minimum wage increase of more than 15.6 percent, which was not only far below the 40 percent of accumulated inflation since the beginning of the year but also *lower* than the 18.5 percent increase offered by the private sector (Aguilar García and Arrieta 1990, 682–83).

18. In May 1983, for example, the Secretary of Labor bestowed the title of "Vanguard of the Labor Movement" on the CROC (Aguilar García and Arrieta 1990, 706).

19. A constitutional reform in December 1986 further centralized the process of wage determination by eliminating regional minimum wage commissions (Franco 1991, 113).

20. Moreover, the government continued to limit contracted wages to annual revisions, despite a shift from annual to need-based adjustments for the minimum wage (Franco 1991, 113).

21. Javier Bonilla (secretary of labor), interview by author, Mexico City, June 18, 1996.

22. Bonilla, interview.

23. Table 5.1 shows that the CTM continued to file strike petitions after 1987, but these petitions were overwhelmingly motivated by collective contract disputes. Out of the strike petitions filed by all unions in federal jurisdiction activities, the share motivated by "other" concerns, including salary adjustments and emergency raises, declined from 52 percent in 1987 to less than 2 percent each year through 1996 (Zedillo 1997).

24. Even after rejecting wage and price controls in the late 1990s, the signatories renewed the institutional form of the *Pacto*. In February 1998, they negotiated the Accord of Cooperation and Consultation of the Productive Sectors to "conserve a permanent space for dialogue in which to monitor the evolution of the principal economic variables at home and abroad" (*La Jornada*, February 25, 1998). Like the *Pacto*, the new accord privileged the CT and the CTM over its rivals in the labor movement (*La Jornada*, March 20, 1998).

25. Pedro Zepeda Martínez (director general of research and development for the Insol), interview by author, Mexico City, December 2, 1994. According to one CTM official, Salinas was using Insol and the FESEBES to put external pressure on the CTM. Antonio Hernández [pseud.], interview by author, Mexico City, November 23, 1994.

26. José Landa (former consultant to the Infonavit), interview by author, Mexico City, December 9, 1994.

27. In a sample based on official figures for seven cities with a high concentration of working-class voters, Cárdenas won an average of 51.4 percent of the vote, compared to only 30.3 percent for Salinas (Trejo Delarbre 1992, 288, n. 9).

28. Raúl Trejo Delarbre, interview by author, Mexico City, December 5, 1994.

29. Bonilla, interview; Cordoba 1994, 241.

30. Jaime Serra Puche, interview by author, Princeton, N.J., May 29, 1996.

31. Carlos Martínez [pseud.] (former high-ranking PRI official), interview by author, Mexico City, December 6, 1994.

32. The CTM was unable, however, to extend its dominance west of the Texas border, where the majority of plants were non-unionized or had protection contracts with other confederations. Moreover, President Salinas used charges of corruption to depose Agapito González, the legendary leader of the CTM's Day Laborers' and Industrial Workers Union in Matamoros, when he made the mistake of challenging U.S. management in the midst of the NAFTA negotiations (*Washington Post*, February 28, 1992).

33. Salinas officially requested the negotiation of a free trade agreement with the United States in August 1990, and Canada joined the negotiations in February 1991 (Lustig 1998, 132). The agreement went into effect in January 1994.

34. Martín Tavarez [pseud.] (CTM official), interview by author, Mexico City, December 7, 1994.

35. Hernández, interview. The CTM also received official backing for the creation of a CTM-affiliated union in the auto parts sector in return for its support for NAFTA (*El Financiero*, August 18, 1992).

36. In December 1987, Cárdenas proposed a unified labor confederation outside the control of the PRI and the government and truly committed to the interests of the working class (*La Jornada*, December 7, 1987). Although Cárdenas avoided explicitly attacking the CTM, this proposal was obviously a direct challenge to both the CTM and the CT.

37. As the son of Lázaro Cárdenas, Mexico's most revered postrevolutionary president, Cuauhtémoc Cárdenas was especially well suited to lay legitimate claim to this doctrine.

38. Claiming to have found two hundred Uzi submachine guns, twenty-five thousand nine-millimeter cartridges, and nineteen high-powered rifles, agents from the federal judicial police, the Federal Public Ministry, and the army arrested La Quina and twenty-five of his associates on January 10, 1989 (Corro and Reveles 1994, 8–11).

39. Just weeks before the Assembly, the CTM also negotiated an accord with the president's

office to appoint a close associate of Velázquez's as the gubernatorial candidate in Nayarit, thereby restoring the CTM's quota of three governorships per *sexenio* (*El Financiero*, April 4, 1993).

40. Specifically, the CTM (1) defeated a previously negotiated proposal to incorporate the Labor and Peasant Sectors into a Territorial Movement; (2) blocked the organizational cells (social base committees) of Pronasol from becoming part of the party's territorial structure; and (3) reduced a Worker-Peasant Alliance from a "structure" to a "strategy" (*El Financiero*, March 30, 1993, April 4, 1993).

41. Landa, interview.

42. Hernández, interview. It is interesting to note that the Labor Ministry initially rejected the FESEBES's petition for registration in December 1990 and did not reverse its decision until after the conclusion of the NAFTA negotiations.

43. Enrique De la Garza Toledo (professor at the Universidad Autónoma de México), interview by author, Mexico City, November 16, 1994. Prior to signing the 1993 *Pacto*, the CTM approved a National Accord for the Elevation of Productivity and Quality and signed a productivity accord with SEDESOL.

44. Hernández, interview.

45. Hernández, interview.

Notes to Chapter 6

1. The Socialists cooperated with the bourgeois Republican Union between 1908 and 1933 and collaborated with the dictatorship of Miguel Primo de Rivera in the 1920s.

2. The Socialists established an anti-imperialist tradition with their campaigns against colonial wars in Cuba and Morocco, but their pacifism was more pragmatic than ideological. After initially opposing World War I as an inter-imperialist conflict, they shifted to qualified support for an Allied victory as the best outcome for the labor movement on both sides (Gillespie 1989, 14–15).

3. This impulse to catch up with the rest of Europe had historical roots. According to Manuel Redero San Román, the reforms proposed by the Socialists during the Second Republic "were motivated by the idea of recuperating lost time for Spain" relative to the other industrialized countries (1992, 55).

4. The PSOE emerged as the largest single party in the parliament elected in June 1931, and three Socialist leaders accepted cabinet positions in the coalition government.

5. The PSOE categorically dismissed a neoliberal solution to Spain's economic crisis in a document issued at its Twenty-ninth Congress in October 1981: "in this [economic] climate, it is not possible to adopt a neoliberal position to overcome the crisis in Spain . . . No political party with a progressive position would be able to deal with the enormous social cost in the form of unemployment that this readjustment would produce" (Hamann 1994, 218, her translation).

6. The UGT's radicalization contributed significantly to the outbreak of the Civil War, which paved the way for Franco's dictatorship. After the failure of the October 1934 Revolution, divisions within the *familia socialista* over the appropriate strategy became an open split between the moderates, led by Indalecio Prieto, and the radicals, led by Largo Caballero. In December 1935, Caballero and his followers resigned from the PSOE executive, leaving the party under the control of the *prietistas* and the UGT under the control of the *caballeristas* (Redero San Román 1992, 30–31).

7. Calculations based on Nájera and González Quintana 1988, 615–18.

8. Manuel Garnacho (secretary general of the UGT's Construction Federation), interview by author, Madrid, July 3, 1995.

9. The USO was a self-proclaimed socialist union that had been founded in 1960 by ex-militants in the UGT and left-wing Catholic workers.

10. Garnacho, interview; José María Zufiaur (director of the Institute of Labor Studies and Confederal Secretary on the executive committee of the UGT), interview by author, Madrid, June 23, 1995. The fusion agreement unleashed a serious internal crisis within the UGT that was ultimately resolved with the help of Felipe González (Santos and Sanchez 1990, 309–26).

11. The UGT's share of the membership of the PSOE's Federal Committee was 57 percent in 1979 and 55 percent in 1982 (Tezanos 1983, 161, 169). In addition, the two executives frequently held joint meetings at the national and provincial levels, as well as organizing mixed committees to manage specific issues (Gunther, Sani, and Shabad 1986, 209).

12. Garnacho, interview.

13. Some UGT members rebelled against this policy of supporting the PSOE in elections, but usually because the PSOE did not select those members' desired UGT candidates for its electoral lists. See Gunther, Sani, and Shabad 1986, 209–10.

14. Based on the Labor Charter of 1938, the corporatist structure established by Franco called for vertical organization of workers and employers under control of the state.

15. It should be noted that the UGT's anti-collaborationist policy was not entirely obeyed. In the early 1970s, nearly one-fifth of all UGT leaders had served in electoral positions in Franco's vertical unions (Fishman 1984, 77).

16. Although the CCOO had participation from various organizations, including the USO, it was dominated by militants from the Spanish Communist Party (PCE).

17. In March 1977, one month before unions were legalized, the government issued a royal decree that replaced the *jurados de empresa* with factory councils *(comités de empresa)* (Wozniak 1992–93, 78; Köhler 1995, 342). In addition to changing their name, the 1977 decree reformed the works councils by expanding their coverage from firms with more than fifty employees to firms with more than ten employees, reducing the role of the state in controlling the electoral system, and abolishing the participation of employers (Escobar 1993, 3).

18. The only sectors in which the UGT gained more votes were hotels and show business. Regionally, the UGT prevailed in Castilla la Vieja, León, Extremadura, Canarias, and the País Vasco (Pérez-Díaz 1979, 17, 19).

19. The UGT also received financial and logistical assistance, especially in small firms, from the UCD government and the CEOE, both of whom viewed the UGT as a bulwark against the creation of a unified labor movement under the leadership of the CCOO (Díaz-Varela and Guindal 1990; Santos and Sánchez 1990).

20. Reflecting the PSOE's strategy of mobilizing the local party apparatus on behalf of the UGT, the UGT did particularly well in firms with fewer than thirty-one employees, in which it led the CCOO by over fifteen percentage points (Führer 1996, 113, 129).

21. The PSOE promised, "through parliamentary action, to advocate legislation regarding union action in the firm and collective bargaining that reinforces the role of the union sections in the firm" while recognizing that "the union sections constitute a novelty that does not have a tradition among workers" (PSOE 1978, 18).

22. Within the firm, a union section could bargain collectively if it controlled the majority of factory council seats. At levels above the firm, the external union could bargain collectively if it controlled at least 10 percent of factory council seats nationwide (or 15 percent within a single region). In addition, the unions were allowed to present closed lists for factory council elections in firms of more than 250 employees *(Estatuto del Trabajador* 1980, 85, 75–76).

23. This arrangement suited the Socialists as well, since it helped reduce the role of the PCE in shaping the legislation. Despite the fact that the factory council system was largely preserved, the CCOO was highly critical of the Worker's Statute and organized demonstrations against it.

24. Francisco Fernández Marugán (PSOE secretary of administration and finance), interview by author, Madrid, June 16, 1995.

25. Garnacho, interview.

26. For an analysis of the disjuncture between PSOE-UGT relations and trends in the working-class vote, see Burgess 1995.

27. One exception to this policy was when the UGT joined the CCOO and the regional unions in opposing the government's plan to reconvert large steel plants in late 1984 *(Cambio 16,* October 8, 1984).

28. Garnacho, interview.

29. According to Zufiaur, the UGT signed the AES "out of inertia" and was convinced by the experience not to negotiate another global pact with the Socialists (Zufiaur, interview).

30. Just as workers were going to the polls in the 1986 factory council elections, the government and employers launched an offensive to flexibilize the labor market through deregulation and decreased employer contributions to social security, which became known as the "27 liberalizing measures" (UGT 1989a, 321).

31. Javier Astudillo Ruiz reinforces this point when he argues that "in contexts of union competitive division, a close relationship to a political party will not pay off for the labor partner when its party is in government and the economy improves" (2001, 284). For a detailed analysis of PSOE-UGT relations by the same author, see Astudillo Ruiz 1998.

32. The Law on Union Patrimony established mechanisms for returning two kinds of patrimony to the unions: (1) "historic" patrimony, which was based on a union's existence prior to the Franco dictatorship; and (2) "accumulated" patrimony, which was determined by the results of the factory council elections, regardless of whether a union was active during the years in question (Baylos 1988, 17–18). This system clearly favored the UGT, since it was the only union to qualify for significant portions of both kinds of patrimony.

33. Luis Martínez Toval, interview by author, Madrid, June 29, 1995.

34. It should be noted that relations between the PSOE and the UGT improved in anticipation of the 1986 elections, prompting Redondo to state that the PSOE's electoral program was "feasible and more socialist than that of 1982" (*El País*, May 22, 1986).

35. The tally was 109 votes in favor, 8 votes in opposition, and 8 abstentions.

36. The final bill contained several amendments introduced by the Socialist Group as a result of discussions with the UGT (*El País*, July 24, 1985).

37. The PSOE, for its part, did not send a single representative to the May Day festivities organized by the UGT in 1985 (Köhler 1995, 350).

38. The delegates to the Congress approved a resolution stating that industrial and political action should be combined to create "a union policy that is independent and not subordinate to the Government" (*El País*, April 6, 1986).

39. Manuel Garnacho, interview.

40. Damborenea stated, "I could not return to Vizcaya saying that I had abandoned Nicolás Redondo. . . . I could not vote against the party but neither could I vote against the UGT, so I preferred to be absent" (*El País*, May 31, 1985).

41. The other unions that participated in the general strike were the USO, the CNT, the ELA-STV, and the regional union from Galicia, the Trade Union Confederation of Galicia (INTG).

42. Just a few years earlier, González had been one of NATO's worst critics, calling it "nothing more than a military superstructure built by the Americans to guarantee the survival of capitalism" (Share 1989, 79).

43. González won both of these victories by narrow margins. He prevailed in the PSOE by only four votes and won the referendum by a vote of 53 percent in favor and 40 percent against.

44. According to Manuel Garnacho, however, the UGT executive did impose sanctions on leaders such as Matilde Fernández who supported the government's position on NATO. Garnacho, interview.

45. Redondo also insisted that his close advisors abandon their posts in the PSOE. Garnacho, interview.

46. Justo Zambrana, interview by author, Madrid, June 20, 1995.

47. Antonio Puerta, the leader of the metal federation, remained in the Federal Committee, and Matilde Fernandez, the leader of the chemical federation, was reelected to the PSOE executive. (*El País*, February 8, 1988). In his closing remarks at the Thirty-first PSOE Congress, González offered Redondo a position on the PSOE executive as a gesture of reconciliation, but Redondo declined.

48. The PSOE also flirted with alternative interlocutors in the labor movement, particularly the Independent Union Confederation of Public Employees (CSIF) and the Democratic Union of Pensioners (UDP).

49. Mariano Guindal (economics editor at *La Vanguardia*), interview by author, Madrid, June 22, 1995. At the end of 1988, 53 percent of young employees already had temporary contracts (Espina 1991, 202).

50. José María Maravall (former minister of education and prominent PSOE leader), interview by author, Madrid, June 27, 1995.

51. Garnacho, interview.

52. Although members of the Socialist Left continued to support the UGT's position, they lacked any real power within the party hierarchy.

53. Garnacho suggests that these leaders remembered the "coup d'etat" against Metal and feared the same outcome in their own federation if they opposed Redondo's leadership. Garnacho, interview.

54. A few cadres sympathetic to the PSOE and the government remained in leadership positions, most notably Garnacho, who was secretary general of construction, and Justo Fernández, who was the secretary general of banking. The secretary general of the Asturian mining federation, José Angel Fernández Villa, also retained his position in the UGT and became the only UGT leader to serve on the PSOE's Federal Committee.

55. According to the CCOO, nearly eight million people, or 94.9 percent of the economically active population (EAP), went on strike (Campos and Alvarez 1990, 105). The government later revised those estimates to 75 percent of the EAP.

56. Spain's other general strikes took place in 1917, 1930, 1934, and 1976.

57. Redondo moved almost immediately after the 1986 factory council elections to cultivate better relations with the CCOO. In January 1987, Redondo wrote a letter to the CCOO's secretary general proposing unity of action in collective contract negotiations, a strategy that had not been advocated since 1979 (*Cambio 16*, January 5, 1987).

58. Zufiaur, interview.

59. It should be noted, however, that Garnacho and Justo Fernández convinced their colleagues to reject a formal prohibition against endorsing the PSOE in elections. Garnacho, interview.

60. Marugán, interview.

61. Ludolfo Paramio (professor, Consejo Superior de Investigaciones Científico), interview by author, Madrid, June 13, 1995.

62. Josefa Pardo, interview by author, Madrid, July 19, 1995.

63. Julián Ariza, interview by author, Madrid, August 1, 1995.

64. For example, in the last line of Redondo's April 1989 letter rejecting any further sharing of organizational responsibilities with the PSOE, he clarified that the UGT would be willing to receive a delegation from the party to discuss issues of concern. This attitude conforms to an attitude of "voice after exit" whereby the two organizations continued to negotiate but as independent entities.

65. Apolinar Rodríguez (former secretary of union action of the UGT), interview by author, Madrid, June 30, 1995.

66. Zufiaur, interview

67. Zufiaur, interview. Apolinar Rodríguez revealed a similar awareness of the futility of seeking hegemony when he stated that "there are no possibilities for imposing an overarching union as in Sweden because of the strength of *Comisiones*." Rodríguez, interview.

68. Relations between the UGT and the CCOO entered into a crisis during the 1990 factory council elections, but they managed to preserve their commitment to unity of action. Rather than breaking their alliance, they supported an electoral norm that made institutional privileges independent from electoral outcomes (Apolinar Rodríguez, interview). This norm was issued as a royal decree by the Labor Ministry on September 9, 1994.

Notes to Chapter 7

1. I am borrowing this term from Jennifer McCoy and William Smith (1995, 121).

2. Although AD first came to power through a military coup in 1945, it took immediate steps to construct a democratic system of government. Some *adecos* supported guerilla movements inspired by the Cuban Revolution in the 1960s, but they had to leave the party to act on their revolutionary views.

3. Real wages rose by 31 percent in 1946 and by another five percent in 1947 (Ellner 1980, 113).

4. Calculations based on Valecillos 1993, 254–55.

5. Between 1961 and 1971, the share of the central government budget devoted to the education ministry increased from 7.8 percent to 14.8 percent, contributing to an increase in the literacy rate from 64.5 percent to 75.9 percent. During the same decade, the share of the budget devoted to the health ministry rose from 6.6 percent to 7.4 percent, and the number of physicians per inhabitant grew from 6.93 to 9.62 (Márquez 1995, 409).

6. The law also stipulated "numerical stability" *(estabilidad numérica)*, which required employers to replace all discharged workers at equal pay regardless of the cause of the dismissal, but this provision was never enforced (Ellner 1993, 206).

7. Strike activity did increase during this period, however, reflecting growing divisions within AD and the CTV that ultimately resulted in defections and the formation of new organizations.

8. Between 1961 and 1983, Venezuela experienced only seventy-eight legal strikes, for an average of 3.4 per year. Even if this figure is combined with "illegal strikes" *(paros intempestivos)*, the average increases to only 113.7 per year. Calculations based on OIT 1991, 119.

9. During the 1980s, three-quarters of the *adecos* in the CTV leadership also held positions in the Labor Bureau (Coppedge 1994, 32).

10. In 1963, the Labor Bureau proposed the candidacy of Raúl Leoni, who had close ties to labor from his tenure as Labor Minister during the *trienio*. Leoni won the nomination over the vehement objections of Rómulo Betancourt, the incumbent president.

11. César Olarte (secretary general of the CTV), interview by author, Caracas, March 30, 1995.

12. AD labor leaders also occupied important elected posts at the state and local levels, which gave them access to a dual power base. The president of the state union federation often served as president of the state legislative assembly (Larrañaga n.d., 11). Likewise, state labor secretaries tapped into the resources of both the labor unions and the state federations, enabling them to act as power brokers in state politics (Coppedge 1994, 33).

13. COPEI won 29 percent of the vote, compared to 27 percent for AD, 22 percent for a coalition of left parties, and 19 percent for the MEP (Ellner 1993, 42).

14. AD helped repentant *mepistas* achieve or maintain important positions within the CTV. César Gil became a member of the CTV executive, and Juan José Delpino and Pedro Brito became substitute members. Likewise, the party helped José Mollegas of Fetrametal and Carlos Pinuera of Fedepetrol keep control of their respective federations (Ellner 1993, 54).

15. Although this figure is comparable to the scope of the Mexican Labor Congress, the CTV was not just an umbrella group whose constituent unions retained their organizational autonomy. Like the CTM and the UGT, the CTV was a confederation with binding authority over its lower-level affiliates.

16. Until 1991, the Venezuelan Peasant Federation (FCV) automatically received 10 percent of the delegates to CTV congresses in recognition of its large constituency (Ellner 1993, 25).

17. It should be noted that this competition took place mostly before the CTV's predecessor was founded in 1947.

18. AD did make major inroads in the oil industry, however. By 1948, Venezuela had three petroleum federations: Fedepetrol, which was dominated by AD and included around fifty unions; Consutrapet, which was dominated by the Communists and included around twenty-five unions; and STOP, a much smaller federation linked to COPEI (Godio 1985, 40).

19. In the 1980s, AD labor leaders occupied the overwhelming majority of the two hundred-odd labor seats on the boards of state-owned companies and agencies (Ellner 1993, 178).

20. According to one source, these subsidies were used in the majority of cases to remunerate union leaders who became "quasi-public employees" (Iturraspe 1993, 277).

21. In addition, affiliates of rival confederations often faced discrimination by labor authorities in the resolution of labor conflicts.

22. In the 1970s, the state also financed construction of the CTV's new headquarters, a fancy high-rise in the cultural district of Caracas.

23. Herrera Campins also dismantled the tripartite commissions formed by Pérez, although he allowed the tripartite commissions established at the subministerial level to continue functioning (McCoy 1989, 54).

24. As Steve Ellner documents, however, the CTV also developed close ties to the AFL-CIO, which often conflicted with the European labor movement (1993, 114–18).

25. In 1984, this approach paid off for blue-collar workers with wages set by collective contracts that nearly tripled in real terms. But this gain was short-lived and in 1985, their real wages fell back nearly to the 1983 level (Valecillos 1993, 71, graph 4).

26. Foreshadowing events in 1989, however, the meeting convinced the CTV leadership to

present the government with a list of demands so as not to lose the initiative to rival unions (Arrieta 1984b).

27. Juan José Delpino, interview by author, Caracas, April 6, 1995.

28. It should be noted that the CTV failed to come to the defense of Matos Azocar's development plan, which was purged of many of its progressive elements after he left Cordiplan (Guevara 1989, 232).

29. Pérez's victory was assured by the presence of around 12,700 trade unionists in AD's 52,000-member electoral college. Following the vote, the Labor Bureau suspended four labor leaders (all of whom were heads or former heads of CTV-affiliated federations) and censured sixteen others for defying the Labor Bureau's decision to support Pérez (Ellner 1993, 79–80).

30. Pérez's margin of victory over his main opponent was the largest in twenty-five years. Unlike Lusinchi, however, he did not enjoy an absolute majority in either house of Congress (Naím 1993, 31).

31. Hector Valecillos (economist and former coordinator of the CTV's Commission of Advisors), interview by author, Caracas, March 24, 1995.

32. According to Moises Naím, who served as Pérez's Minister of Industry, the president was influenced by the success of the economic reforms in Spain as carried out by his close friend, Felipe González (1993, 46).

33. Valecillos, interview.

34. As they had under Lusinchi, AD labor leaders demanded that the austerity package be accompanied by measures to compensate less-privileged sectors.

35. This situation is analogous to the conflicts in Spain that developed within the UGT during the negotiation of the AES and eventually broke out into the open, contributing to a strategic shift to norm-breaking voice.

36. According to a CTV leader from MAS, the February riots provided an opening for Delpino to pursue his more combative agenda. Rodrigo Penso (MAS Labor Secretary), interview by author, Caracas, March 14, 1995.

37. Although the party broke quorum in the Chamber of Deputies to avoid a vote on the reforms in early March, it subsequently voted against a proposal to request a revision of the president's policies (*El Nacional*, March 17, 1989, March 30, 1989).

38. While expressing sympathy for Rios's complaints regarding the reforms, Barrios proposed the traditional remedy of organizing a meeting between the AD executive and the president.

39. AD labor leaders also agreed to exempt state-owned industries such as electricity and steel in return for the government's promise not to withhold the salaries of state workers who participated in the strike (Ellner 1993, 83).

40. Juan José Delpino, interview by author, Caracas, March 30, 1995. Delpino himself admitted that frustration with the lack of viable alternatives contributed to his decision to leave the CTV.

41. Delpino, interview, April 6, 1995.

42. AD's main complaint against Pérez was his appointment of non-AD technocrats to his cabinet and his unwillingness to consult regularly with the party leadership regarding his policies. The party had had similar problems with Pérez during his first presidency in the 1970s (Karl 1982, 517–50), but the conflict was much worse in the context of scarcity rather than abundance.

43. In May 1991, rumors began appearing in the press that Celli, the secretary general of AD, was circulating a draft document that called for the formal withdrawal of the party's support from the government (*El Nacional*, May 2, 1991).

44. In September 1991, the *ortodoxos* won 53 percent of the vote for party delegates to the national convention. Under the strong-arm leadership of Alfaro (and with the help of electoral rules that diluted the votes of the rank and file), they were able to transform this margin into 86 percent at the convention. As a result, they took control of all top party positions and the majority of secretariats (*Veneconomía*, September 1991, October 1991; Corrales 2002).

45. These costs would not have brought any policy benefits, moreover, because the Venezuelan Congress can overturn a veto with a simple majority (Crisp 1998, 2).

46. In a practice that became increasingly common under Pérez, AD labor leaders withheld their vote for subsequent delivery to the parliamentary leadership under protest. This option,

known as "vote-saving" *(salvar su voto),* enabled them to conform to party discipline while register-ing their objections to the outcome.

47. The proposed law never made it off the back burner during subsequent legislative sessions, largely because the government was thrown into crisis in 1992 by two attempted military coups (in February and November) and a dramatic rise in civil disobedience.

48. In the same vote, Congress approved Decree 1585, which raised the minimum wage but was much less controversial.

49. The alternative language, proposed by César Gil, would have committed Congress to ap-proving a general wage increase if the president did not decree a scaled pay raise ranging from 15 to 30 percent. This effort failed, however, because of a prior agreement among the parties *(Diario de Caracas,* May 30, 1991).

50. Javier Corrales, E-mail to author, August 1997. The party reinforced this unwritten pact in favor of labor mobilizations when it approved the participation of AD teachers in a national strike backed by the CTV (Urquijo and Bounilla 1992, 104).

51. Matos Azócar was expelled from AD for his act of indiscipline.

52. Several AD labor leaders avoided the pitfalls of this "double discourse" by remaining absent on the day of the vote, which earned them the congratulations of the labor secretary of COPEI *(El Nacional,* March 29, 1992).

53. Another incentive for AD to oppose Pérez was polling data showing that only 13 percent of the population identified themselves as *adecos* (Grindle 2000, 74).

54. For example, the value-added tax was never fully implemented under Velásquez and was partially repealed by the next administration (McCoy and Smith 1995, 138).

55. According to Hector Valecillos, union candidates did defect from AD at the local level to-ward the end of Pérez's administration. This outcome illustrates the greater punishing power of workers at the level of the firm.

Notes to Chapter 8

1. In Britain, these changes followed an episode of norm-breaking voice by unions in the Trade Unions Congress when they unleashed the so-called "Winter of Discontent" by staging wildcat strikes against the Labour government in the late 1970s. On the British case, see Dorey 1999; McIlroy 1998; Reid 2000; and Taylor 1993. On the Argentine case, see Levitsky 2003.

2. For example, UGT membership increased by 80 percent between 1987 and 1993 according to affiliation figures collected by Jacint Jordana (1996, 216). Although these gains can be partly at-tributed to the rapid job creation that accompanied Spain's economic boom in the late 1980s, most new workers during this period were on temporary contracts and therefore unlikely to join unions. Moreover, several studies suggest that factors linked to the UGT's assertiveness toward the PSOE and unity of action with the CCOO contributed to the increase. For more detail, see Burgess 1999, 16–17.

3. The PRI's plurality in the Chamber of Deputies was somewhat misleading, moreover, be-cause the PAN ran in a coalition with the Mexican Green Ecology Party and, together, they had 213 seats compared to 209 for the PRI (La Botz 2001).

4. For a detailed analysis of the impact of democratization on the Mexican labor movement, see Samstad 2002.

5. The PRI was also wracked by increasingly high-level defections, especially when party officials imposed their candidates for elected office without consulting the bases. For example, the PRD won its first governorship in 1998 when a PRI candidate rejected by the party hierarchy ran instead under the PRD banner.

6. Perhaps to encourage Fox's cooperation, they took steps to improve the CTM's corrupt image by announcing an investigation of eighty national union affiliates for the sale of protection con-tracts.

7. It should be noted that the CTM was not the only labor organization with a seat on the new Council, which also included the UNT (see note 9). James Samstad, E-mail to author, August 26, 2002.

8. They had less reason to be pleased, however, with the party's new secretary general, Elba Es-

ther Gordillo, who had been a thorn in the CTM's side as secretary general of the National Teachers' Union (SNTE).

9. The UNT grew out the Forum of Unionism Before the Nation *(Foro)*, which was created in September 1995 by a group of important unions, including the FESEBES, the SNTE, the Union of National Autonomous University of Mexico Workers (STUNAM), the National Social Security Workers' Union (SNTSS), and the Revolutionary Labor Confederation (COR). The *foristas* initially tried to promote democratization from within the CT, but they met with fierce resistance by the CT leadership (Samstad 2002).

10. Several important unions withdrew from the Assembly, but sixty other worker and peasant organizations indicated their desire to join the UNT in the following weeks *(Mexican Labor News and Analysis*, September 1997).

11. In a less momentous but similar development, eight federations claiming to represent 350 unions and 500,000 workers formed the National Alliance for Democratic Unionism (ANSD) in August 1998 to represent workers from small and medium-sized firms. Like the UNT, the ANSD committed itself to operating in a horizontal, democratic, and participatory fashion (National 1998).

12. The same unions organized another large demonstration against privatization of the electrical power industry in Mexico City in August 1999.

13. The success of the FNRCPIE's campaign and the election of Vicente Fox to the presidency inspired several major unions, including the SME, the STPRM, and the SNTE, to propose the creation of a new labor confederation that would act as a counterweight to both the CT and the UNT (Major 2000).

14. While the SME represents workers at Light and Power, which serves Mexico City and central Mexico, SUTERM represents workers at the Federal Electrical Commission, which serves the rest of the country.

15. These leaders include Alejandra Barrales of the UNT, who became a PRD deputy, and Bertha Luján, of the Authentic Labor Front (FAT), who became controller of the new PRD government of Mexico City. In Luján's case, FAT statutes required her to resign her post in the union (Bertha 2000). The FAT has played a leading role in forming cross-border alliances with U.S. unions and social movements, particularly since the NAFTA debate, and has had close ties with the PRD since the late 1980s.

16. While allowing for the exclusion clauses in collective contracts, the PRD proposal would require that union members vote to authorize their leaders to negotiate such clauses (Cook 1998, 16, n. 27).

17. Concerned by the administration's pro-business stance, the UNT sent its own proposal to Congress that called for replacing the JCAs with new labor courts, establishing a public registry of labor unions and collective bargaining agreements, and requiring unions to report their economic assets and activities (National 2002).

18. For example, during an interview with an official in the technical office of the Labor Ministry in 1994, I was informed that basic data on union membership was not public information.

19. The registry indicated that there were ninety-five thousand contracts on deposit with the JLCA, and that the CTM accounted for 45 percent of the unions and 70 percent of unionized workers in local jurisdiction activities in the Federal District (Federal 1999).

20. A report issued by the Labor Ministry several months after the May 1999 ruling indicated that 108 new unions had been registered in the public sector, with 56 belonging to the old labor federations and 52 registered as independent (New 1999).

21. Serious discussions of political decentralization began under Lusinchi, who created the Presidential Commission for Reform of the State (COPRE). The commission presented a set of proposals to Lusinchi in 1986, but no action was taken until Pérez expressed support for COPRE's recommendations during the presidential campaign in 1988 (Grindle 2000, 52–64).

22. For a detailed discussion of the struggle for control of SUTISS, see Ellner 1993, 153–62.

23. Caldera's vote share compared to 23.6 percent for Fermin (AD), 22.7 percent for Oswaldo Alvarez Paz (COPEI), and 22.0 percent for Velásquez (Causa R). His coalition, National Convergence, fared less well in the legislative elections, winning only 26 out of 203 seats in the Chamber

of Deputies and six out of 50 seats in the Senate (Political Database of the Americas 2001).

24. AD's share of governors and mayors fell, respectively, from 55 percent and 55.9 percent in 1989 to 31.8 percent and 42.9 percent in 1992 (Grindle 2000, 88).

25. AD's recent gains at the state level evaporated, leaving the party with only 34.8 percent of the governorships (Grindle 2000, 88). It still held the most governorships of any single party, however (Buxton 2000, 14).

26. AD expelled Alfaro from the party in late November 1998 for refusing to resign his candidacy and join AD in its support for Salas Romer (*El Nacional*, December 1, 1998).

27. The other remaining seats went to five opposition leaders and three representatives of indigenous groups. It is worth noting, however, that 54 percent of the electorate abstained, and 35 percent of the voters opposed Chávez but were too dispersed to win a comparable share of seats (Corrales 2000, 41).

28. *Poder ciudadano* includes the offices of public ombudsman, attorney general, and comptroller general (Corrales 2000, 45).

29. A group of former *adecos* formed a new party, National Encounter *(Encuentro Nacional)*, which supported the candidacy of Claudio Fermín for president. But Fermín received only 2.7 percent of the vote and subsequently returned to AD.

30. The CTV also agreed to eliminate the notorious "employment commissions" in oilworkers' unions that required each member to pay the union a share of his or her salary in return for securing employment (*El Nacional*, February 4, 1999).

31. The CTV never held the elections it had promised to have after reforming its statutes in April 1999. Originally scheduled for September 1999, the elections were postponed indefinitely after the National Electoral Council requested that the CTV wait until the new constitution went into effect (*El Mundo*, October 26, 2001).

32. It should be noted, however, that abstention rates were remarkably high for these elections, in which voters also selected local officials. Abstention was over 78 percent nationally and 85 percent in Caracas (*El Nacional,* December 4, 2000).

33. Venezuela's new constitution gives the CNE the authority to convene, organize, and supervise union elections.

34. Steve Ellner, E-mail to author, August 8, 2002.

35. One indication of the government's change of attitude was its acceptance of the Supreme Court's decision to designate Ortega as leader of Venezuela's most representative labor central and therefore the country's official delegate to the Ninetieth International Labor Conference (*El Nacional*, May 31, 2002).

36. Unless otherwise indicated, the discussion of the AIEE is based on Burgess 1999, 21–22.

37. A prime example is the telephone workers' union, which has been plagued by frequent accusations by dissident factions that Francisco Hernández Juárez has stifled internal democracy to perpetuate his long tenure as secretary-general.

38. For an interesting example of the fragmentation of Venezuela's neighborhood associations, see Ellner 1999a.

39. Parties or party factions have also participated in these alliances, but they are not the main organizers nor do they necessarily have other ties with the unions.

References

Acedo Angulo, Blanca Margarita. 1990. En la construcción y consolidación del estado cardenista. 1936–1940. In *Historia de la CTM: 1936–1990*, edited by Javier Aguilar García. México, DF: Instituto de Investigaciones Sociales, UNAM.

AD (Democratic Action Party). 1977. *Estatutos*. Caracas: Secretaria Nacional de Organización.

———. 1993. *Estatutos*. Caracas: Secretaria Nacional de Organización.

Aguilar Camin, Hector. 1988. *Después del milagro*. México, DF: Cal y arena.

Aguilar García, Javier, and Lorenzo Arrieta. 1990. En la fase más aguda de la crisis y en el inicio de la reestructuración o modernización. In *Historia de la CTM: 1936–1990*, edited by Javier Aguilar García. México, DF: Instituto de Investigaciones Sociales, UNAM.

Albarracín, Jesús. 1991. La política de los sindicatos y la dinámica del movimiento obrero. In *La reestructuración del capitalismo en España, 1970–1990*, edited by Miren Etxezarreta. Barcelona: ICARIA.

Aldrete-Haas, José A. 1991. *La deconstrucción del Estado Mexicano*. México, DF: Alianza Editorial.

Alonso, Enrique. 1991. Conflicto laboral y cambio social. In *Las relaciones laborales en España*, edited by Faustino Miguélez and Carlos Prieto. Madrid: Siglo veintiuno editores.

Alvarez Béjar, Alejandro. 1991. Economic Crisis and the Labor Movement in Mexico. In *Unions, Workers, and the State in Mexico*, edited by Kevin Middlebrook. La Jolla, Calif.: Center for U.S.–Mexican Studies, UCSD.

Alvarez, Sonia E., Evelina Dagnino, and Arturo Escobar, eds. 1998. *Cultures of Politics, Politics of Cultures: Re-Visioning Latin American Social Movements*. Boulder, Colo.: Westview Press.

Anuario El País, 1983–1992.

Arismendi, León, and Francisco Iturraspe. 1990. Sistemas electorales sindicales. In *Mandato político, evolución electoral, comunicación y sociedad*, edited by Manuel Vicente Magallanes. Caracas: Publicaciones del Consejo Supremo Electoral.

Arrieta, José Ignacio. 1984a. El pacto social: parto o aborto? *SIC* 47, no. 467: 301–4.

———. 1984b. Sindicatos, crisis, gobierno, empresarios. *SIC* 47, no. 470: 443–44.

Arter, David. 1994. "The War of the Roses": Conflict and Cohesion in the Swedish Social Democratic Party. In *Conflict and Cohesion in the Western European Social Democratic Parties*, edited by David Bell and Eric Shaw. London: Pinter Publishers.

Astudillo Ruiz, Javier. 1998. *Los recursos del socialismo: Las cambiantes relaciones entre el PSOE y la UGT (1982–1993)*. Madrid: Centro de Estudios Avanzados en Ciencias Sociales.

———. 2001. Without Unions, but Socialist: The Spanish Socialist Party and Its Divorce from Its Union Confederation (1982–1996). *Politics and Society* 29: 273–96.

Aziz Nassif, Alberto. 1989. *El Estado Mexicano y la CTM*. México, DF: Ediciones de la Casa Chata.

Bar, Antonio. 1988. Spain. In *Cabinets in Western Europe*, edited by Jean Blondel and Ferdinand Müller-Rommel. London: Macmillan.

Barry, Brian. 1974. Review Article: Exit, Voice, and Loyalty. *British Journal of Political Science* 4: 79–107.

Basañez, Miguel. 1990. *El pulso de los sexenios*. México, DF: Siglo veintiuno editores.

Baylos, Antonio. 1991. La intervención normativa del estado en materia de relaciones colectivas. In *Las relaciones laborales en España*, edited by Faustino Miguélez and Carlos Prieto. Madrid: Siglo veintiuno editores.

Benegas, José María. 1990. *La razón socialista*. Barcelona: Editorial Planeta.

Bennett, Brian Timothy. 1988. Recent U.S.–Mexico Trade Relations: Positive Results and Increased Cooperation. In *Mexico and the United States: Managing the Relationship*, edited by Riordan Roett. Boulder, Colo.: Westview Press.

Bensusan, Graciela. 1997. Estrategias sindicales y relaciones laborales frente al TLC: El caso de México. Paper presented at the 19th International Congress of the Latin American Studies Association, April 17–19, Guadalajara, Mexico.

Bensusan, Graciela, and Samuel León. 1990. *Negociación y conflicto laboral en México*. México, DF: Fundación Friedrich Ebert.

Bergquist, Charles. 1986. *Labor in Latin America*. Stanford: Stanford University Press.

Bermeo, Nancy. 1990. The Politics of Public Enterprise in Portugal, Spain, and Greece. In *The Political Economy of Public Sector Reform and Privatization*, edited by Ezra N. Suleiman and John Waterbury. Boulder, Colo.: Westview Press.

———. 1994. Sacrifice, Sequence and Strength in Successful Dual Transitions: Lessons from Spain. *Journal of Politics* 56: 601–27.

Bertha Lujan of FAT Becomes Controller in PRD Government in Mexico City. 2000. *Mexican News and Labor Analysis* 5, no. 9: on-line.

Bertranou, Julian. 1994. Decisiones públicas y formulación de políticas en el México contemporaneo. Tesis para obtener el grado de maestro, FLACSO.

Bizberg, Ilán. 1990. *Estado y sindicalismo en México*. México, DF: El Colegio de México.

Blank, David Eugene. 1984. *Venezuela: Politics in a Petroleum Republic*. New York: Praeger.

Blinkhorn, Martin. 1990. Spain. In *The Working Class and Politics in Europe and America, 1929–1945*, edited by Stephen Salter and John Stevenson. London: Longman.

Boeckh, Andreas. 1972. Organized Labor and Government under Conditions of Scarcity: The Case of Venezuela. Ph.D. diss., University of Florida.

Bolivar Espinoza, Agusto, and Luis Antonio F. Bonifaz Moreno. 1992. Las reformas constitucionales. *El Cotidiano* 50: 36–43.

Bonime, Andrea R. 1985. The Spanish State Structure: Constitution Making and the Creation of the New State. In *Politics and Change in Spain*, edited by Thomas D. Lancaster and Gary Prevost. New York: Praeger.

Bouza, Fermín et al. 1989. *Perfil, actitudes y demandas del delegado y afiliado a UGT*. Madrid: Fundación Largo Caballero.

Brenan, Gerald. 1978. *The Spanish Labyrinth*. Cambridge: Cambridge University Press.

Burgess, Katrina. 1995. Un divorcio a medias: reforma económica y políticas laborales en España. *Política y gobierno* 2: 207–42.

———. 1998. Alliances under Stress: Economic Reform and Party-Union Relations in Mexico, Spain, and Venezuela. Ph.D. diss., Princeton University.

———. 1999. Unemployment and Union Strategies in Spain. *South European Politics and Society* 4: 1–31.

Buxton, Julia. 2000. Realignment of the Party System in Venezuela? Paper presented at the 22nd International Congress of the Latin American Studies Association, Hyatt Regency Hotel, Miami, Florida, March 16–18.

Calvo, Mauricio. 1990. Análisis de los factores que han permitido acuerdos en la concertación. *Claridad* 35/36: 63–69.

Camacho, Manuel. 1980. *El futuro inmediato*. Edited by Pablo González Casanova. Vol. 15, *La clase obrera en la historia de México*. México, DF: Siglo Veintiuno Editores.

Campos, Angel, and José Manuel Alvarez. 1990. *Ayer, hoy y mañana del 14-D*. Madrid: Comisiones Obreras.

Cerny, Philip G. 1990. *The Changing Architecture of Politics: Structure, Agency, and the Future of the State*. London: Sage Publications.

Chalmers, Douglas A., Scott B. Martin, and Kerianne Piester. 1997. Associative Networks: New Structures of Representation for the Popular Sectors? In *The New Politics of Inequality in Latin America*, edited by Douglas A. Chalmers, Scott B. Martin, Kerianne Piester, Carlos M. Vilas, Katherine Hite, and Monique Segarra. New York: Oxford University Press.

Chávez, C. R. 1988. *Dos líderes, dos tormentas*. Caracas: Imprenta Nacional y Gaceta Oficial.

CNE (National Electoral Council). 2001. Elecciones Sindicales. [database online]. <http://www.cne.gov.ve/Elecc_sindicales.asp>.

Collier, Ruth Berins, and David Collier. 1979. Inducements versus Constraints: Disaggregating Corporatism. *American Political Science Review* 73: 967–86.

———. 1991. *Shaping the Political Arena*. Princeton, N.J.: Princeton University Press.

Cook, Maria Lorena. 1998. The Politics of Labor Law Reform: Comparative Perspectives on the Mexican Case. Paper presented at the 20th International Congress of the Latin American Studies Association, Chicago, Illinois, September 24–26.

Coppedge, Michael. 1993. Parties and Society in Mexico and Venezuela: Why Competition Matters. *Comparative Politics*, 25: 253–74.

———. 1994. *Strong Parties and Lame Ducks*. Stanford: Stanford University Press.

Corbo, Vittorio. 2000. Economic Policy Reform in Latin America. In *Economic Policy Reform: The Second Stage*, edited by Anne Krueger. Chicago: University of Chicago Press.

Cordoba, José. 1994. In *The Political Economy of Policy Reform*, edited by John Williamson. Washington, D.C.: Institute for International Economics.

Corona Armenta, Gabriel. 1995. La burocracia sindical mexicana ante la sucesión presidencial: los procesos recientes. *Estudios Políticos* Nueva Época 8: 128–42.

Corrales, Javier. 1997. El presidente y su gente: cooperación y conflicto entre los ámbitos técnicos y políticos en Venezuela, 1989–1993. *Nueva Sociedad*, November–December: 93–107.

———. 2000. Hugo Chávez Plays Simon Says: Democracy without Opposition in Venezuela. *Hopscotch: A Cultural Review* 2: 38–49.

———. 2002. *Presidents without Parties. Economic Reforms in Argentina and Venezuela in the 1990s*. University Park, Pa.: Penn State Press.

Corriente Democrática. 1989. Documentos de Trabajo No. 1. In *Las elecciones de 1988 y la crisis del sistema político*, edited by Jaime González Graf. Mexico, DF: Editorial Diana.

Corro, Salvador, and José Reveles. 1994. *La Quina: El lado oscuro del poder*. México, DF: Editorial Planeta Mexicana.

Crisp, Brian. 1998. Presidential Decree Authority in Venezuela. In *Executive Decree Authority*, edited by John M. Carey and Matthew Soberg Shugart. New York: Cambridge University Press.

CSE (Commission for Monitoring and Evaluation). 1994. *Pacto para el bienestar, la estabilidad y el crecimiento y sus antecedentes, 1987–1994*. México, DF: Comisión de Seguimiento y Evaluación del Pacto para el Bienestar, la Estabilidad y el Crecimiento.

CTM (Confederation of Mexican Workers). 1942. Informe del Comite Nacional de la C.T.M. Al Primer Congreso Nacional Ordinario de la misma. In *C.T.M. 1936–1941*. México, DF: Talleres Tipográficas Modelo.

———. 1986a. Informe de la Secretaría General, No. 212. In *CTM: Cincuenta años de lucha obrera*. México, DF: Instituto de Capacitación Política, PRI.

———. 1986b. Dictamen sobre el punto 10 del temario de la convocatoria: la CTM y el PRI, No. 273. In *CTM: Cincuenta años de lucha obrera*. México, DF: Instituto de Capacitación Política, PRI.

———. 1986c. Congreso Nacional de Empresas y Organismos de Sector Social. In *CTM: Cincuenta años de lucha obrera*. México, DF: Instituto de Capacitación Política, PRI.

CTV (Confederation of Venezuelan Workers). 1987a. Informe del Comite Sindical Unitario Nacional al III Congreso de Trabajadores, Documento No. 5. In *Antecedentes y testimonios de los congresos de la CTV*. Caracas: Inaesin/Ildis.

———. 1987b. III Congreso de Trabajadores de Venezuela: Declaración de Principios. In *Antecedentes y testimonios de los congresos de la CTV, Documento No. 4*. Caracas: Inaesin/ILDIS.

————. 1987c. Discurso del Presidente de la Confederación de Trabajadores de Venzuela (C.T.V.) Juan José Delpino, Capítulo II, Documento No. 6. In *Antecedentes y testimonios de los congresos de la CTV*. Caracas: Inaesin/ILDIS.

————. 1990. Manifiesto de Soberanía. *Revista de Investigaciones sobre Relaciones Industriales y Laborales* 26.

Dalton, Russell J. 1999. Reflections on the Historical Development of Class Voting in OECD Party Systems. Paper presented at the Workshop on Political Parties and Working Class Constituencies, May 1, at University of California, Berkeley.

Dávila Capalleja, Enrique Rafael. 1997. Mexico: The Evolution and Reform of the Labor Market. In *Labor Markets in Latin America*, edited by Sebastian Edwards and Nora Lustig. Washington, D.C.: The Brookings Institution Press.

Davis, Charles L. 1989. *Working-Class Mobilization and Political Control*. Lexington: University Press of Kentucky.

De la Garza Toledo, Enrique. 1993. *Reestructuración productiva y respuesta sindical en México*. Mexico, DF: Universidad Nacional Autónoma de México.

Dehesa, Guillermo. 1994. Spain. In *The Political Economy of Reform*, edited by John Williamson. Washington, D.C.: Institute for International Economics.

Deutsch, Haydée. 2001. Elecciones sindicales en Venezuela 2001 [online]. Coordinadora Democrática de Acción Cívica. <http://www.geocities.com/caciv_ve/hd_sindicat.htm>.

Díaz, Rolando. 2002. Revolución sin sindicatos? [online]. Portal Latinoamericano en Globalización.<http://www.globalizacion.org/venezuela/SindicatosVzDiaz.htm>.

Díaz-Varela, Mar, and Mariano Guindal. 1990. *A la sombra del poder*. Barcelona: Tibidabo Actualidad.

Documentos. 1990. *Revista de investigaciones sobre relaciones industriales y laborales* 26: 99–150.

Donaghy, Peter J., and Michael T. Newton. 1987. *Spain: A Guide to Political and Economic Institutions*. Cambridge: Cambridge University Press.

Dorey, Peter. 1999. The Blairite Betrayal: New Labour and the Trade Unions. In *The Impact of New Labour*, edited by Gerald R. Taylor. New York: St. Martin's Press.

Durand Ponte, Victor Manuel. 1991. The Confederation of Mexican Workers, the Labor Congress, and the Crisis of Mexico's Social Pact. In *Unions, Workers, and the State in Mexico*, edited by Kevin Middlebrook. La Jolla, Calif.: Center for U.S.–Mexican Studies, UCSD.

Eguiagaray Ucelay, Juan Manuel. 2002. Ecos de una huelga general. *Cinco Días*, June 3.

Electrical Workers and Allies March against Privatization of Electric Power Industry. 1999. *Mexican Labor News and Analysis* 4, no. 13: on-line.

Ellner, Steve. 1980. Los partidos políticos y su disputa por el control del movimiento sindical en Venezuela, 1936–1948. Caracas: Universidad Catolica Andres Bello.

————. 1993. *Organized Labor in Venezuela, 1958–1991*. Wilmington, Del.: Scholarly Resources.

————. 1996. Political Party Factionalism and Democracy in Venezuela. *Latin American Perspectives* 23: 87–109.

————. 1999a. Obstacles to the Consolidation of the Venezuelan Neighborhood Movement. *Journal of Latin American Studies* 31: 75–97.

————. 1999b. The Impact of Privatization on Labor in Venezuela. *Political Power and Social Theory* 13: 109–45.

Encarnación, Omar. 2001. Civil Society and the Consolidation of Democracy in Spain. *Political Science Quarterly* 116: 53–79.

Escobar, Arturo, and Sonia E. Alvarez, eds. 1992. *The Making of Social Movements in Latin America*. Boulder, Colo.: Westview Press.

Escobar, Modesto. 1993. Works or Union Councils? The Representative System in Medium and Large Sized Spanish Firms. Estudio/Working Paper 1993/43. Madrid: Instituto Juan March.

España, Luis Pedro. 1989. El futuro político de las minorias partidistas. *SIC* 52, no. 511: 13–15.

Espina, Alvaro. 1991. Trade Unions and Spanish Democracy. In *Social Concertation, Neocorporatism and Democracy*, edited by Alvaro Espina. Madrid: Ministerio de Trabajo y Seguridad Social.

Esping-Andersen, Gøsta. 1985. *Politics against Markets*. Princeton, N.J.: Princeton University Press.

Estatuto del trabajador. 1980. Madrid: Grafex, S.A.

Ewell, Judith. 1984. *Venezuela: A Century of Change.* London: C. Hurst and Company.

Fagan, Stuart. 1977. The Venezuelan Labor Movement: A Study in Political Unionism. Ph.D. diss., University of California, Berkeley.

Fajardo Cortez, Victor, and Miguel Lacabana. 1993. Programa de ajuste y reestructuración del mercado de trabajo. In *II Congreso Americano de Relaciones de Trabajo,* edited by Hector Lucena. Caracas: Universidad de Carabobo.

Febres, Carlos Eduardo. 1985. El movimiento sindical: ¿Actor social o gestor institucional? In *El caso venezolano: Una ilusión de armonía,* edited by Moisés Naím and Ramon Piñango. Caracas: IESA.

Federal District Creates Union Register to Prevent Phoney Unions, Contracts. 1999. *Mexican Labor News and Analysis* 4, no. 15: on-line.

Fernández Marugán, Francisco. 1992. La década de los ochenta: Impulso y reforma económica. In *La década del cambio,* edited by Alfonso Guerra and José Felix Tezanos. Madrid: Editorial Sistema.

Fundación FIES. 1985. Representatividad y organización de CCOO y UGT: Una comparación europea. *Papeles de economía española* 22: 235–43.

Fishman, Robert. 1984. El movimiento obrero en la transición. *Revista Española de Investigaciones Sociológicas* 26: 61–112.

———. 1990. *Working-Class Organization and the Return to Democracy in Spain.* Ithaca, N.Y.: Cornell University Press.

Foweraker, Joe. 1987. Corporatist Strategies and the Transition to Democracy in Spain. *Comparative Politics* 20: 57–72.

———. 1995. *Theorizing Social Movements.* London: Pluto Press.

Fox Praises CTM Old Guard. 2001a. *Mexican Labor News and Analysis* 6, no. 3: on-line.

Fox to Continue Pacts, Wage Ceilings. 2001b. *Mexican Labor News and Analysis* 6, no. 3: on-line.

Franco, G. S., and J. Fernando. 1991. Labor Law and the Labor Movement in Mexico. In *Unions, Workers, and the State in Mexico,* edited by Kevin Middlebrook. La Jolla, Calif.: Center for U.S.–Mexican Studies, UCSD.

Fülnei, Ilse Marie. 1996. *Los sindicatos en España.* Madrid: Consejo Económico y Social.

Garrido, Luis Javier. 1982. *El Partido de la Revolución Institucionalizada.* México, DF: Siglo Veintiuno Editores.

———. 1993. *La ruptura: La Corriente Democrática del PRI.* Mexico, DF: Grijalbo.

Gillespie, Richard. 1989. *The Spanish Socialist Party.* Oxford: Clarendon Press.

———. 1990. The Break-up of the "Socialist Family": Party-Union Relations in Spain, 1982–89. *West European Politics* 13: 47–62.

———. 1992. Factionalism in the Spanish Socialist Party. Barcelona: Institut de Ciències Polítiques i Socials.

Godio, Julio. 1985. *El movimiento obrero Venezolano, 1945–1964.* Caracas: ILDIS.

González Casanova, Pablo. 1981. *El estado y los partidos políticos en México.* México, DF: Ediciones Era.

Gourevitch, Peter, Andrew Martin, George Ross, Christopher Allen, Steven Bornstein, and Andrei Markovits. 1984. *Unions and Economic Crisis: Britain, West Germany and Sweden.* London: George Allen and Unwin.

Grayson, George. 1989. *The Mexican Labor Machine.* Washington, D.C.: CSIS.

———. 1998. *From Corporatism to Pluralism.* Forth Worth, Tex.: Harcourt Brace Publishers.

———, ed. 1990. *Prospects for Democracy in Mexico.* New Brunswick, N.J.: Transaction Publishers.

Gregory, Peter. 1986. *The Myth of Market.* Washington, D.C.: The World Bank.

Grindle, Merilee. 2000. *Audacious Reforms: Institutional Invention and Democracy in Latin America.* Baltimore: The Johns Hopkins University Press.

Guevara, Pedro. 1989. *Concertación y conflicto.* Caracas: Universidad Central de Venezuela, Facultad de Ciencias Jurídicas y Políticas, Escuela de Estudios Políticos y Administrativos.

Guindal, Mariano, and Rodolfo Serrano. 1986. *La otra transición.* Madrid: Unión Editorial.

Gunther, Richard, Giacomo Sani, and Goldie Shabad. 1986. *Spain after Franco: The Making of a Competitive Party System*. Berkeley: University of California Press.

Gutiérrez, José Luis, and Amando de Miguel. 1990. *La ambición del César*. Madrid: Ediciones Temas de Hoy.

Hagopian, Frances. 1998. Democracy and Political Representation in Latin America in the 1990s: Pause, Reorganization, or Decline? In *Fault Lines of Democracy in Post-Transition Latin America*, edited by Felipe Agüero and Jeffrey Stark. Miami: North-South Center Press.

Hamann, Kerstin. 1994. Regime Change and Public Policy: Labor Legislation in Spain, 1970–1990. Ph.D. diss., Washington University.

Hamilton, Nora. 1982. *The Limits of State Autonomy*. Princeton, N.J.: Princeton University Press.

Hellinger, Daniel. 1991. *Venezuela: Tarnished Democracy*. Boulder, Colo.: Westview Press.

Hernández Alvarez, Oscar. 1990. La propuesta de concertación social y sus perspectivas. In *Las relaciones de trabajo en los noventa*, edited by Hector Lucena. Caracas: ILDIS.

————. 1993. La privatización y sus efectos en las relaciones laborales. Paper presented at the Segundo Congreso Americano de Relaciones de Trabajo, Valencia, Venezuela.

Hernández Juárez, Head of UNT, Resigns From PRI. 2002. *Mexican Labor News and Analysis* 7, no. 3: on-line.

Hernández Rodríguez, Rogelio. 1991. La reforma interna y los conflictos en el PRI. *Foro Internacional* 32: 222–49.

Heywood, Paul. 1987. Mirror Images: The PCE and the PSOE in the Transition to Democracy. *West European Politics* 10: 193–210.

Hirschman, Albert. 1970. *Exit, Voice, and Loyalty*. Cambridge, Mass.: Harvard University Press.

Howell, Chris. 1992–93. Family or Just Good Friends? The Changing Labour Party-Trade Union Relationship in Britain since 1979. *International Journal of Political Economy* 22: 17–35.

Howell, Chris, and Anthony Daley. 1992–93. The Transformation of Political Exchange. *International Journal of Political Economy* 22: 3–16.

IDB (Inter-American Development Bank). 1997. *Latin American After a Decade of Reforms: Economic and Social Progress*. Washington, D.C.: Inter-American Development Bank.

ILO (International Labour Organization). 1997–98. *World Labour Report*. Geneva: International Labour Organization.

INEGI (National Institute of Geographic and Statistical Information). 1995. *Anuario estadístico*. México, DF: Instituto Nacional de Estadística, Geografía e Informática.

————. 2000. *Anuario estadístico*. México, DF: Instituto Nacional de Estadística, Geografía e Informática.

Iranzo, Consuelo. 1991. La política de reconversión y el sector laboral. *Cuadernos de CENDES* 17/18 (April–December): 67–90.

Iturraspe, Francisco. 1993. Sindicatos y crisis política y social en Venezuela. *Politeia* 16: 269–82.

Jenson, Jane, and Rianne Mahon. 1993. Representing Solidarity: Class, Gender and the Crisis in Social-Democratic Sweden. *New Left Review* 201: 76–100.

Jordana, Jacint. 1996. Reconsidering Union Membership in Spain, 1977–1994: Halting Decline in a Context of Democratic Consolidation. *Industrial Relations Journal* 27: 211–24.

Karl, Terry. 1982. The Political Economy of Petrodollars: Oil and Democracy in Venezuela. Ph.D. diss., Stanford University.

Kaufman, Robert R., Carlos Bazdresch, and Blanca Heredia. 1994. Mexico: Radical Reform in a Dominant Party System. In *Voting for Reform*, edited by Stephan Haggard and Steven B. Webb. New York: Oxford University Press.

Kelley, R. Lynn. 1986. Venezuela Constitutional Forms and Realities. In *Venezuela: The Democratic Experience*, edited by John D. Martz and David J. Myers. New York: Praeger.

Kitschelt, Herbert. 1990. New Social Movements and the Decline of Party Organization. In *Challenging the Political Order*, edited by Russell J. Dalton and Manfred Kuechler. New York: Oxford University Press.

————. 1994. *The Transformation of European Social Democracy*. Cambridge: Cambridge University Press.

Klesner, Joseph L. 1987. Changing Patterns of Electoral Participation and Official Party Support in

Mexico. In *Mexican Politics in Transition*, edited by Judith Gentleman. Boulder, Colo.: Westview Press.

Koelble, Thomas A. 1991. *The Left Unraveled: Social Democracy and the New Left Challenge in Britain and West Germany*. Durham, N.C.: Duke University Press.

Köhler, Holm-Detlev. 1995. *El movimiento sindical en España*. Madrid: Editorial Fundamentos.

Kornblith, Miriam. 1991. Constitutions and Democracy in Venezuela. *Journal of Latin American Studies* 23: 61–89.

———. 1995. Public Sector and Private Sector: New Rules of the Game. In *Venezuelan Democracy under Stress*, edited by Jennifer McCoy et al. New Brunswick, N.J.: Transaction Publishers.

Kornblith, Miriam, and Daniel H. Levine. 1993. Venezuela: The Life and Times of the Party System. In *Building Democratic Institutions: Party Systems in Latin America*, edited by Scott Mainwaring and Timothy R. Scully. Stanford: Stanford University Press.

Krasner, Stephen D. 1983. Regimes and the Limits of Realism. In *International Regimes*, edited by Stephen D. Krasner. Ithaca, N.Y.: Cornell University Press.

La Botz, Dan. 1992. *Mask of Democracy*. Boston: South End Press.

———. 2001. Mexico's Labor Year in Review: 2000—The End of the System, The Beginning of the Future. *Mexican Labor News and Analysis* 6, no. 1: on-line.

La Botz, Dan, and Sam Smucker. 1997. National Workers' Assembly Decides to Establish New Labor Federation. *Mexican Labor News and Analysis* 2, no. 17: on-line.

Lander, Edgardo. 1996. The Impact of Neoliberal Adjustment in Venezuela, 1989–1993. *Latin American Perspectives* 23: 50–73.

Langston, Joy. 2001. Why Rules Matter: Changes in Candidate Selection in Mexico's PRI, 1988–2000. *Journal of Latin American Studies* 33: 485–511.

Larrañaga V., Juan Carlos n.d. Venezuela Competitiva: Legislación, Sindicatos y Relaciones Laborales. Caracas.

Lazcano, José A. 1989. Los números electorales. *SIC* 52, no. 511: 4–7.

Lechner, Norbert. 1998. The Transformation of Politics. In *Fault Lines of Democracy in Post-Transition Latin America*, edited by Felipe Agüero and Jeffrey Stark. Miami: North-South Center Press.

Levine, Daniel M. 1978. Venezuela since 1958: The Consolidation of Democratic Politics. In *The Breakdown of Democratic Regimes: Latin America*, edited by Juan J. Linz and Alfred Stepan. Baltimore: The Johns Hopkins University Press.

Levitsky, Steven. 2003. *Transforming Labor-Based Parties in Latin America: Argentine Peronism in Comparative Perspective*. New York: Cambridge University Press.

Levitsky, Steven, and Lucan Way. 1998. Between a Shock and a Hard Place. *Comparative Politics* 30: 171–92.

LFT (Federal Labor Law). 1931. México, DF: Ediciones Botas.

———. 1990. México, DF: Editorial Alco.

López, Mussot, María Luisa, and Guadalupe González Cruz. 1990. En la posguerra. Reestructuración de la CTM y formación de un nuevo proyecto sindical. 1947–1952. In *Historia de la CTM: 1936–1990*, edited by Javier Aguilar García. México, DF: Instituto de Investigaciones Sociales, UNAM.

López Maya, Margarita, Luis Gómez Calcaño, and Thaís Maingón. 1989. *De Punto Fijo al pacto social*. Caracas: Fondo Editorial Acta Científica Venezolana.

López Maya, Margarita, and Nikolaus Werz. 1981. *El estado y el movimiento sindical (1958–1980)*. Caracas: Ediciones CENDES.

López Villegas, Virginia. 1990. El periodo de la unidad nacional y de la segunda guerra mundial. In *Historia de la CTM: 1936–1990*, edited by Javier Aguilar García. México, DF: Instituto de Investigaciones Sociales, UNAM.

Lopez-Claros, Augusto. 1988. *The Search for Efficiency in the Adjustment Process*. Washington, D.C.: International Monetary Fund.

Lowenthal, Abraham F. 2000. Latin American at the Century's Turn. *Journal of Democracy* 11: 41–55.

Lucena, Hector. 1982. *El movimiento obrero petrolero*. Caracas: Ediciones Centauro.

Lustig, Nora. 1998. *The Remaking of an Economy.* 2d ed. Washington, D.C.: The Brookings Institution Press.

Madrid, Raul. 2003. Laboring against Neoliberalism: Unions and Patterns of Reform in Latin America. *Journal of Latin American Studies* 35: 53–88.

Mainwaring, Scott, and Timothy R. Scully. 1995. Introduction to *Building Democratic Institutions: Party Systems in Latin America*, edited by Scott Mainwaring and Timothy R. Scully. Stanford: Stanford University Press.

Major Mexican Unions Plan to Create New Labor Federation. 2000. *Mexican Labor News and Analysis* 5, no. 6: on-line.

Maravall, José María. 1978. *Dictadura y disentimiento político: obreros y estudiantes bajo el franquismo.* Madrid: Ediciones Alfaguara.

———. 1992. From Opposition to Government: The Politics and Policies of the PSOE. In *Socialist Parties in Europe*, edited by José María Maravall et al. Barcelona: Institut de Ciencies Politiques i Socials.

Marks, Gary. 1989. *Unions in Politics: Britain, Germany, and the United States in the Nineteenth and Early Twentieth Centuries.* Princeton, N.J.: Princeton University Press.

Márquez, Gustavo. 1995. Venezuela: Poverty and Social Policies in the 1980s. In *Coping with Austerity: Poverty and Inequality in Latin America*, edited by Nora Lustig. Washington, D.C.: The Brookings Institution Press.

Martínez Lucio, Miguel. 1992. Spain: Constructing Institutions and Actors in a Context of Change. In *Industrial Relations in the New Europe*, edited by Anthon Ferner and Richard Hyman. Oxford: Basil Blackwell.

Martz, John. 1966. *Acción Democrática: Evolution of a Modern Political Party in Venezuela.* Princeton, N.J.: Princeton University Press.

Mateos López, Abdón. 1986. Sindicalismo socialista y movimiento obrero durante la dictadura franquista (1939–1976). In *El socialismo en España*, edited by Santos Juliá. Madrid: Editorial Pablo Iglesias.

McCoy, Jennifer. 1988. Las consecuencias de la política de ajuste en las relaciones de trabajo en Venezuela. *Revista Relaciones de Trabajo* 10/11: 204–26.

———. 1989. Labor and the State in a Party-Mediated Democracy. *Latin American Research Review* 24: 35–67.

———. 1999. Chavez and the End of Partyarchy in Venezuela. *Journal of Democracy* 10: 64–77.

McCoy, Jennifer, Andrés Serbin, William C. Smith, and Andrés Stambouli, eds. 1995. *Venezuelan Democracy under Stress.* New Brunswick, N.J.: Transaction Publishers.

McCoy, Jennifer, and William C. Smith. 1995. Democratic Disequilibrium in Venezuela. *Journal of Interamerican Studies and World Affairs* 37: 113–79.

McIlroy, John. 1998. The Enduring Alliance? Trade Unions and the Making of New Labour, 1994–1997. *British Journal of Industrial Relations* 36: 537–64.

Medina, Luis. 1978. Del Cardenismo al Avilacamachismo. Volume 18, *Historia de la Revolución Mexicana.* México, DF: El Colegio de México.

———. 1979. Civilismo y modernización del autoritarismo. Vol. 20, *Historia de la Revolución Mexicana.* México, DF: El Colegio de México.

Mendez, Luís, and José Othón Quiroz. 1993. El proyecto cetemista y la modernidad laboral. *El Cotidiano* 56: 8–17.

Mesa-Lago, Carmelo. 1978. *Social Security in Latin America.* Pittsburgh: University of Pittsburgh Press.

Mexican News and Labor Analysis. On-line at <http://www.ueinternational.org>.

Mexican Supreme Court Rules Rodríguez Alcaine Must Repay Two Billion Pesos to Union Welfare Fund. 2000. *Mexican Labor News and Analysis* 5, no. 8: on-line.

Mexican Supreme Court Rules that Workers Have Right to Organize Independent Unions in the Public Sector. 1999. *Mexican Labor News and Analysis* 4, no. 10: on-line.

Mexican Workers March on May Day against Fox, Abascal. 2002. *Mexican Labor News and Analysis* 7, no. 4: on-line.

Middlebrook, Kevin. 1981. Political Change and Political Reform in an Authoritarian Regime: The Case of Mexico. Washington, D.C.: Latin American Program of the Woodrow Wilson International Center for Scholars, Smithsonian Institution.

———. 1989. The Sounds of Silence: Organized Labor's Response to Economic Crisis in Mexico. *Journal of Latin American Studies* 21: 195–220.

———. 1995. *The Paradox of Revolution*. Baltimore: The Johns Hopkins University Press.

Miguélez Lobo, Faustino. 1991. Las organizaciones sindicales. In *Las relaciones laborales en España*, edited by Faustino Miguélez and Carlos Prieto. Madrid: Siglo veintiuno editores.

MTAS (Ministry of Labor and Social Affairs). 1982–1996 *Anuario de estadísticas laborales y de asuntos sociales*.

———. 2002. *Boletín de estadísticas laborales*.

MTSS (Ministry of Labor and Social Security). 1983–1992. *Anuario de estadísticas laborales*.

Murillo, María Victoria. 2001. *Labor Unions, Partisan Coalitions, and Market Reforms in Latin America*. New York: Cambridge University Press.

Myers, David J. 1986. The Venezuelan Party System: Regime Maintenance under Stress. In *Venezuela: The Democratic Experience*, edited by John D. Martz and David J. Myers. New York: Praeger.

Nacional Financiera. 1995. La economía mexicana en cifras. México, DF.

Naím, Moisés. 1993. *Paper Tigers and Minotaurs: The Politics of Venezuela's Economic Reforms*. Washington, D.C.: The Carnegie Endowment.

Nájera, Aurelio Martín, and Antonio González Quintana, eds. 1998. *Fuentes para la historia de la Unión General de Trabajadores*. Madrid: Editorial Pablo Iglesias.

National Alliance of Unionism (ANSD) Founded to Represent Workers in Small and Medium Sized Industry. 1998. *Mexican Labor News and Analysis* 3, no. 14: on-line.

National Union of Workers (UNT) Calls for Alternative Economic Agenda. 1999. *Mexican Labor News and Analysis* 4, no. 14: on-line.

National Union of Workers (UNT) Shifts Debate on Labor Law. 2002. *Mexican Labor News and Analysis* 7, no. 5: on-line.

Navarro, Juan Carlos. 1994. Reversal of Fortune: The Ephemeral Success of Adjustment in Venezuela Between 1989 and 1993. Working paper, Caracas.

Navarro, Miguel. 1990. *Política reconversión: Balance crítico*. Madrid: Eudema.

New Unions Proliferate in Public Sector as Result of Supreme Court Decision. 1999. *Mexican Labor News and Analysis* 4, no. 14: on-line.

Offe, Claus. 1987. Challenging the Boundaries of Institutional Politics: Social Movements since the 1960s. In *Changing Boundaries of the Political*, edited by Charles S. Maier. Cambridge: Cambridge University Press.

OIT (International Labour Organization). 1991. Informe de la Misión de la Oficina International del Trabajo sobre el diagnóstico de la relaciones laborales en Venezuela. Geneva: Oficina Internacional del Trabajo.

Ortega, Max, and Ana Alicia Solís. 1990. Estado, capital y sindicatos. In *Los saldos del sexenio*, edited by Esthela Gutiérrez Garza. México, DF: Siglo Veintiuno Editores.

Pacheco, Guadalupe. 1991. La XIV Asamblea Nacional del PRI. *Estudios Políticos* 3, Octubre–Diciembre: 71–88.

Palacio Morena, Juan Ignacio. 1991. La política de empleo. In *Las relaciones laborales en España*, edited by Faustino Miguélez and Carlos Prieto. Madrid: Siglo veintiuno editores.

Palma, Pedro A. 1989. La economía venezolana en el período 1974–1988. In *Venezuela contemporanea, 1974–1989*. Caracas: Fundación Eugenio Mendoza.

PAN (National Action Party). 1995. Iniciativa de decreto que reforma la Ley Federal del Trabajo. México, DF: Partido de Acción Nacional.

Paralelismo o subversión en la CTV. 1984. *SIC* 47, no. 467: 301–4.

Paramio, Ludolfo. 1992. Los sindicatos y la política en España, 1982–1992. In *La década del cambio*, edited by Alfonso Guerra and José Felix Tezanos. Madrid: Editorial Sistema.

Party of Democratic Revolution (PRD) and National Union of Workers (UNT) Form Alliance. 2001. *Mexican Labor News and Analysis* 6, no. 2: on-line.

Pascual Moncayo, Pablo, and Raúl Trejo Delarbre. 1993. *Los sindicatos mexicanos ante el TLC*. México, DF: Sindicato Nacional de Trabajadores de la Educación.

Pérez Ledesma, Manuel. 1987. *El obrero consciente*. Madrid: Alianza Editorial.

Pérez-Díaz, Victor. 1979. Elecciones sindicales, afiliación y vida sindical local de los obreros españoles de hoy. *Revista Española de Investigaciones Sociológicas* 6: 11–52.

————. 1987. *Retorno de la sociedad civil*. Madrid: Instituto de Estudios Económicos.

Pereznieto Castro, Leonel. 1990. Algunos cambios probables en los estatutos del PRI, de acuerdo a las resoluciones de la XIV Asamblea Nacional. In *El partido en el poder*. México, DF: IEPES, PRI.

Piore, Michael J., and Charles F. Sabel. 1984. *The Second Industrial Divide*. New York: Basic Books.

Pizzorno, Alessandro. 1978. Political Exchange and Collective Identity in Industrial Conflict. In *The Resurgence of Class Conflict in Western Europe since 1968*, edited by Colin Crouch and Alessandro Pizzorno. New York: Holmes and Meier Publishers.

Political Database of the Americas. 2001. Venezuela: Electoral Results [database online]. Georgetown University and Organization of American States. <http://www.georgetown.edu/pdba/Elecdata/Venezuela/ven.html>.

Pontusson, Jonas. 1992. Introduction to *Bargaining for Change*, edited by Miriam Golden and Jonas Pontusson. Ithaca, N.Y.: Cornell University Press.

————. 1994. Sweden: After the Golden Age. In *Mapping the West European Left*, edited by Perry Anderson and Patrick Camiller. New York: Verso.

PRI (Institutional Revolutionary Party). 1981. *Historia documental*. Vol. 5. Mexico, DF: Partido Revolucionario Institucional.

————. 1982a. Pacto de las centrales que constituyen el PRI. In *Historia documental del Partido de la Revolución*. México, DF: Instituto de Capacitación Política, PRI.

————. 1982b. Declaración de Principios, Programa de Acción y Estatutos del PRI. In *Historia documental del Partido de la Revolución*. México, DF: Instituto de Capacitación Política, PRI.

Prieto, Carlos. 1994. Sindicalismo. In *Tendencias sociales en España*, edited by Salustiano del Campo. Bilbao: Fundación BBV.

Progressive Step for Mexican Labor. 1997. *Mexican Labor News and Analysis* 2, no. 22: on-line.

Przeworski, Adam, and John Sprague. 1986. *Paper Stones*. Chicago: University of Chicago Press.

PSOE (Spanish Socialist Workers' Party). 1978. Estrategia sindical del PSOE.

————. 1981. Anexo del Acta del 29 Congreso.

————. 1983. Informe elecciones sindicales 1982.

————. 1984. Resoluciones, 30 Congreso.

————. 1990. 32 Congreso Federal: Resoluciones.

Puhle, Hans-Jurgen. 1986. El PSOE: Un partido predominante y heterogeneo. In *Crisis y cambio*, edited by Juan J. Linz and José R. Montero. Madrid: Centro de Estudios Constitucionales.

Ramírez Cuéllar, Héctor. 1992. *Lombardo: Un hombre de México*. México, DF: El Nacional.

Redero San Román, Manuel. 1992. *Estudios de historia de la UGT*. Salamanca: Ediciones Universidad de Salamanca.

Redondo, Nicolás. 1984. Una aproximación a la transición sindical española. *Claridad* No. 1: 11–17.

————. 1989. Discurso de clausura de las jornadas de reflexión sobre el giro social. *Claridad* Nos. 29–30, 49–56.

Regini, Marino. 1987. Industrial Relations in the Phase of Flexibility. *International Journal of Political Economy* (fall): 8–107.

Reid, Alstair. 2000. Labour and the Trade Unions. In *Labour's First Century*, edited by Duncan Tanner, Pat Thane, and Nick Tiratsoo. Cambridge: Cambridge University Press.

Reyes del Campillo, Juan. 1990. El movimiento obrero en la Cámara de Diputados (1979–198). *Revista Mexicana de Sociología* 52: 139–60.

Rhodes, Martin. 1997. Spain. In *The New Politics of Unemployment*, edited by Hugh Compston. London: Routledge.

Rigby, Mike, and Teresa Lawlor. 1994. Spanish Trade Unions 1986–1994; Life After National Agreements. *Industrial Relations Journal* 25: 258–71.

Roberts, Kenneth. 1998. *Deepening Democracy? The Modern Left and Social Movements in Chile and Peru.* Stanford: Stanford University Press.

———. 1999. Class Inequality without Class Cleavages? Paper presented at the Workshop on Political Parties and Working Class Constituencies, May 1, at University of California, Berkeley.

Rodríguez, Samuel Freije, Keila Betancourt, and Gustavo Márquez. 1995. Venezuela. In *Reforming the Labor Market in a Liberalized Economy,* edited by Gustavo Márquez. Washington, D.C.: Inter-American Development Bank, The Johns Hopkins University Press.

Rodrik, Dani. 1994. Comment in *The Political Economy of Reform,* edited by John Williamson. Washington, D.C.: Institute for International Economics.

Romero, Anibal. 1997. Rearranging the Deck Chairs on the Titanic: The Agony of Democracy in Venezuela. *Latin American Research Review* 32: 7–36.

Sabando Suárez, Pedro, Ignaicio Cruz Roche, Eduardo Gutiérrez, and Jaime Frades Pernas. 1989. Protección social. *Claridad* 29–30: 23–27.

Sabel, Charles. 1987. A Fighting Chance. *International Journal of Political Economy* (fall): 26–56.

Samstad, James. 2002. Corporatism and Democratic Transition: State and Labor Relations during the Salinas and Zedillo Administrations. *Latin American Politics and Society* 44: 1–28.

Santos, Roberto, and José Antonio Sánchez. 1990. *La conjura del zar.* Madrid: Ediciones Tema de Hoy.

Saracíbar, Antón. 1986. El reto sindical de la participación obrera en España. *Claridad* 3, no. 13: 5–23.

———. 1988. Las razones que se quieren ocultar. In *La desavenencia,* edited by Santos Juliá. Madrid: Ediciones El País.

Satrústegui, Miguel. 1992. PSOE: A New Catch-All Party. In *Socialist Parties in Europe.* Barcelona: Institut de Ciencies Politiques i Socials.

Schneider, Ben Ross. 1990. The Politics of Privatization in Brazil and Mexico: Variations on a Statist Theme. In *Political Economy of Public Sector Reform and Privatization,* edited by Ezra Suleiman and John Waterbury. Boulder, Colo.: Westview Press.

Segura, Julio. 1990. Del primer gobierno a la integración en la CEE: 1983–1985. In *Economía española de la transición y la democracia,* edited by José Luis García Delgado. Madrid: CIS.

Share, Donald. 1989. *Dilemmas of Social Democracy.* New York: Greenwood Press.

Smith, Peter. 1979. *Labyrinths of Power: Political Recruitment in Twentieth-Century Mexico.* Princeton, N.J.: Princeton University Press.

STDF (Subsecretaría del Trabajo del Distrito Federal). 1999. *Informe de política laboral.*

Stinchcombe, Arthur L. 1968. *Constructing Social Theories.* New York: Harcourt, Brace and World.

STPS (Ministry of Labor and Social Welfare). 1995. Internal database. México, DF: Secretaría de Trabajo y Previsión Social.

———. 2000. Información Estadística Laboral. México, DF: Secretaría de Trabajo y Previsión Social.

———. 2002. Información Estadística Laboral. Secretaría de Trabajo y Previsión Social.

Streek, Wolfgang. 1987. The Uncertainties of Management in the Management of Uncertainty. *International Journal of Political Economy* 17: 57–87.

Supreme Court Ruling Changes Labor Law. 2001. *Mexican Labor News and Analysis* 6, no. 5: on-line.

Supreme Court Upholds Union Democracy: "Official" Unions Attack Decision. 1996. *Mexican Labor News and Analysis* 1, no. 10: on-line.

SUTERM (Sole Union of Electrical Workers of the Mexican Republic). 2001. The Principles of the Opposition Movement in the Electrical Workers Union (SUTERM). *Mexican Labor News and Analysis.* 5, no. 9: on-line.

Taylor, Andrew. 1993. Trade Unions and the Politics of Social Democratic Renewal. *West European Politics* 16: 133–55.

Tezanos, José Felix. 1983. *Sociología del socialismo español.* Madrid: Editorial Tecnos.

————. 1984. Sociología del sindicalismo español. *Claridad* 1: 61–75.

————. 1989. Continuidad y cambio en el socialismo español: El PSOE durante la transición democrática. In *La transición democrática española*, edited by José Felix Tezanos, Ramón Cotarelo, and Andrés de Blas Guerrero. Madrid: Editorial Sistema.

Thousands of SUTERM Members Rally against Privatization; Dissidents Threaten Split in Union Unless Union Changes Line. 1999. *Mexican Labor News and Analysis* 4, no. 10. on-line.

Trejo Delarbre, Raúl. 1992. Sexenio de cambios aplazados. In *México: Auge, crisis y ajuste*, edited by Carlos Bazdresch et al. México, DF: Fondo de Cultura Económica.

Tuñon de Lara, Manuel. 1992. El movimiento obrero de 1981 a 1991. In *La década del cambio*, edited by Alfonso Guerra and José Felix Tezanos. Madrid: Editorial Sistema.

UGT (General Workers' Union). 1976. XXX Congreso. Madrid: Unión General de Trabajadores.

————. 1978. Memoria que presenta la Comisión Ejecutiva al XXXI Congreso de la Unión General de Trabajadores. Barcelona: Unión General de Trabajadores.

————. 1982. UGT ante el triunfo electoral socialista. Madrid: Oficina de Prensa Confederal, Coordinación Informativa.

————. 1983a. Gestión de la C.E.C. Al XXXIII Congreso Confederal. Madrid: Unión General de Trabajadores.

————. 1983b. Resoluciones del XXXIII Congreso Confederal. Madrid: Unión General de Trabajadores.

————. 1984. Manifiesto electoral. In *Materiales para el estudio del sindicato*, edited by Luis Enrique de la Villa. Madrid: MTSS.

————. 1985a. Carta-Circular. Madrid: Comisión Ejecutiva.

————. 1985b. Redondo: No hay problemas personales entre UGT y gobierno. Madrid: Oficina de Prensa Confederal.

————. 1985c. Reunión de la Comisión Ejecutiva Confederal de UGT. Madrid: Oficina de Prensa Confederal, Coordinación Informativa.

————. 1986a. Resoluciones del XXXIII Congreso Confederal. Madrid: Unión General de Trabajadores.

————. 1986b. 10 años haciendo futuro. Madrid: Unión General de Trabajadores.

————. 1987a. Circular No. 13. Madrid: Comisión Ejecutiva.

————. 1987b. Circular No. 14. Madrid: Comisión Ejecutiva.

————. 1988a. Carta/Circular. Madrid: Comisión Ejecutiva.

————. 1988b. Objetivos y criterios de actuación ante las movilizaciones generales. Madrid: Unión General de Trabajadores.

————. 1989a. A la sección de economía y laboral. Madrid: Comisión Ejecutiva.

————. 1989b. Carta a Ramón Rubial. 18 April 1987. Madrid: Comisión Ejecutiva.

————. 1989c. Gestión de la C.E.C. Al XXXV Congreso Confederal. Madrid: Unión General de Trabajadores.

————. 1989d. N. Redondo contesta a la invitación del PSOE. Madrid: Comisión Ejecutiva.

————. 1989e. Propuesta sindical de progreso. Madrid: Unión General de Trabajadores.

————. 1989f. UGT ante resultados elecciones parlamento europeo. Madrid: Comisión Ejecutiva.

————. 1990. Resoluciones del XXXV Congreso Confederal. Madrid: Unión General de Trabajadores.

————. 1991. Iniciativa sindical de progreso. Madrid: Unión General de Trabajadores.

————. 1994. Gestión de la C.E.C. Al 36 Congreso Confederal. Madrid: Unión General de Trabajadores.

UNT, SME, FSM Sign Unity Pact. 1999. *Mexican Labor News and Analysis* 4, no. 15: on-line.

Urquijo, José I., and Josué Bonilla G. 1992. Crónica laboral documentada. *Revista de investigaciones sobre relaciones industriales y laborales* 28: 63–144.

USAID (United States. Agency for International Development). 1996. *Latin America and the Caribbean: Selected Economic and Social Data*. Washington, D.C.: U.S. Agency for International Development.

Valecillos, Hector. 1990. Problemas y perspectivas del sindicalismo venezolano en una época de crisis. In *Economía y política del trabajo en Venezuela*. Caracas: Academia Nacional de Ciencias Económicas.

———. 1992. *El reajuste neoliberal en Venezuela*. Caracas: Monte Avila Editores.

———. 1993. Estadísticas socio-laborales de Venezuela, series históricas 1936–1990. 2 vols. Caracas: Banco Central de Venezuela.

Von Bülow, Marisa. 1994. Reestructuración productiva y estrategias sindicales: El caso de la Ford en Cuautitlán, 1987–1993. Tesis de maestría, FLACSO.

Wilson, Richard R. 1981. The Corporatist Welfare State: Social Security and Development in Mexico. Ph.D. diss., Yale University.

Woodruff, Christopher. 1997. Inflation stabilization and the vanishing size-wage effect. Working paper.

Works Council Elections Results. 1996. *European Industrial Relations Review* 267: 26.

Wozniak, Lynne. 1991. Industrial Restructuring and Political Protest in Socialist Spain. Ph.D. diss., Cornell University.

———. 1992–93. The Dissolution of Party-Union Relations in Spain. *International Journal of Political Economy* 22: 73–90.

Zamora, Gerardo. 1990. Hacia la inestabilidad económica. Apertura democrática e insurgencia obrera. In *Historia de la CTM: 1936–1990*, edited by Javier Aguilar García. México, DF: Instituto de Investigaciones Sociales, UNAM.

Zaragoza, Ángel. 1989. *Partits polítics, sindicats i patronal*. Barcelona: PPU.

Zazueta, César, and Ricardo de la Peña. 1984. *La estructura del Congreso de Trabajo*. México, DF: FCE.

Zedillo, Ernesto. 1997. 3 informe de gobierno, anexo gráfico y estadístico. Mexico, DF.

Zufiaur, José María. 1989. Presentación. *Claridad* Nos. 29–30.

———. 1990. Concertación social. *Claridad* 35/36: 5–9.

Index